"Leadership and management guides too often propose some narrow technique as a new way to workplace success. In this book, however, the authors take exactly the opposite approach, on the basis that work relationships are best handled through a knowledge of how to balance and apply emotions, intellect and intuition, sometimes together, sometimes apart, to work through work problems with colleagues and clients.

This is a style of leadership different from sectoral skill: it is the professional as rounded human being. I particularly enjoyed the chapter of dealing with difficult people, a skill rarely taught."

Ian, Lord Blair of Boughton, Commissioner of Police of the Metropolis, 2005–2008

"As a reader you are holding an exceptional book in your hands. I know of no other generic work that addresses the universal challenges that face all professionals and, regardless of specialisation, aims to support them in performing their tasks, to serve their customer/clients in as efficient a manner as may be possible given particular contexts and configurations. Understanding the human attributes and relationships that underpin professionalism and being reminded of and taught about its salient implications, will make all of us more effective and better able to perform our obligations to provide the best possible service we are able to deliver. That is the value of this book."

Peter Fonagy, OBE, PhD, Professor of Psychoanalysis and Developmental Science and Head of the Division of Psychology and Language Sciences at University College London

Psychology, Emotion and Intuition in Work Relationships

Psychology, Emotion and Intuition in Work Relationships: The Head, Heart and Gut Professional highlights the increasing importance of human relations in professional life. In modern society, all those who work with or provide services to others are increasingly called upon to be not just technical experts, but also 'head, heart and gut professionals' – who can work and relate to others with their head, heart and gut.

The book explains and synthesises these elements in an accessible way, based on a sound theoretical perspective combined with practical guidance. The authors address how to manage client expectations; how to deal with risk, uncertainty and imperfection, as well as how to improve communication and interpersonal skills. Attention is also given to the central role of empathy and rapport in professional relationships, while recognising the need for proper professional boundaries.

Psychology, Emotion and Intuition in Work Relationships will be a valuable guide for all modern practising and training professionals in a broad range of fields, including mental health, law, social and healthcare, teaching and academia, technology, financial and other services – indeed, for anyone who provides services and has working relationships of any kind.

Henry Brown, a retired solicitor, mediator and trainer, co-established a law firm in London, Waterloo and subsequently became a partner in a City of London firm. He co-founded and is a Vice-President of the Family Mediators Association and was Director of Mediation of the family lawyers' organisation Resolution.

Neil Dawson and Brenda McHugh are consultant systemic psychotherapists, lecturers and mediators. Having worked for over thirty years in child adolescent mental health services they are now programme directors at the Anna Freud National Centre for Children and Families where they have co-founded The Family School, London for children excluded from mainstream schools. They are internationally recognised trainers and have recently created an online training programme for mental health and school-based professionals.

Consultants to the work are: Peter Fonagy, Professsor of Contemporary Psychoanalysis and Developmental Science, UCL and CEO of the Anna Freud Centre, London and Rohan de Silva, a reader in neuroscience at UCL.

Psychology, Emotion and Intuition in Work Relationships

The Head, Heart and Gut Professional

Henry Brown, Neil Dawson and Brenda McHugh

Consultants: Peter Fonagy and Rohan de Silva

Routledge
Taylor & Francis Group

LONDON AND NEW YORK

First published 2018
by Routledge
2 Park Square, Milton Park, Abingdon, Oxon OX14 4RN

and by Routledge
711 Third Avenue, New York, NY 10017

Routledge is an imprint of the Taylor & Francis Group, an informa business

British Library Cataloguing in Publication Data
A catalogue record for this book is available from the British Library

Library of Congress Cataloging in Publication Data
A catalog record for this book has been requested

ISBN: 978-1-138-30273-0 (hbk)
ISBN: 978-1-138-30274-7 (pbk)
ISBN: 978-0-203-73171-0 (ebk)

Typeset in Times New Roman
by Keystroke, Neville Lodge, Tettenhall, Wolverhampton

MIX
Paper from
responsible sources
FSC
www.fsc.org   FSC™ C013985

Printed in the United Kingdom
by Henry Ling Limited

Contents

Foreword

Peter Fonagy, PhD FMedSci FBA FAcSS OBE, Professor of Contemporary Psychoanalysis and Developmental Science, Research Department of Clinical, Educational and Health Psychology, University College London; Chief Executive Officer, Anna Freud National Centre for Children and Families, London.

I have been most unprofessional in relation to writing this Foreword. I promised to deliver it by a certain date only to be overwhelmed by other demands and in the process let the authors, and myself, down. I stopped acting in their best interest and am guilty of having acted selfishly. I became unempathic and failed to listen to their reasonable and moderate demands for me to prioritise this task. My integrity slipped; I was less than fully transparent in relation to the opportunities I have to read the book sufficiently thoroughly to provide a reflection. My communications, or rather lack of them, further reflected this failure of professionalism. The underlying disappointment was the absence of professional energy, not turning my attention to the task required of me. Broadly, my behaviour fell significantly short of the expectation of skill and expertise that the authors had every right to anticipate on the basis of prior undertakings I made.

This brief analysis, painful and somewhat shaming, is based on Chapter 9 ("Professional Relationships and Expectations") of this extraordinary book. As specialisms and technical complexity grow within our communities, we are increasingly dependent on others who have the relevant skills and competencies to enable us to adapt to the multifaceted demands that survival in the twenty-first century requires.

The authors cite Francis Bacon's exclamation from the sixteenth century "knowledge is power". We know from Machiavelli (Chapter 21 in *The Prince*) that power corrupts and we are all familiar with Lord Acton's elaboration, "Power tends to corrupt and absolute power corrupts absolutely". The increased complexity of our world with its narrow specialisms has all but eradicated the renaissance ideal of a single individual with comprehensive expertise. We are all in the hands of a cadre of potential tyrants of expertise – the ubiquitous *professional*. There is urgent need for a guide, a code of conduct if you like, which cuts across specific domains of knowledge and speaks to the generic skill set of the individual whose training has prepared them to wield the Baconian power.

What should such a book cover? What is the essential knowledge that every professional should possess? The authors make it rapidly and abundantly clear that *the client–professional relationship entails almost every aspect of human functioning.* To be well equipped as a professional, whether a dentist or a lawyer, an IT professional or a plumber, a surgeon or a psychotherapist, it is essential to the appropriate conduct of daily business to have an understanding of the way individuals and the way organisations function. This means psychology and neuroscience and systems theory and sociology.

The immodest ambition of this monograph, and one that it achieves in an extraordinarily successful way, is to present a comprehensive toolkit to the professional to help her or him to manage effectively their daily responsibility for transmitting information, empowering their client to make adaptive and productive decisions, to assist them or deliver for them the outcomes they wish for which would not have been possible without their intervention. It is of course this capacity to assist that makes them professionals, for good or ill.

Why do I think this book is so special? Because, perhaps for the first time, it makes it explicit that being a professional lies at the very heart of what it means to be a human being.

As socio-biology has taught us, at the core of being human is the notion of accumulation of knowledge within a system we term *culture.* Tomasello et al. (2005) argue that the emergence of culture is based on the "ratchet effect" (one idea being discarded in favour of another) generating the accumulation of knowledge within a social group transmitted through social learning for which evolution has prepared us. The idea is retained within the social group until such time as a better solution to the same problem comes along.

In a recent book entitled *The Cultural Lives of Whales and Dolphins* Hal Whitehead and Luke Rendell (2015) identified a number of features of culture, only some of which are specific to homo sapiens. A particular culture adopts a specific characteristic technology that necessarily engenders a moral component with rules to protect that adaptation. The morality defines the group: "this is the way that we do things here". The rule is further buttressed by appropriate punishment for infraction. In human as well as in non-human mammalian culture this creates an acquired distinction between "insiders" and "outsiders" (those con-specifics who do not follow this rule). In humans this then permits a cumulative character to be established with knowledge built up and elaborated across a range of domains, in a manner reminiscent of the working of a ratchet, adopting new elements that are superior to and enable the dispensing of prior solutions. The mechanism that we have evolved to maintain this process is *teaching.* This is the biological mechanism that has evolved to sustain human professionalism, *homo peritun* (Latin for expert).

The role of the expert fits into the revolutionary and unique neuro-developmental structure that has emerged in a small species of humanoids (sapiens) in East Africa perhaps no more than 70,000 years ago. This innovative adaptation was for the transmission of knowledge between generations based on learning and teaching. The efficiency of pedagogy in place of natural selection mediated by DNA is extraordinary and accounts for the astonishing progress of our species at the expense of most other classes of living organisms over this period. However, our unique dependence on learning from other humans in order to acquire knowledge of the bewildering array of tools that surround us creates exceptional and substantial challenges.

What is the biological challenge? The young human is required to distinguish trustworthy, benevolent and reliable sources of knowledge from communicators who are either poorly informed or bad-intentioned. In either case the latter are the purveyors of useless or deceptive information. Thus to make adequate use of the tremendous power that the transmission of knowledge as culture via teaching creates, humans needed to evolve a reliable way of distinguishing who could and who should not be trusted. Trust in knowledge (what we may call *epistemic trust*) is at the heart of what it means to be a professional. Clients come and see their advisor/professional with appropriate *epistemic vigilance*. In a sense they are like all young humans at the mercy of a knowledge differential, uncertain about the trustworthiness of the information they are about to receive. Thus professionals could learn a lot from those who are able to rapidly establish epistemic trust in order to create a rapid and efficient system of knowledge transfer.

So how do children do it? How can a young human infant, completely naïve about the complex and potentially dangerous world he or she was brought into, know who to trust? Two developmentalists, Gergely Csibra and George Gergely (2011), discovered the answer, at least for infants. They demonstrated that if the communicator made a special effort to show that they recognised the infant as an individual, calling them by their name, smiling at them, responding sensitively to their actions in an attuned manner, then and mostly then the knowledge they communicated was taken by the infant as relevant to them, to be remembered and generalisable to other similar situations. With Patrick Luyten, Liz Allison and Chloe Campbell, we have advanced the view that all professional relationships depended on the effective use of this mechanism (Fonagy et al., 2017).

John Hattie, the New Zealand educationalist researcher, in a unique comprehensive analysis of what made an effective educational process, demonstrated that students learned most effectively from teachers who they felt were able to see the specific learning problem from the student's perspective, to recognise them as individuals sometimes struggling to acquire skills and ideas that were new to them (Hattie, 2013). Gergely and Csibra would label the behaviours effective teachers are able to use in their communication of knowledge as *ostensive cues*. This may be a helpful term to designate the capacity for marking ideas as potentially relevant to the learner.

We take a slightly broader view and suggest that what is essential for the establishment of epistemic trust, for the efficient transfer of information, so it is listened to and not just heard, is the recognition by the communicator that the individual they are communicating to is an *agent*. The term agent in this context comes from the German sociologist Max Weber ([1923] 1968), who identified a sense of control or agency as essential for an individual to experience full humanity.

To be an effective professional, to have the trust of one's clients, those of us practising a particular speciality must also acquire the capacity to recognise the essential humanity of individuals we are setting out to assist.

This is why this book, which sets out how to be a professional, has by necessity also to be a generic text of neuroscience, psychology and sociology. Regardless of the skill and knowledge of a nurse, a radiologist, a lawyer or a mediator, the professional who hopes to be trusted is obliged to understand the context and personal situation of the individual they hope to advise in order for the views of that individual to be taken seriously, outside of the room in which the advice is being given. In other words, to generalise to other contexts and meaningfully affect the behaviour of the individual who is being offered advice, the professional attitude must first and foremost link meaningfully to the thoughts, feelings, wishes, hopes and desires of the individual who lacks the essential knowledge to help themselves in the particular context where they depend on professional assistance. They need to feel respected and recognised so that their mind can genuinely open to receive a new understanding. In later chapters of the book, the authors consider individuals in some ways at odds with professional help. They favour conflict over learning. They may be given advice but they appear not to be able to listen. They are in a state of epistemic hypervigilance where prior disappointments have led to the disorganisation of the very mechanism that could help them open their minds to alternative perspectives. They may be relatively few in number. But they consume a vast proportion of professional resources across a range of specialities. Learning how professions can adapt to their needs and offer them effective help may be the next challenge.

But let us get back to where we started. Why was my behaviour "unprofessional" in the terms of this book and the terms I just elaborated? I behaved unprofessionally by not responding in a timely manner to the request for my assistance with this Foreword. By not communicating effectively and enabling my colleagues to act as effective agents, I disempowered them and made whatever contribution I was going to offer ultimately potentially of limited value. However, by writing about this process in this way, stating openly my failure of professionalism and respectfully acknowledging the personal value of the forbearance of the authors, I hope to have been able to restore such epistemic trust that might have previously characterised our long-standing relationship.

As a reader you are holding an exceptional book in your hands. I know of no other generic work that addresses the universal challenges that face all professionals and, regardless of specialisation, aims to support them in performing their tasks, to serve their customers/clients in as efficient a manner as may be possible given particular contexts and configurations. Understanding the human attributes and relationships that underpin professionalism, and being reminded of and taught about its salient implications, will make all of us more effective and better able to perform our obligations to provide the best possible service we are able to deliver. That is the value of this book.

Peter Fonagy
January 2018

References

Csibra, G. and Gergely, G., "Natural Pedagogy as Evolutionary Adaptation", *Philosophical Transactions of the Royal Society of London B: Biological Sciences*, 366 (2011), 1149–57.

Fonagy, P., Luyten, P., Allison, E. and Campbell, C. "What We Have Changed Our Minds About: Part 2. Borderline Personality Disorder, Epistemic Trust and the Developmental Significance of Social Communication", *Borderline Personal Disord Emot Dysregul*, 4 (2017), 9.

Hattie, J., *Visible Learning: A Synthesis of Over 800 Meta-Analyses Relating to Achievement* (Routledge, 2013).

Tomasello, M., Carpenter, M., Call, J., Behne, T. and Moll, H., "Understanding and Sharing Intentions: The Origins of Cultural Cognition", *Behavioral and Brain Sciences*, 28 (2005), 675–91.

Weber, M., *Economy and Society* (Bedminster Press, [1923] 1968).

Whitehead, H. and Rendell, L., *The Cultural Lives of Whales and Dolphins* (University of Chicago Press, 2015).

Preface

In writing this book, we have been largely motivated by our awareness that the world has become increasingly complex, uncertain and challenging. The need for understanding of human behaviour and the ability to respond and act appropriately has never been greater. For professionals (by which we mean not only those in traditional professions but a much wider group of people, as outlined in Chapter 1) technical expertise and skill are of course essential, but these alone are not enough; we also need to have knowledge, insights, interpersonal skills and other attributes that will help us to understand and manage demanding relationships, difficult people, conflict, uncertainty, imperfection, frustration, stress and a wide range of other challenges in our professional as well as personal lives.

In one way we have more technical and technological support than ever before. Information technology is at our fingertips, online encyclopaedias and reference material are instantly available. Modes of communication have proliferated and are instantaneous wherever we might be – through smartphones, laptops, tablets, social media, video and many other links. These are developing in sophistication by the day.

However, these advanced and sophisticated modes of communication do not in themselves enhance a better quality of communication between people, and indeed they may sometimes have the opposite effect. What we need is the ability to listen and respond effectively, to have genuine empathy and rapport within carefully maintained and understood boundaries, and to communicate meaningfully.

We have used the theme of "head, heart and gut" as the cornerstone for this work and the core aspects to be understood and incorporated into professional life and practice. "Head" involves a basic understanding of psychology, neuroscience, behaviour and personality, the factors that affect cognitive function and the ways in which we establish empathy and rapport. "Heart" involves understanding emotions, one's own and one's clients' or patients', how this affects decision-making and functioning, and having "boundaried empathy": emotional intelligence. "Gut" speaks of our intuitions, which we need to trust but, paradoxically, we also need to monitor with an awareness of their potential flaws and unreliability. Understanding and using this "head, heart and gut" approach in one's professional life, relationships and work will not only enhance the way one works, but should have positive implications for one's personal life.

Various practical aspects are related to these understandings, such as negotiation, conflict and dispute resolution, understanding and managing client expectations, systemic tensions and transitions, and dealing with risk, uncertainty and imperfection. Equally important is self-awareness: understanding and accepting ourselves, as individuals and professionally, exploring and recognising personal values, meaning and purpose, authenticity, and the importance of care and self-nurturing.

Having worked with, trained and taught many people over the years, from a wide range of working backgrounds and levels of experience – those in training and young professionals through to those approaching or in retirement – we have observed the dearth of attention given to these matters in most professional training, usually because there is so much technical expertise to learn that these elements are regarded as "soft" and non-essential, to be picked up over the years rather than formally taught. Consequently, there is a "hit-and-miss" nature to people's awareness of them and their ways of learning about them.

We are also mindful of the predicament of young professionals employed in the current market-driven economy, where the sense is that few jobs are permanent or secure and there is little notion of a defined career path. With progression uncertain, some people may feel the need to move on after a few years to get the experience of "promotion". In these circumstances, they need to develop themselves and their "competencies" as marketable commodities and to gain personal insights into what is required of them to become fully functioning competent professionals very quickly.

But the concepts that we cover are applicable to every stage of professional life and are intended to support experienced practitioners just as much as those entering the field. Mature practitioners are likely to have accumulated knowledge, experience and wisdom, but may appreciate the theoretical underpinning of what they know and may find satisfaction in coming across the "aha" factor, as well, perhaps, as discovering something new.

Our aim in this book is to draw all these strands together and synthesise them into a coherent outline guide to professionals, with some suggestions for further reading at the end of each chapter. Although in doing so we have drawn on academic writings and concepts, our perspective on these matters is based not only on theoretical understandings, but more importantly on many years of professional experience in actual practice of law, psychotherapy and counselling, mediation and teaching.

In this work we have generally used gender-neutral words such as "his or her" but sometimes we have just used one gender to avoid the text becoming too cumbersome; however, we want to emphasise that all our comments are gender-neutral, save of course where we specifically refer to men or women in any particular context.

We have a number of people to acknowledge and thank. In particular, we appreciate the support and expertise of Professor Peter Fonagy, who was also the consultant to our 2006 book and DVD on managing difficult divorce relationships, and who contributed to the concepts that we developed about working with high conflict personalities. More than a decade on and Peter's support for our new work remains invaluable. We also wish to thank neuroscientist Rohan de Silva, who reviewed our references to the brain and neuroscience. Rohan, too, was a contributor to our 2006 work. Some of the ideas in this book were bounced around with Lawrence Kershen QC at an earlier stage – thank you, Lawrence. The title was in part inspired by Frank Lazarus in the course of discussion about the opening chapters – thank you, Frank; and thanks also to Leonard Weinreich for his creative contribution. We want to acknowledge the late Arthur Marriott QC, co-author with Henry of *ADR Principles and Practice*, from which aspects regarding negotiation and dispute resolution were drawn and adapted. Our thanks, too, go to Joanne Forshaw, Charlotte Taylor and Kristina Siosyte at Routledge/Taylor & Francis and Kelly Winter, Maggie Lindsey-Jones, Geraldine Lyons, Neil Dowden and the team at Keystroke for their help and support. Finally, we want to acknowledge all the people whose words we have quoted or images we have used. We have sought permission wherever possible and appropriate but if we have missed any we will be happy to remedy this in any later printing or edition.

We hope that readers will enjoy the synthesis of all the elements in this book and will share our enthusiasm for the matters that we have covered. Our hope is that all professionals everywhere will eventually be "head, heart and gut professionals" – for the mutual benefit of their clients or patients and themselves.

Henry Brown, Neil Dawson and Brenda McHugh
January 2018

Acknowledgements

Thanks to the following for their cartoon and illustration contributions:

123RF (www.123rf.com) for the photograph introducing Chapter 1 and the brain diagram in Chapter 2.

CartoonStock (www.cartoonstock.com) for the cartoons introducing Chapters 2, 4, 7, 8, 9, 13 and 16.

Blifaloo.com (www.blifaloo.com) for the cartoon introducing Chapter 5.

Peretz Partensky from San Francisco, USA for the picture introducing Chapter 6 (which was artistically adapted for publication) and Pixabay.com

John Richardson, cartoonist and illustrator, for the cartoon introducing Chapter 14.

Glasbergen Cartoon Service (www.glasbergen.com) for the cartoon introducing Chapter 10.

Grantland Cartoons (www.grantland.net) for the "Grantland" cartoon in Chapter 11.

Len Weinreich (www.wordbright.com) for the illustrations introducing Chapters 3 and 12.

Chapter 1

On being a professional

Credit: Andrey Popov 123RF

The concept of "professional" in this work

There are different kinds of professionals.

Traditional professions are occupations that require extensive education and training leading to specialised knowledge and a formal qualification, regulated by professional bodies that seek to ensure that members comply with prescribed and expected standards and ethics of practice and conduct. These include medicine, law, dentistry, accountancy, architecture, teaching and academia, social work, psychotherapy and counselling, nursing, engineering, surveying, librarianship and religious ministry.

Other professions include expert service fields such as complementary health-care, banking, financial and insurance services, information technology (IT), management, human resources and public relations, the creative arts, media and publishing, journalism, advertising, marketing, the military, police, fire, ambulance and other emergency services, and many forms of advisory and consultancy services.

A "professional" may also mean someone who earns a living from an activity, as distinct from someone who follows similar activities for pleasure as an unpaid amateur. Hence, we may refer to an amateur sportsman has having "turned professional".

Those who provide expert skilled services in crafts or trades, such as plumbing, electrical work, carpentry, motor repairs, hairdressing and others may not traditionally be viewed as members of a "profession", but they too are professionals in relation to the issues outlined in this book, which are relevant to all these different forms of professionalism and skilled services, especially where working relationships need to be maintained.

A more effective professional role and understanding

The focus on substantive education and training

In most fields of professional activity there is a vast amount to learn. Educators are faced with stark choices as to what aspects are fundamental and what can be left to be developed after qualification. It is not surprising that primary attention is given to substantive knowledge and that anything considered peripheral or "soft" and unquantifiable knowledge is placed lower down the chain of learning or – more usually – omitted entirely.

So, for example, while aspects concerning psychology, neuroscience or relationships may be fundamental to some professions such as counselling, psychotherapy and social work, these have relatively low priority for most other professions and, where included at all, tend to be addressed on a minimal or optional basis.

Consequently, many people qualify as professionals without any insights into why people behave and respond the way they do, how to manage expectations or how to work with high conflict personalities or people with different and perhaps challenging personality traits, notwithstanding the profound impact that such understanding has on the work that they do; nor does training generally aim to outline how best to cope with competing systemic tensions or with uncertainty or imperfection. "We are not counsellors or therapists" becomes a common defensive mantra.

Practical matters flowing from these aspects such as effective communication, rapport and negotiation and dealing with conflict and disputes are similarly often left unaddressed.

The aspiration of this book is to cover these topics and others of professional and personal interest and relevance such as purpose and meaning, reflective practice and self-nurturing, support resources, and managing change, transitions and endings. It aims to do so by way of a concise but reasonably comprehensive introduction. For those who wish to probe further into any particular aspect, there is a further reading section at the end of each chapter.

Gaining some understanding of the behaviour of others

All working relationships are important, some profoundly so, whether with clients, patients, colleagues, support personnel, students or others. However, it would be unrealistic to expect, in the course of an ordinary professional relationship, to develop any deep understanding as to why individuals behave the way they do, or to know what may have influenced them and helped carve out their fundamental and innermost beliefs or *world views*.

> In *Mediation: A Psychological Insight into Conflict Resolution*, Freddie Strasser and Paul Randolph describe "world views" as "the meanings, values and belief systems that [people] create in order to survive the uncertainties of existence".

However, we can develop better understandings of the factors that influence people in their decision-making, why some people may be more prone to certain kinds of behaviour than others and what the best way to respond may be – in often imperfect circumstances. We can learn about personality differences and patterns of behaviour that will make our work more effective and our reactions more relevant.

We can learn what practices enhance our relationships and what are more likely to damage them; what communications are effective and what are more likely to be negatively received; when acting like a friend in a working relationship is likely to be counter-productive; and how everyday strategies can improve working relationships.

Whatever our field of work we can learn how to manage stress, anger, distress, panic and high conflict more effectively. We can develop rapport with our clients and more readily defuse volatile situations. We can develop better ways of communicating, help people to express themselves more clearly and minimise the risk of inappropriate responses and over-reaction to provocative or challenging situations.

Gaining some understandings about ourselves

As professionals, gaining greater understanding about ourselves and the unconscious forces that shape how we function can have a significant importance for the way we work, how effective we are in what we do and the level of fulfilment that our work provides.

- For many people, having a sense of purpose and meaning in their lives and work is a luxury that they cannot necessarily afford – yet it is an important element of well-being. Reflection, understanding and self-awareness may help clarify what is important and how one's work may perhaps be done or adapted to incorporate some element of this.

- Some people feel that they need to adopt a professional image or *persona* to reflect the way that they believe a professional should look and behave. Of course, clients or patients will have certain expectations of professional conduct but there are many ways to achieve this without compromising personal authenticity. Some reflective self-awareness, understandings and insights may help bring this into consciousness and help to achieve greater personal and professional authenticity.
- We need to understand more about our own personality, motivation and style so that we can work to our strengths. Perhaps we may need to bring greater balance into the relationship between our working lives and our personal and family lives.
- Cognitive dissonance theory, proposed in 1957 by social psychologist Leon Festinger, proposes that people are sensitive to inconsistencies between their beliefs and their actions, which causes dissonance that will result in their changing their beliefs, their actions or their perceptions of their actions, for example by rationalising them. An understanding of this and its implications may help us to cope better with such situations.
- Another issue that affects some people, even those who are highly regarded, is that they may experience huge levels of secret anxiety, may feel occasional panic, or may have a secret fear of failure, of "being found out". Petrūska Clarkson refers in *The Achilles Syndrome: Overcoming the Secret Fear of Failure* to a mismatch between their abilities and their confidence.

This book will try to make some sense of the ways in which we can understand ourselves better and of our working lives and relationships.

So it is said that if you know your enemies and know yourself, you will fight without danger in battles.

If you know only yourself, but not your opponent, you may win or may lose.

If you know neither yourself nor your enemy, you will always endanger yourself.

(From Sun Tzu's classical sixth-century
Chinese treatise *The Art of War*)

What does the public expect from professionals?

Individual expectations may vary, but there are undoubtedly some common themes:

- In all cases, the common thread is undoubtedly that there has to be an acceptable level of qualification, skill, judgement and up-to-date expertise.

- Clients will expect personal conduct appropriate to the service provided, involving some form of professional demeanour (which does not imply excessive formality, but rather an appropriate way of relating to the client, even if this is informal).
- For traditional professionals, and in various other fields, there will generally be some kind of ethical and/or practice code and a regulatory body to whom complaints can be directed, which will have powers and sanctions to discipline the person and, in the most extreme failings, withdraw their right to work in that field.
- Professional relationships should embody mutual respect, with relevant communications and language. Some clients will expect the professional to maintain a professional distance, others may prefer the professional to be more like a friend.
- Invariably, clients will expect professionals to act and advise them responsibly in their best interests, understanding their needs and responding appropriately.

Professional and personal authenticity

This book will develop a number of themes to help the professional towards better relationships with clients and to function effectively and in a personally satisfying way. One of these themes will be the need for personal and professional authenticity; that is to say, practising one's profession in a way that provides a genuinely good service to the client while also maintaining one's own integrity and values.

> In his book *On Becoming a Person*, psychotherapist Carl Rogers uses the term *congruent* to describe authenticity. It lies in being trustworthy, dependable or deeply consistent, not only in a practical sense, but also by being true to oneself. Rogers calls this being "dependably real".

Professional authenticity may manifest itself in many ways. It involves genuineness in the services one provides, and for example in not pretending to a level of expertise that one does not have. This does not mean never stretching oneself or developing new skills, but rather being realistic and straightforward about what can be done. It involves practical matters such as doing effectively what one undertook to do, indicating when additional expertise is needed, and generally providing the expertise and skill that the client is entitled to expect. It also involves understanding the client's concerns and needs and responding appropriately and honestly; dealing with clients in a way that is genuinely respectful and empathetic; and communicating clearly.

Clients will generally be able to detect authenticity – or otherwise. Professionals who can deal with and respond to their clients appropriately and authentically are likely to gain their trust and support. Those who do not may find it difficult to establish an effective relationship.

Personal and professional authenticity is of course interrelated. As a personal attribute, it involves simply "being oneself" and honouring one's own values and beliefs – not "putting on a show" to meet others' expectations. This does not mean developing an uncompromising approach to every aspect of personal and professional life, which would be impracticable as well as potentially intolerable to others, but rather living one's life and practising one's profession with personal integrity and self-belief, firm in one's convictions, but without a need to "bang tables" or to deny one's own vulnerability. The need for personal authenticity does not license intolerance, rudeness, insensitivity or hurt to others.

> This above all: to thine own self be true,
> And it must follow, as the night the day,
> Thou canst not then be false to any man.
>
> (Polonius, in Shakespeare's *Hamlet*)

Some people may be fortunate enough, whether through nature or nurture, to have a strong sense of their own self, and may have no difficulty with establishing their own authenticity. For others, the path to authenticity may involve a period of self-awareness, self-actualising and support.

Professional jargon, mystification and patronisation

Conspiracy against the laity

One of the common attributes of a professional body or group is a tendency to develop its own language and – wittingly or unwittingly – to "mystify" its process. This arises in different ways including through specialist language, terminology, processes and systems. Laymen may be baffled by some forms of legal drafting, by IT instructions or if they try to get feedback between doctors' surgeries and hospitals or to penetrate local authority labyrinths.

> Franz Kafka's disturbing existential novel *The Trial* illustrates an extreme example of an individual lost in the web of an unknowable bureaucracy.

Practitioners are at risk of becoming so used to their own language, system and culture that they can lose sight of the fact that their clients may find these challenging and often incomprehensible. Little wonder that George Bernard Shaw's 1911 line in *The Doctor's Dilemma*, "all professions are a conspiracy against the laity", remains so well known.

The patronising professional

Some professionals may unwittingly patronise their clients by their language, tone or demeanour and their attitudes may appear condescending.

Although an increasing number of professionals are sensitive to their clients, the charge of professionals being patronising remains commonly heard. Some seem not to realise that clear and simple language, explanations and advice can be provided in a supportive, helpful and empathetic way. They do not appreciate the client's ability to be a part of the "team" addressing the issue, nor perhaps the negative effect that they are having on their clients; or if they do, they either do not care or simply do not know how to overcome their difficulty.

Clients' reactions and empowerment

There have been significant reactions against these professional attitudes, real or perceived. These have come both from the clients themselves and also from professionals and their representative bodies. The following are some examples:

- There has been a reaction against the dominance of some members of the medical profession. The patient empowerment movement places greater emphasis on self-reliance, safety awareness and patients' rights and encourages more effective communication with doctors. This has emanated both from patients' organisations and from the medical profession and, in the United Kingdom (UK), from the National Health Service (NHS).

> In a 2015 Institute for Public Policy Research report entitled "Powerful People: Reinforcing the power of citizens and communities in health and care", Rick Muir and Harry Quilter-Pinner make a strong argument for the value of patient power as a key driver for change in the UK's NHS, with a shift from a paternalistic to a co-productive model of care, and citizens taking greater responsibility for their own health. This would produce better health outcomes, improved patient satisfaction and could be economically beneficial.

- The establishment of mediation has at least in part been attributed to the need for people to be empowered to deal with their own disputes, albeit with professional support. Empowerment means the increase in the parties' ability to make their own decisions and the corresponding reduction of their dependence on third parties including professional advisers and the courts.
- There is a trend towards personal empowerment, involving a greater awareness and assumption of individual and group power, self-reliance and self-confidence. In this climate of empowerment, there is inevitably less willingness

to bow to professional form or to hold back on questioning and challenging professional views.

- There is also a trend towards reducing jargon in law and other fields. For example, Clarity, an international organisation, promotes the use of plain legal language, as does the Plain Language Association International.
- Cases against lawyers, doctors and financial institutions involving malpractice, negligence, breach of duty or wrongdoing have also had an effect in undermining confidence in professionals and shifting them from their pedestals.

Another factor is that whereas in the past professionals may have been reluctant to challenge their colleagues, for example by giving evidence against them in professional negligence cases, many more are now readier to do so where they perceive standards falling below an acceptable level.

This in turn has led to a climate in which greater accountability is quite properly expected of professionals. Those perceived to have performed their duties unsatisfactorily can expect to face disciplinary proceedings from their professional bodies and/or negligence actions by their clients. Teachers, social workers and others who have a more public function may face members of the public to whom they are responsible and/or administrative committees and/or the glare of public enquiry with vigilant and sometimes highly critical media.

> Opposition to patient empowerment often focuses on the pushy patient who tiresomely challenges the doctor's years of education on the basis of an afternoon on Google. But the bigger issue is the much larger group of patients who simply don't want to hold their doctors to account or get involved in decisions about their care.
>
> (The King's Fund, Think Differently Blog, Roger Taylor, 4 April 2013: www.kingsfund.org.uk/time-to-think-differently/blog/giving-power-patient)

This, then, is the environment in which professionals function in many countries: with continuing regard from the public, but an increasing willingness to challenge and to seek clarification, less patience with pompousness and jargon, and a greater need for introspection and self-discipline in a more contentious and less respectful world.

Helping and healing professions

Defining the helping professions

Some professions are viewed as "helping professions". There is no accepted definition of this term but, based on common usage and publications, these are generally considered to be medicine and healthcare, nursing, teaching, social work, the clergy, psychotherapy and counselling, and any others that have as their core helping people to manage their lives and to deal with problems – to learn, to recover, to heal, to cope.

One may speculate why other professions that have similar helping aspects are not included in this definition. After all, most professions that provide services will address problems and are "helping" in their nature: the emergency services, the legal profession, financial and tax advisers, to mention just a few. Perhaps a distinguishing feature is the element of physical, mental or emotional support that the helping professions provide, though this does not entirely satisfactorily explain why other professions that also do so are excluded.

Healing professions

While clearly there is an overlap between the helping and the healing professions, with medicine, nursing, counselling and therapy falling into both, the general view is that healing professions deal primarily with personal issues of a physical, emotional or mental kind.

A range of complementary and alternative health professions are generally also included here, such as acupuncture, chiropractic, osteopathy, homeopathy, naturopathy and Ayurveydic medicine.

Here again, questions arise as to whether the general view of "healing professions" is an adequate one. Can law, for example, be a healing profession? Although the words "law" and "healing" are not commonly juxtaposed, there is a view that law can be healing when practised with humanity. If law and other professions can work with wounded people and can help them towards recovery, might they not also qualify as "healing professions"?

> In *Re-rooted Lives: Inter-disciplinary Work within the Family Justice System*, the chapter "Visions of Excellence – Law, Healing and Humanity" by Henry Brown refers to the "infinite variety of ways that law can be practised, that humanity can be expressed and that healing can take place".

The concept of the wounded healer

In Greek mythology, the centaur Chiron was a noted healer and teacher who when poisoned by an arrow was unable to heal himself. Carl Jung used this as an archetype in situations in which an analyst's own emotional wounds are activated by the patient's references to similar issues, which need to be addressed in the analysis. The analyst's response to this stimulation may affect the way in which the relationship with the patient develops and may be used to effect a therapeutic outcome.

The concept of the wounded healer can also refer to situations in which a person who experiences illness, trauma, addiction or emotional crisis becomes a practitioner working in the field of that experience, helping others. This may or may not be a conscious decision. For example, a person who has experience of a conflictual relationship, directly or by observing others such as his or her parents, may take up a vocation that involves working with conflicted parties, such as therapy, counselling or family law.

Further reading

Specific relevant reading suggestions are set out at the end of each chapter.

On the subject of professionalism, books tend largely to be profession-specific rather than broadly generic, though some are geared to particular aspects of professionalism such as ethics, sociology or self-help style works for successful practice.

By way of random example, books about medical and healthcare professionalism include *Measuring Medical Professionalism* edited by David Thomas Stern; *Patient Care and Professionalism* edited by Catherine D. DeAngelis; and Jill Thistlethwaite and Judy McKimm's *Healthcare Professionalism at a Glance.* Or professionalism in education is addressed in Jane Green's *Education, Professionalism and the Quest for Accountability: Hitting the Target but Missing the Point*, which looks at issues of managerial accountability in education and more widely in other professions, particularly in the public sector.

The psychotherapeutic profession provides books that are aimed at its members, but which can sometimes be of wider application, a notable example being Carl Rogers' *On Becoming a Person: A Therapist's View of Psychotherapy.* The Rogerian humanistic approach and principles about client relationships have been absorbed into other professions; and David Howe's *On Being a Client: Understanding the Process of Counselling and Psychotherapy* contains principles that are applicable to many other professions.

More generic works relevant to this subject include Susie Kay's short and easy-to-read *Professionalism: The ABC for Success* and Alan Cribb and Sharon Gewirtz's reflective work *Professionalism.* There is also a comprehensive analysis of professional conduct cases – regulatory and disciplinary in all professional fields – coming before the English courts in Kenneth Hamer's *Professional Conduct Casebook.*

Chapter 2

Head, heart and gut

Head – brain and mind

"Always use your head, follow your heart
and go with your gut feeling."

Credit: CartoonStock.com

Head, heart and gut in functioning and decision-making

Like the boy in the cartoon, one can be forgiven for being somewhat confused by advice to:

- follow your heart: that is, trust your emotions, feelings and values;
- use your head: that is, be guided by rational logic and intellect not by emotions;
- go with your gut feelings: that is, follow your intuition and instinct rather than logic.

At first sight, these are contradictory messages. However, they may not necessarily be inconsistent with one another. The question is whether one can have regard to intuition and know when to trust it and when it may be unreliable, and whether logical and rational thought can complement emotional feelings and values to provide a "joined-up" reaction.

> You have to master not only the art of listening to your head, you must also master listening to your heart and listening to your gut.
> (Carly Fiorina, former President of Hewlett-Packard)

To provide a better understanding of these three components – head, heart and gut – and to facilitate integrating them in practice, three chapters will address them separately, starting in this chapter with the head – the brain and mind.

This will be relevant both to the professional's own understandings and actions, and also to a better awareness of the factors at play in relation to a client's functionality and decision-making process, and will help to inform aspects discussed in later chapters.

The brain: central to understanding and functioning

Developments in neuroscience and insights now possible through functional brain imaging and other technology into the workings of the human brain and nervous system have exponentially increased our understanding of how we think and function, how our rational and logical processes can be overwhelmed, why and how we operate as social beings, why some people lack understanding and empathy – and a host of other matters relevant to us as functioning human beings and more particularly as professionals.

Fortunately, we do not need to be neuroscientists to gain a basic understanding of the human brain and how it functions. But it is relevant and indeed exciting to understand how we all respond to primitive parts of our brains, and how the relatively more recently developed parts can mediate those responses – and when they fail to do so.

We may know or work with people, whether clients or colleagues, who have huge difficulty in relating sensitively and empathetically to others, who can't read the signs being given to them and who may indeed not even comprehend how others can be thinking. We now know that there are kinds of brain cells that have this function, and which may be malfunctioning – these may be new and relevant insights for us.

From neuroscience and from psychology we are developing understanding and theories of behaviour, including a better sense of why some people have difficulty with relationships and why some people have high conflict personalities – and how best to deal with them, and generally with people in panic or under stress, in our personal and professional capacities.

The range of this information, both established and newly available, is vast and we cannot hope – and this work doesn't aspire – to get to grips with it all.

We should also be aware that neuroscience cannot provide all the answers. It can provide data, but it remains necessary to formulate understandings from that data, which allow for different conclusions. New discoveries and insights continue to emerge: this is a work in progress.

Accepting these limitations and imperfections – and we will reflect later on the issue of imperfection – we can nevertheless gain an awareness of the brain and its functioning sufficient to enhance our professional practices and our personal relationships.

> Surely, the brain must hold the key to human nature: understanding it will allow us to make sense of so much that puzzles us about ourselves.
>
> (Adam Zeman, *A Portrait of the Brain*)

Basic neuroscience: the brain and nervous system

Introduction to 100 billion neurons

In the age of the computer, it is extraordinary to think that we humans – *Homo sapiens sapiens* – have at our disposal a mechanism and system that rival and generally outperform the most sophisticated computers in existence.

The human brain is the centre of the nervous system, and is probably the most complex biological structure in existence. Almost inconceivably, it has an average of 100 billion neurons, which are nerve cells that process and electrically transmit information from one part of the body to another (though the vast majority are within and interconnected in the brain). That is 100,000,000,000 neurons.

Each neuron may have up to 10,000 synapses, which are tiny gaps that serve as connection points to other neurons, across which messages fly (through chemicals called neurotransmitters). That is, up to 1,000,000,000,000,000 synapses.

So there are potentially trillions of paths that messages can take between the neurons of one person's brain.

Merely reading this page involves brain and neural activity which may for example include coordinating hand movements that organise turning the page and holding the book or device, eye movements in reading the words and carrying the information to the brain, brain function in absorbing and making sense of what is written, memory functions that on the one hand give meaning and put into context what is being read and on the other hand store (or choose not to store) the information for future use, perhaps also combined with adjusting optical focus and light, maintaining balance in a chair, and perhaps also watching the time if there are other priorities to be attended to, and remembering or keeping on one side other matters that may be competing for attention. Alongside this the body needs to breathe and function and to be alert for and manage any unexpected interruptions or crises.

> In the preface to his book *The Tell-tale Brain: Unlocking the Mystery of Human Nature*, on attempts to crack the code of the human brain, V. S. Ramachandran describes the human brain, with its vast number of connections and modules, as "infinitely more enigmatic than any Enigma machine".

The nervous system

The nervous system consists of:

*   *The central nervous system*, which comprises the brain and the spinal cord, which in turn comprises a bundle of nerves running from the brain down the backbone. Its primary functions are to relay information between the brain and the body, in both directions, as well as information processing with stimuli relating to cognition, response to environment and memory. It also coordinates with the peripheral nervous system.
*   *The peripheral nervous system*, which comprises the nerves and nerve cells outside the central nervous system, but connected to that system and relaying information between it and the body's limbs and organs. It controls voluntary body movements primarily through muscle contraction (the *voluntary* or *somatic nervous system*) and involuntary and unconscious actions through the *autonomic nervous system*.
*   *The autonomic nervous system*, which controls many organs and muscles so as to maintain normal internal functions on an involuntary visceral basis, including heart rate, respiration, and the contraction and relaxation of muscles. It helps us to deal with emergencies by creating a "fight or flight" reaction (technically the *sympathetic sub-system*), and in non-emergencies provides a "rest and digest" reaction (the *parasympathetic sub-system*), slowing the heartbeat, reducing blood pressure and allowing digestion.

The human brain: old and new

A convenient starting point for consideration of the brain is the concept of a *Triune Brain* conceived by neurologist Paul MacLean in the 1960s. Although now considered to be an inappropriate way of viewing the brain, it nevertheless provides a useful opening view in order to see how ideas started, and have developed since then.

MacLean's concept was that the human brain had three brain layers, each functioning like a separate computer, which had developed on top of one another sequentially. On this view, the earliest, and innermost, is the reptilian brain, rigid, compulsive and repetitive. The next layer is concerned with emotions and instincts, feeding, fighting, fleeing and sexual behaviour. The third, newest, outer layer is the cerebral neocortex, found in higher animals, viewed as the superior or rational brain.

This theory is now widely considered to be erroneous, as it now seems clear that the brain works as a unified whole. However, MacLean's concept seems to have provided a helpful stepping stone towards subsequent understanding. There is now a broad consensus that the basic (inner) design of the human brain is perhaps 200 million years old and shared by all other mammals, whereas the outermost prefrontal lobes (pre-frontal cortex) are less than 1 million years old. These inner and outer parts of the brain have different functions, and their inter-relationship is critical to the way we behave as individual humans.

The pre-frontal cortex is responsible for executive functions such as resolving conflicting thoughts, making choices, and predicting and planning future events. It governs conscious thoughts, feelings, language, memories, voluntary actions and social control.

> Sue Gerhardt, author of *Why Love Matters: How Affection Shapes a Baby's Brain*, describes the pre-frontal cortex as "the thinking part of the emotional brain, where emotional experience is held on line and alternative courses of action considered".

The range of activities that the brain and nervous system control is vast and includes:

- *The limbic system:* comprising brain structures supporting functions such as emotions, long-term memory, and the sense of smell. It includes the *hypothalamus* (controlling areas such as body temperature, chemical levels, hunger and thirst), the *thalamus* (which addresses data received from the senses other than smell), the *hippocampus* (memory and learning) and the *amygdala* (fear, arousal and other strong emotions).
- *Biochemistry of the body:* the brain continuously processes data from our five senses to determine what chemicals are required to deal with any situation. Among these are the neurotransmitters *dopamine* (which affects processes that control movement, emotional responses including love and euphoria, and the ability to experience pleasure and pain) and *serotonin* (which affects mood, aggression, the sex drive and the sleep cycle); and the hormones *oxytocin* (connected with bonding, love, trust and generosity), *adrenaline* (the "fight or flight" hormone released when danger threatens) and *cortisol* (secreted in response to physical or psychological stress).
- *Left- and right-brain activity:* each hemisphere of the brain has a different function, which is relevant to an understanding of behaviour, as dealt with below.

The efficient functioning of the brain and nervous system involves all these complex systems working effectively in coordination with one another. When

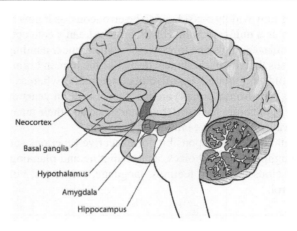

Neocortex

Basal ganglia

Hypothalamus

Amygdala

Hippocampus

Credit: 123RF Stock Photo

elements get out of kilter, physical, personal, behavioural or psychological problems may arise.

Neuroscience has developed into a complex field, involving the integration of neurological function, body and brain chemistry, psychology, genetics, social context and other factors.

The brain's hemispheres: left and right brain

The brain is divided into two large cerebral hemispheres, each of which controls the muscle movements in the opposite side of the body: the left brain makes the right arm move and vice versa. Each hemisphere is divided into four *lobes*: *frontal*, *temporal*, *parietal* and *occipital*.

The left and right hemisphere each controls different ways of thinking, which has given rise to a somewhat simplistic notion that the left brain controls logic and the right brain controls intuition and creativity. The position is rather more complex and some practitioners have a greater regard for the influence of other systems and neurochemical mechanisms.

However, the relevance of these hemispheres cannot be overstated. Nobel Prize winner Roger Sperry and psychologist Robert Ornstein both demonstrated that the left and right hemispheres specialise in different tasks, and many others have elaborated on this.

The left side of the brain takes care of analytical and verbal tasks, processing information in a detailed, analytical and sequential way, looking first at the pieces then putting them together to get the whole. Its tasks include words and language, reason, logic and analysis, numbers and sequences.

The right side is visual, taking care of space perception tasks and processing information in an intuitive and simultaneous way, looking first at the whole picture and then the details. Its tasks include imagination, daydreaming, spatial cognition (navigation or face recognition), rhythm, colour and dimension.

People may tend to use one side more than the other, which becomes dominant. However, all activity involves both sides working in concert, connected by a network of nerve fibres, the *corpus callosum*.

A clear example of the need for both sides to coordinate with one another arises when deciding whether to trust someone. This requires memory, information and logic on the one hand, and also intuition and judgement on the other. It seems almost inconceivable that one might make an effective decision on this without both sides of the brain working in concert.

Two ways of thinking

One aspect of the human brain is fundamental to behaviour. This relates to the two different ways in which the human brain functions: the immediate, spontaneous and automatic response to any experience, and the more attentive, conscious response that may follow. This distinction has been described in different ways, but the fundamental principles are the same: one part of our brain provides the automatic response and a different part provides the conscious attentive element.

Nobel Prize winning psychologist Daniel Kahneman adopted a simple way of distinguishing these two systems, namely System 1 and System 2 as detailed in his best-selling book *Thinking Fast and Slow*. Each of these ways of thinking will be separately considered.

Automatic processing

At a fundamental level, the brain operates automatically in relation to our basic bodily functions such as breathing, eating, drinking and sleeping. Here, *homeostasis* is relevant – that is, the ability and tendency of a body or organism to regulate its internal conditions so as to maintain a stable and broadly constant equilibrium within itself. The human body maintains homeostasis in relation to its temperature, blood pressure, blood sugar levels, water balance and other bodily variables. This is largely done through the autonomic nervous system.

At another level the brain functions automatically in relation to tasks that a person may carry out that don't require conscious attention. This may, for example, apply when a cyclist mounts and rides his or her bicycle or when one performs a daily ritual such as washing dishes. It can also relate to simple cognitive tasks such as knowing how many pence there are in a pound, or singing the words of a familiar song. This falls into Kahneman's System 1 – thinking fast.

There is, however, another level at which the brain functions automatically that is particularly relevant to professionals: the "fight or flight" response. In this regard the starting point is the limbic system, with particular reference to the thalamus and the amygdala.

The thalamus addresses data received from the senses other than smell. It acts a sensory regulator, receiving signals and relaying them to the amygdala and to the frontal cortex, from where the second system of conscious attention operates.

The amygdala's functions include dealing with fear, arousal and other strong emotions. It stores memories of emotionally significant events and automatically responds to stimuli that recall those events and their related emotions, in turn producing an instinctive response from the body – a somatic response – such as sweating or increased heart rate and a sense of aversion towards the stimuli in question.

The fear reaction or other strong emotion generated by the amygdala results in the fight or flight response, though there is also a third reaction, namely dissociate or "freeze".

If the body's stress response is activated too often and for too long, chronic stress can result. This can have detrimental effects including loss of sleep and fatigue, raised blood pressure, suppression of the immune system, forgetfulness, anxiety and potentially depression, heart attack or stroke. Other physical symptoms may vary, but can include headaches, muscle tension, loss of sexual desire or functionality and gastro-intestinal disorders such as irritable bowel syndrome, peptic ulcers or gastroesophageal reflux disease (GERD).

Even if not currently in fight, flight or freeze mode, a chronically stressed person is likely to find it difficult to make effective decisions, partly because thinking about the original stressor may rekindle the response mode, and also because chronic stress decreases memory function and cognitive flexibility.

Conscious attentive processing

Here again, a range of activities fall into this category, starting at the one end with light attentive function, such as conscious awareness that someone is looking at you and reflecting momentarily on whether to look back or look away, through to intensive and complex cognitive demands, such as considering a complicated chess position in order to evaluate the permutations of possible moves, assessing the subtleties of personal and social relationships or engaging in sophisticated problem-solving.

The key part of the brain responsible for this conscious processing is the *neocortex* and in particular the *pre-frontal cortex* (or *prefrontal lobes*). One of its main functions is to inhibit and regulate the instinctive reactions of the amygdala – to prevent "amygdala hijacking".

Neuropsychologist Mark Solms and Oliver Turnbull in their work *The Brain and the Inner World: An Introduction to the Neuroscience of Subjective Experience* say: "Free will consists in freedom *not* to act in an automatic and preprogrammed fashion."

All mammals have a neocortex, but what distinguishes primates from other mammals in this regard is the relative size of the prefrontal lobes, with humans having relatively the largest sized prefrontal lobes of all primates. It is this factor that has enabled humans to develop in the way that they have, including in particular acquiring a sophisticated language facility and, with that, sophisticated thought processes including abstract thought.

But Mark Solms has issued a warning. In his insightful essay "Neurobiological Foundations" published in J. W. de Gruchy (ed.) *The Humanist Imperative in South Africa*, after analysing humans' main instinctual behaviour – and that of other mammals – he says:

> We are rightly proud of our highly developed prefrontal capacity. However, I would like to … [point] out that increased inhibition and thinking (and all the flexible artifices and other benefits that flow from them) also come at a price. The price is this. Because the prefrontal lobes necessarily inhibit not only instinctual actions but also the affects (feelings) that accompany them, we humans are *uniquely ignorant of our own motivations*. We do not know why we do what we do. Our actions are so far removed from the instincts that motivated them (and unconsciously guide them) that we no longer know what we are trying to achieve.

Intelligence

The meaning of this word remains enmeshed with the methods used to measure it. The original intelligence test, the Binet–Simon Scale, evaluated functions such as reasoning, imagination, insight, judgement and adaptability, but this has been significantly extended.

IQ (intelligence quotient) testing is a measure of assessing the level of a person's intelligence relative to his or her peers. It is used to evaluate intellectual and cognitive abilities and can help diagnose learning difficulties and cognitive disorders. It may cover matters such as general knowledge and comprehension, verbal reasoning skills or visual and spatial skills.

Professor Howard Gardner developed the concept of multiple intelligences which he set out in his book *Frames of Mind: The Theory of Multiple Intelligences*. He challenged the concept that intelligence could simply be assessed by answering a series of short questions that might predict academic success. Intelligence could be manifested in a wide variety of ways and in his view the whole concept of human intellect needed to be thought about in a different way, to be expanded and reformulated.

Having reviewed earlier studies, Gardner came to the view that different intellectual strengths or competences existed, supported by corresponding neural organisation. He refuted the concept of one single universally accepted criterion for human intelligence. From this he developed his theory of multiple intelligences, which include the following:

Linguistic intelligence: For Gardner, poetry reflects sensitivity to words with an appreciation of subtle differences in words and meaning as well as their sounds, rhythms and inflections. Linguistic intelligence also includes the use of rhetoric and the facilitation of explanation.

Musical intelligence may manifest in performance or composing and having a sense of pitch, rhythm and timbre.

Logical-mathematical intelligence is the ability to appreciate logical and mathematical thought, as also scientific understanding.

Spatial intelligence involves an ability to perceive the visual world accurately and to draw on that to re-create or modify those perceptions without physical observation. So, for example, one may imagine how an object may look if seen from a different angle, or one may have a facility for working with graphic depictions of three-dimensional objects or scenes.

Bodily kinesthetic intelligence attaches to those people who are able to master their bodies' actions and movements or who are able to manipulate objects with skill and finesse. Dancers, actors and footballers would for example fall into this category.

Personal intelligences: This covers intrapersonal intelligence (understanding and having access to one's personal and emotional life) and interpersonal intelligence (reading and understanding one's relationship with others, their moods and intentions).

Intelligence may also be judged differently according to cultural differences. Behaviour that may be considered intelligent in one culture may be quite differently viewed in another. This gives rise to the concept of *cultural intelligence*, which is the ability to relate and work effectively across cultures.

And as outlined in Chapter 3, there is also the concept of *emotional intelligence*, which concerns the relationship between emotions and rational thought and decision-making and the role of self-awareness, impulse control, empathy and other qualities in our lives.

Quite clearly, intelligence has a range of meanings and contexts and one can understand the continuing difficulty in trying to give it a simple and clear meaning.

Some specialist views of the brain

In addition to the commonly understood neuro-biological and technical aspects of the brain there are also various specialist views and concepts concerning the brain, such as the following.

The mindful brain

Developed by Daniel J. Siegel in *The Mindful Brain: Reflection and Attunement in the Cultivation of Well-being*, the mindful brain has a number of aspects, but the one on which Siegel focuses concerns the relationship between mind and brain, with particular reference to mindfulness – or being aware of our everyday experiences by paying attention to them rather than functioning largely on automatic. It also means that we are aware that we are aware.

The social brain

This refers to the regions of the brain involved in understanding others. A number of people have proposed ideas based on it. Harvard psychologist Matthew D. Lieberman, for example, has written about the social brain and the hypothesis that evolution has made us more social, more connected to and dependent on the social world as the best way to thrive as a species.

Psychology professor Louis Cozolino has written about the brain as a social organ in *The Neuroscience of Human Relationships: Attachment and the Developing Social Brain*. Taking the synapse (being the gap between neurons) as a metaphor, he postulates a social synapse – a gap that exists between people, and which also links us together as social beings in our families, communities, societies and as a species. He examines how people, like neurons, interconnect and link together to create relationships and how brains develop (and have indeed evolved) in the context of social and personal relationships.

Professor Cozolino refers to a social engagement system, developed in early childhood, which regulates the social behaviour of individuals in complex situations. Our ability to attune to others, to empathise and to respond appropriately is a function of the social brain.

> No man is an island,
> Entire of itself,
> Every man is a piece of the continent,
> A part of the main …
>
> (John Donne)

The ethical brain

In the developing field of cognitive neuroscience, Professor Michael Gazzaniga's book *The Ethical Brain* considers the ethical concerns arising from an understanding of the basics of brain development, ageing, belief systems emanating from the brain and other issues. Fascinating questions arise, such as that of free will, and how far legal and criminal responsibility can be attributed to a person whose brain function has become distorted. Can he plead, "My brain made me do it"?

Other ethical issues that are considered in the context of neuroscience and the brain include brain and memory enhancement by the use of drugs (forbidden in sport but are they acceptable in relation to brain function?); embryonic stem-cell research and the moral status of an embryo; whether dementia qualifies as a state in which life-saving measures should no longer be taken; and the role of the brain in arriving at our values.

The spiritual brain

The highly evolved human brain has the capacity for abstract thought and spiritual belief. Neuroscientist Mario Beauregard and Denyse O'Leary consider the question whether religious experiences come from God or are merely the random firing of brain neurons.

Dr Beauregard is a nonmaterialist who does not doubt the possibility of someone having a mystical experience and whose work explores the neural correlates of that experience. In his research with contemplative nuns, he demonstrated that a mystical state of consciousness really existed. His book with Denyse O'Leary, *The Spiritual Brain: A Neuroscientist's Case for the Existence of the Soul*, reviews that study and more generally provides what they describe as a neuroscientific approach to understanding religious, spiritual and mystical experiences.

The mommy brain

A study by leading neuropsychologist Alan Schore shows that during the early period of infancy, mother and child communicate at right-brain level; that is, on an intuitive rather than verbal basis. The mother's right brain serves the infant's developing neural circuitry.

In right-brain mode the mother's body increases the production of the bonding hormone *oxytocin* (one of the side effects of which is some impairment of memory functions) and *endorphins* (neurotransmitters in the brain with pain-relieving qualities). So when a baby's mother feels that her "brain has stopped working", there may be a physiological basis for this. Her body is trying to ensure that she can attune to her baby, connect effectively right brain to right brain, and give the baby's brain function a healthy start.

Katherine Ellison, a Pulitzer Prize winner and author of *The Mommy Brain: How Motherhood Makes Us Smarter*, believes that motherhood enhances the mother's brain function as she copes with myriad different tasks. Traits such as perception, efficiency, resiliency, motivation and emotional intelligence, she says, are present whether one is a good mom or "a CEO of a Fortune 500 company".

The "new" brain

Richard Restak in his 2004 work *The New Brain: How the Modern Age Is Rewiring Your Mind: Research from the Frontiers of Brain Science* raises issues that still warrant consideration. The "new" brain is now accessible through sophisticated computer-driven imaging techniques capable of providing insights that were unimaginable in the past.

There has been a new awareness of brain *plasticity* – the brain's capacity for change by reorganising neural pathways as new experiences and learning are introduced. We are now aware that plasticity continues throughout adult life. Understandings are also developing as to the impact of computers, mobile phones, the Internet and other technological developments on the evolution of the brain. Some of the aspects raised in the book are now dated but the idea of a new and more rapid evolution of the brain remains relevant.

The mind

Is the mind the same as the brain? Or is it something different and if so what is it, where does it reside and what are its functions?

The Penguin Dictionary of Psychology (3rd edition, 2001) describes the mind as "the battered offspring of the union of philosophy and psychology" and includes viewing the mind as separate from the mechanistic systems of the brain, seeing it as a metaphor for neurophysiological brain processes, treating the term as equivalent to the brain, and treating it as synonymous with intelligence.

The view that the mind is different from the brain seems compelling. Whereas the brain is physically visible and tangible, the mind is intangible and has an almost metaphysical aspect, which includes the capacity for thought, consciousness and free will. Without conscious awareness, we refer to the mind as something different from the brain. When we say "I've changed my mind" we don't mean that we've substituted a new brain.

There are different views about the mind's relationship to the brain, for example the *computational theory of mind*, which views the brain and mind as comprising an information-processing system. In this metaphor, the brain may be seen as computer hardware and the mind as the software and its inputs.

In *Five Minds for the Future* Professor Howard Gardner defines five kinds of cognitive abilities by reference to the disciplinary mind, the synthesising mind, the creating mind, the respectful mind and the ethical mind. Clearly these are not different kinds of brain, but rather different ways in which brains may function.

Daniel J. Siegel's book *The Mindful Brain* relates to the brain but in essence deals with the workings of the mind. He defines the mind as "a process that regulates the flow of energy and information" – both within the individual and between people. This is distinct from the brain, which comprises the neural connections and their complex patterns of firing.

Siegel reflects on the fact that the brain and mind correlate their functions, and he considers how this happens, as the brain may create the mind but the mind can activate the brain. The energy and information flow is a two-way process. For

Siegel, evolution has involved not only the development of the brain, but also mental evolution in the way we as a species pass energy and information from one generation to another.

Although the terms "brain" and "mind" may be used interchangeably, the distinction in meaning, often subtle, may need to be noted.

> The mind is its own place, and in itself
> Can make a heaven of hell, a hell of heaven.
> (John Milton (1608–1674), Paradise Lost)

Further reading

The following brain and neuroscience books will help to provide a fuller picture of the matters outlined in this chapter:

Amthor, Frank, *Neuroscience for Dummies* (Wiley, 2012). An informative technical work containing a high level of detail. Certainly not for dummies.

Beauregard, Mario and O'Leary, Denyse, *The Spiritual Brain: A Neuroscientist's Case for the Existence of the Soul* (HarperOne, 2007).

Cozolino, Louis, *The Neuroscience of Human Relationships: Attachment and the Developing Social Brain* (Norton, 2006). Fascinating thoughts about the brain as a social organ – and the relevance of attachment.

Ellison, Katherine, *The Mommy Brain: How Motherhood Makes Us Smarter* (Basic Books, 2006).

Gardner, Howard, *Frames of Mind: The Theory of Multiple Intelligences* and *Five Minds for the Future* (Harvard Business School Press, 2006). Both compelling and well worth reading.

Gazzaniga, Michael S., *The Ethical Brain* (Dana Press, 2005).

Gerhardt, Sue, *Why Love Matters: How Affection Shapes a Baby's Brain* (Brunner-Routledge, 2004). This excellent book effectively outlines how love and attunement are vital to brain development in the early years of life.

Gibb, Barry J., *The Rough Guide to the Brain* (Rough Guides Ltd, 2007).

Goleman, Daniel, *Emotional Intelligence: Why It Can Matter More Than IQ* (Bloomsbury, 1996). A classic work, still relevant.

Kahneman, Daniel, *Thinking Fast and Slow* (Penguin, 2011). A brilliant read.

Pink, Daniel J., *A Whole New Mind: Why Right-Brainers Will Rule the Future* (Marshall Cavendish Business, 2008).

Ramachandran, V. S., *The Tell-Tale Brain: Unlocking the Mystery of Human Nature* (Windmill Books, 2012).

Restak, Richard, *The New Brain: How the Modern Age Is Rewiring Your Mind: Research from the Frontiers of Brain Science* (Rodale, 2004).

Seth, Anil (ed.), *The 30-Second Brain: The 50 Most Mind-Blowing Ideas in Neuroscience, Each Explained in Half a Minute* (Ivy Press, 2014). A succinctly and clearly written work.

Siegel, Daniel J., *The Mindful Brain* (W.W. Norton & Co., 2007). How mindfulness and attunement affect brain function: a study in the field of contemplative neuroscience.

Solms, Mark and Turnbull, Oliver, *The Brain and the Inner World: An Introduction to the Neuroscience of Subjective Experience* (Karnac, 2002).

Zeman, Adam, *A Portrait of the Brain* (New Haven, CT: Yale University Press, 2008).

Chapter 3

Head, heart and gut

Heart – emotions

Credit: Len W

The heart as metaphor?

From time immemorial, the heart has been seen as the symbolic and metaphoric seat of emotions including in particular the symbol of love.

> "He gave her his heart"
> "She wears her heart on her sleeve"
> "He must have a heart of stone"

Other emotions and states associated symbolically with the heart include *courage and will*: "He fought with all his heart"; *kindness*: "She has a heart of gold"; *sympathy*: "My heart goes out to him"; *trust and belief*: "I believe that with all my heart"; *sincerity*: "I'm speaking to you from the heart"; *fear and dread:* "It was a heart-stopping moment" or "My heart was in my stomach"; and *sadness*: "I do this with a heavy heart" or "My heart bleeds for him."

This apparently multi-functional organ of love and emotion is actually, rather prosaically, a muscle that pumps blood around the body. So how has it acquired this widespread metaphorical and symbolical usage and meaning? And how far is there any factual validity in these usages? Do these emotions in some way actually reside in the heart?

Cultural and biblical heritage

People from a wide range of backgrounds and cultures have throughout history had a view of the heart as more than just an organ pumping blood.

In Ancient Egypt, emotions, thought and morality were believed to emanate from the heart, which held a person's mind and soul. In the afterlife, the heart gave evidence for or against the person (and was weighed against a feather to assess its immortality).

The fourth-century BC Greek philosopher and scientist Aristotle considered the heart to be the seat of both intelligence and emotions, and the source of consciousness.

Biblical references to the heart tend to be metaphorical, for example "The wise in heart will receive commandments" (Proverbs 10:8); and "and their heart failed them, and they were afraid" (Genesis 42:28).

By the Renaissance the structures of the heart were better understood, and in the following centuries its functions were increasingly accurately reflected; but this did not stop it also being viewed as a spiritual centre and the seat of the emotions.

Current religions widely refer to the heart in this spiritual and metaphorical sense. So for example, a Christian perspective is likely to include "letting God (or Jesus) into your heart". The Understand Quran Academy provides an Islamic perspective on the heart: its functions include understanding, reflection and reason. "What will save you on the Day of Judgement is *qalbun saleem*—a sound heart." And Judaism's primary prayer, the *Shema*, requires one to "love God with all your heart".

So with millennia of this usage in culture, religion, poetry and everyday language, perhaps it isn't surprising that virtually all modern cultures, while recognising the physiological functions of the heart as a pump, also view it metaphorically as a spiritual and emotional centre.

> When the heart (the center, core and epitome of the entire body being) is intensified in the process of Communion with Life, then Life is magnified, pervading the body–mind universally.
>
> (Adi Da Samraj, *Enlightenment of the Whole Body*)

The heart's physiological role in relation to the brain and emotions

It now seems that some ideas about the heart as metaphor have re-established themselves as possible truisms.

First, neuroscience has developed a picture of the heart as indeed having its own nervous system independent of the brain. This has been described as the heart's own intelligence and as "the brain in the heart" – so that referring to the wisdom of the heart may not simply be metaphor. Whether this may be overstating the case is a matter of some dispute between medical experts. One of the reasons for this is that the heart does indeed have its own network of neurons – cells that electrically transmit information from one part of the body to another. However, not all neurons are brain cells, so the existence of neurons doesn't necessarily mean that there is "brain" function.

There is also a view that the heart's hormonal, chemical and other data are sent to the brain through neural pathways, providing a regulatory role over many autonomic nervous system signals and also cascading into the brain's higher centres, where they may influence perception, decision-making and other cognitive processes.

This leads to the second perspective, which is that at a neurological level there is certainly a two-way communication between heart and brain. For example, when the amygdala reacts to an experience causing a strong emotion such as fear, adrenaline is generated into the blood supply, increasing blood pressure and accelerating the heart rate. The effect of an increasing heart rate is to create or increase anxiety. So these reactions reinforce one another.

In a world of developing understandings, it is clear that the brain is where emotions are based but it seems that there may be an inter-relationship with the heart, which supplements the brain in both influencing and responding to the emotions we experience. But the primary neurological perspective appears to be that the heart is an autonomous robot, obeying signals from elsewhere and that everything else is a metaphor.

To help towards gaining a complete picture of our effective functioning, we should consider the emotions themselves.

Emotions and feelings

Emotional intelligence

Daniel Goleman's seminal 1995 work *Emotional Intelligence* is sub-titled *Why It Can Matter More Than IQ*.

There seems little doubt that intelligence, as ordinarily understood in relation to cognitive thought, logic and reasoning, is a critical factor in enabling a person to adapt to his or her environment, to plan and solve problems, to understand complex ideas and to learn from experience. For well over a century, tests have been devised and used to measure intelligence and to indicate a person's intelligence quotient or IQ.

Yet intelligence clearly embraces more than logic and reasoning. Professor Howard Gardner propounded the Theory of Multiple Intelligences, pointing out that there are different kinds of natural human intelligence in addition to logical-mathematical intelligence including, for example, linguistic intelligence, musical intelligence, spatial intelligence and bodily kinesthetic intelligence. He also mentions personal intelligences – knowledge of self and others.

Emotional intelligence may be viewed against this background. The thesis of Goleman's book is that the rational and the emotional minds mostly work in har-mony "exquisitely coordinated", but that (especially in the light of our evolutionary nature) the emotional mind can prevail, allowing the emotional centres huge power to influence the functioning of the rest of the brain. This of course crucially affects decision-making and all aspects of life.

An outline awareness of emotions and the role that they play is a critical component of professional, and indeed human, understanding. Emotional intelligence involves the understanding and recognition of emotions and feelings, self-awareness, the influences of emotions on decision-making, awareness of feelings and how best to manage them, impulse control and managing social skills.

Kinds of emotions

In seeking to define emotions, the *Penguin Dictionary of Psychology* doubts whether any other term in psychology shares its combination of difficulty to define and frequency of use.

Neuroscientist Antonio Damasio refers to three kinds of emotions, namely primary or universal emotions, secondary or social emotions and background emotions. He considers that these emotions would all share the phenomenon of constituting chemical and neural responses that have a regulatory role in maintaining life and advantageous circumstances.

There is a broad consensus that we have certain basic (or primary or universal) emotions, namely anger, fear, joy (or happiness), sorrow or distress (or sadness), surprise and disgust. Some view happiness and sadness as moods rather than emotions, distinguishing moods as background states that affect one's susceptibility to emotional stimuli.

A second category of emotions has been variously described as secondary emotions, social emotions or higher cognitive emotions. These include, for example, love, shame, guilt, embarrassment, pride, compassion, envy and jealousy.

A third category proposed by Damasio is that of background emotions, such as well-being or malaise, calm or tension, enthusiasm or discouragement, stability or instability. These are closely related to moods, which are sustained low-level emotional states.

The purpose and effect of emotions

Although there may be cultural differences in the way that people express (or hide) their emotions, there is a universality of the six basic emotions in virtually all peoples, nationalities and cultures. This is not surprising, as emotions emanate from the brain, and brain structure and function are the same for all members of the human race.

Some of these basic emotions date back hundreds of millions of years. When facing a sabre-tooth tiger, our ancestor needed a mechanism that would prime the brain and body into an immediate appropriate reaction: fear shifted him from any cognitive response into a spontaneous fight, flight or freeze response, appropriate to the danger.

The amygdala still serves this purpose, providing an immediate bodily response to fear. The autonomic nervous system is activated, the body is primed for action, and the stress hormones adrenaline and cortisol are released. In this condition, the rational part of the brain, the pre-frontal cortex, is temporarily superfluous and is bypassed.

Although we no longer have sabre-tooth tigers, many other things in modern life may induce fear. Encountering a group of hooded youths in a dark road could prepare the body for fight or flight. Other frightening situations may produce the same response, for example giving evidence in court – or for some people even engaging with a professional, who should not be surprised to find some clients not functioning from their optimal cognitive base.

Other emotions such as shame and humiliation may engender the same primitive response in people as fear, making it difficult for them to function entirely rationally while in this state.

Anger, too, had – and continues to have – its role in preparing a person to meet a hostile situation, primed for action, which is more likely to be fight than flight. Like fear, it activates the sympathetic autonomic nervous system, and creates a somatic, often visible, response that may override rational, cognitive processes. Arguably, anger motivates responses to transgression and deters further transgression.

The origins of love and joy lie in the need for the species to reproduce; but this cannot be the complete answer, as love exists widely in a non-sexual context, such as in a mother's love for a child. Again, the body's responses in producing chemicals play a part. In romantic love, the chemical dopamine is released which is associated with the "reward" system of the brain, providing a rush of pleasure. In other kinds of love, arising from recognition and attachment, the chemicals vasopressin and oxytocin (which also enhances bonding) are released.

Other emotions had similar evolutionary purposes. Surprise as a reaction to an unexpected event or threat provided a bodily response that might be needed for survival; and disgust is widely understood to have originated as a survival response to coming across putrid food.

Emotions have an invaluable role in human life. At a biological level, they help to provide appropriate responses to stimuli that we constantly face, whether threatening or pleasurable. In particular, they regulate the bodily state. They also combine with our cognitive functions to enable us to make effective decisions. And emotions inform us, helping us to interpret communications and relationships, and provide similar information to others about us.

In his book *The Feeling of What Happens: Body, Emotion and the Making of Consciousness* Antonio Damasio dismisses the notion of emotions as some sort of optional luxury and describes them rather as an inherent part of the mechanisms regulating survival. Despite being old in evolution he calls them "a fairly high-level component of the mechanisms of life regulation".

Feelings and consciousness

Understandably, we may regard emotions and feelings as synonymous but there is a distinction. A feeling is the conscious awareness of an emotion. The body state may be changed by the production of chemicals, by neural signals and by muscular contraction, all of which combine to bring the emotion into consciousness. Without having the feeling, we may be experiencing the emotion without awareness of its presence.

Emotionally sensitive people may readily find their emotions converted into feelings, but many others may experience emotions without actually being aware of them. Counselling and psychotherapy may have as one of its objectives bringing these unconscious emotions into consciousness so that they can be understood and addressed.

Consciousness, it may be said, embodies a greater sense of non-verbal knowing and feeling, of integration of perceptions, thoughts, sensations and emotions, and a subjective understanding of one's own existence.

Emotions: reality and myths

A professional is expected to maintain objectivity and a rational, thoughtful and clinical approach rather than a purely emotional one. To take a somewhat clichéd example, one would not want one's brain surgeon to become emotional during brain surgery.

However, professionals are also generally expected to be sensitive and responsive to the feelings and needs of their clients and patients, caring and "human". One would not want an oncologist informing his patient that she has irreversible and imminently life-threatening cancer, in a cold and offhand manner (though alas, this may happen).

From the professional's perspective, we would like our clients and patients to be reasonable, rational and realistic in relation to whatever we have been asked to deal with. We can understand that some aspects may perhaps evoke an emotional response, but we will want and expect them to get past those emotions and deal in a proper way with their issues.

However, the reality is that emotions, perhaps unconscious, are commonly likely to influence professionals and clients: purely rational decision-making may in many cases be a myth.

The myth of rational decision-making

It is comforting to believe that all important decisions will be made on a considered and rational basis. The pros can be carefully weighed against the cons and a balanced and well-considered decision made.

The problem, however, is that many important issues involve personal and emotional elements that can't be easily separated from the rational aspects, particularly, for example, with issues involving conflict, health, financial concerns, relationship problems, educational concerns and indeed most decisions on which professionals might be consulted.

In practice, few such decisions can be made entirely unemotionally, either by the professional or more especially by the client. In most cases there may be a struggle between emotional and rational forces, "between head and heart".

Many decisions involve a balance between rational, emotional and intuitive responses. The classic example is whether or not one can trust somebody – imagine making this judgement on the basis of either facts and logic alone, or emotion and intuition alone. Clearly this judgement needs to be made on the basis of all of these factors working in harmony.

Dan Ariely, Professor of Behavioural Economics and founder of the wonderfully named Center for Advanced Hindsight, in his book *Predictably Irrational: The Hidden Forces that Shape our Decisions*, believes that we are not only irrational, but predictably so, consistently overpaying, underestimating and procrastinating. He believes that we systematically and predictably fail to understand the profound effects of our emotions on what we want.

> The only real surprise is not that people, and the professionals who minister to them in their difficulties in varied capacities, are predictably irrational, but that we should expect them to be calm rational actors in such circumstances. More often than not, momentary bouts of reason and reflection are interspersed with spats and bursts of irrationality—emotional responses sometimes seemingly out of nowhere, illogic of varying degrees, faulty or skewed memories of events, and perceptions of people infiltrated by a multitude of biases, some blatantly apparent and many others more subtle and unwittingly in play.
>
> (Robert Benjamin, *On Becoming a Rationally Irrational Negotiator/Mediator: The 'Messy' Human Brain and the 'Myth of Rationality'*)

The myth that "negative emotions" are bad

The concept of "positive" and "negative" emotions is widely accepted. Love, happiness and joy, serenity and contentment are generally considered to be positive because they indicate well-being, have a pleasant subjective feel and have positive social implications. Anger, fear, sadness, hate, disgust and jealousy are examples of what are generally considered to be negative emotions, so called because they indicate some form of distress, are subjectively unpleasant and often painful, are viewed as inimical to rational thinking, and have some negative social implications.

There is a commonly held view that negative emotions are bad for us and hence are to be avoided or overcome. This is largely implicit in calling them "negative".

Negative words are not uncommonly seen as being related to negative attitudes, which in turn are perceived as limiting and damaging one's life. One recognises intuitively that there is validity in this proposition; but this may disguise and distort the fact that so-called negative emotions may be appropriate, valuable and, paradoxically, even positive.

For example, anger may be entirely appropriate where one's own – or indeed others' – rights, feelings or boundaries have been deliberately violated or abused, or where one faces an unacceptable attack or threat, physically, verbally or emotionally. The anger may be a necessary precursor to appropriate action: without it one may not be motivated to act effectively. This is equally applicable at a micro level to one's own life, where one may be responding angrily to a false accusation, and at a macro level, where communal anger has brought about necessary social and political change.

Sadness is of course an entirely appropriate emotional response to loss. The loss may be of any kind: death of a loved one, or loss of physical capacity through illness. Observing an act of depravity or receiving rancid food would disgust most people. Envy may be a motivator to taking steps to achieve for oneself whatever has been identified as the object of that emotion. Hatred may be a natural and appropriate emotional reaction to evil.

Other considerations may further complicate these issues:

- In all cases, proportionality may be relevant. Disproportionate anger may be inappropriate and may require anger management and interminable grief may become pathological.
- The brain's pre-frontal cortex has the task of mediating emotional reactions, and importing some rational element into emotional responses. We thus have the capacity over time to check that our emotional reactions are well based and proportionate and to moderate our responses where necessary. That of course is not always easy or possible where the emotions are strong or wholly unconscious.
- Attitudes are also affected by people's world views: their belief systems whether personal, religious, ethical or ideological. So for example, a religious injunction may be that "Thou shall not hate"; and the Ten Commandments instruct people not to covet others' property (or wives) which would affect some attitudes towards envy.

The myth that "venting" an emotion will resolve it

There is a widely held belief that allowing a person to express anger or other emotion will help to clear it, often referred to as "venting" the emotion – obtaining some sort of cathartic relief. It is even encouraged by some mental health professionals as an end in itself.

Like many other misconceptions, there is some basis of validity in this. There may be some cathartic relief in expressing an emotion like anger (the term "venting" has a patronising quality), which in some cases will allow the person to move on temporarily. Where the emotion is spontaneous and not deeply rooted, the cathartic release may well be lasting.

However:

- Deep-seated emotional responses that have become problematic can't be resolved simply by expressing or "venting" them and may need skilled professional support, possibly over time, to help move through the underlying issues. Otherwise the emotion is likely to re-surface as soon as the beliefs that generated it return.
- Venting anger can have the opposite effect to that intended: the memory may rekindle the experience and reinforce the anger. Various tests have found that "venting" is actually a very poor anger-management strategy.
- The pre-frontal cortex needs time to assimilate and assess data. Having time and space for reflection may often be a better way to help someone deal with anger or any other strong emotion than expressing and reinforcing it. Writing reflectively (but without "ranting") can sometimes also be beneficial in gaining better insights and understandings.
- If someone is caught up in expressing their anger or any other emotion, it may be helpful to allow them to do so for a little while rather than trying to cut them off mid-stream. However, this should generally be time-limited. While allowing a person to express anger can sometimes be beneficial, helping the person back into a cognitive process may be the best way forward, unless working with them in a therapeutic context.

The myth that women are emotional but men are not

On television, there was a stereotypical response by one woman to another enquiring whether her boyfriend had discussed certain relationship problems that she had raised: "Of course not – he's a bloke, isn't he?"

Here again, the myth is based on some solid observations. Anyone working professionally with couples in conflict is likely to notice that in many cases – though by no means all – the woman is likely to be more overtly emotional than the man, readier to show her feelings. There is almost an expectation that this will be the case.

John Gray's *Men Are from Mars, Women Are from Venus* identifies some of the differences of language and communication between men and women. Barbara and Allan Pease's *Why Men Don't Listen and Women Can't Read Maps* explains some of the emotional and linguistic differences between the sexes leading to miscommunication.

While there are some gender differences in the way people present and communicate their emotions and demonstrate their feelings, the generalised myth distorts the complex reality of the position.

- During the first four to five years or so of childhood, boys and girls experience and express the full range of human emotions without gender distinction.
- As children mature into adulthood, socialisation takes place and expectations may influence gender roles. For example, in Western societies, women tend more commonly to have nurturing roles, whereas men tend to have a role of providing material resources. Of course, there are many and increasing exceptions to this. However, that is broadly still the dominant cultural position.
- Part of this socialisation involves men refraining from expressing intense emotions publicly. However, this relates to expressing the feelings of those emotions, and does not mean that men do not have the same emotions, albeit that these may commonly be buried at some level or expressed privately.
- While men may suppress many of their feelings, some interesting research has shown that there is a gender-specific pattern in the way men and women respond to emotions. It seems that there is a correlation between emotions that demonstrate power, such as anger and contempt, which men are ready to display, and emotions that indicate powerlessness and inability to cope with negative events, such as fear, sadness, guilt and blame, which women may be more prone to display. Men are not readily expected to show vulnerable, tender and powerless emotions, save in some very specific contexts.
- There may be some cross-cultural variation in this experience, depending on the different roles women play in different societies. There are, however, indications that even where there is greater gender equality, this does not necessarily result in men adopting the emotions demonstrating powerlessness, whereas in such cases women are more able to express powerful emotions such as anger.
- Of course, these are generalisations, and there are likely to be many variations between individuals. We no doubt all know men who are able to express their feelings readily and conversely women who do not find it easy to do so.

Further relevance of emotions

This basic outline of emotions will serve partly as an introduction to the subject and partly as a foundation for addressing some of these concepts in greater detail in other chapters.

> If your emotional abilities aren't in hand, if you don't have self-awareness, if you are not able to manage your distressing emotions, if you can't have empathy and have effective relationships, then no matter how smart you are, you are not going to get very far.
>
> (Daniel Goleman, *Emotional Intelligence: Why It Can Matter More Than IQ*)

Further reading

Many of the books mentioned in Chapter 2 are likely to be relevant to emotions, inasmuch as the brain is also the emotional centre. In addition, the following books may be of interest:

Ariely, Dan, *Predictably Irrational: The Hidden Forces that Shape our Decisions* (HarperCollins, 2009). This book is also relevant to the subject of intuition.

Damasio, Antonio, *The Feeling of What Happens: Body, Emotion and the Making of Consciousness* (Vintage, 2000). This book provides wonderfully clear explanations of consciousness and emotions, with technical detail.

Damasio, Antonio, *Self Comes to Mind: Constructing the Conscious Brain* (Vintage, 2012).

Evans, Dylan, *Emotion: The Science of Sentiment* (Oxford University Press, 2001).

Gardner, Howard, *Frames of Mind: The Theory of Multiple Intelligences* (Fontana Press, 2nd edition, 1993).

Goleman, Daniel, *Emotional Intelligence: Why It Can Matter More Than IQ* (Bloomsbury, 1996).

Gray, John, *Men Are from Mars, Women Are from Venus* (HarperCollins 2002; also new edition HarperElement, 2012). Lightly written, this uses metaphor and humour to illustrate common gender conflicts. Gray has written other books with a similar theme.

Pease, Allan and Pease, Barbara, *Why Men Don't Listen and Women Can't Read Maps* (Orion, 2001).

Tannen, Deborah, *You Just Don't Understand: Women and Men in Conversation* (Virago, 1992).

Head, heart and gut

Gut – intuition

Credit: CartoonStock.com

Gut as metaphor?

In the same way that the heart is commonly used by way of metaphor for emotions, so "gut" is a universal metaphor for intuition.

"I feel it in my gut"
"Gut feelings don't lie"
"My gut reaction is to leave"

Once again, as with the heart, we may reflect on whether "gut" is just a metaphor, or whether it is based on any bodily reality.

Columbia University Professor Michael Gershon researched this question extensively over decades. His book *The Second Brain* led to some radical new understandings about the relationship between the brain and the stomach and intestines and how this linked to gastrointestinal illness and influenced our mental states.

The "second brain" – technically the "enteric nervous system" – consists of some 100 million neurons contained within the alimentary canal, using neurotransmitters (chemicals that transmit signals between neurons) including dopamine, which is relevant to the body's reward system, and serotonin, which contributes to a feeling of well-being. The enteric nervous system enables the gut to control the digestive system independently of the brain; and significantly it also carries messages between the gut and the brain.

Although the gut does not have any cognitive function nor does it hold or directly regulate emotions, all of these being functions of the brain, everyday emotional well-being and mood may be affected by messages from the gut to the brain.

Various physical feelings, such as stress, fear and excitement may all be reflected by gut reactions, including for example "butterflies in the stomach" or diarrhoea. Stress affects the links between brain and gut and in many cases may lead to a range of gastrointestinal disorders including inflammatory bowel disease, irritable bowel syndrome (IBS) and other gastrointestinal diseases, peptic ulcer and GERD (gastroesophageal reflux disease).

The concept of a "gut feeling" seems to have originated because of the effect that an intuition may have on us: the automatic, unconscious and perhaps visceral reaction that we may experience, a "feeling in the pit of the stomach". So although it may be metaphorical, it does indeed have a basis in reality.

> There is a voice that doesn't use words. Listen.
>
> (Rumi)

Intuition

Intuition and gut feelings have a profound influence on our decisions and actions, affecting us as professionals and in our daily lives, and of course affecting the decisions, actions and lives of our clients and patients. It is vital for a well-rounded professional to have an understanding of intuition and its value, and, equally, its limitations and dangers.

What do we mean by intuition?

Intuition is "a mode of understanding or knowing characterised as direct and immediate and occurring without conscious thought or judgment" (*Penguin Dictionary of Psychology*, 3rd edition). It is the sense of feeling spontaneously that we know something, that we recognise what to do, or feel whether something is right or wrong, without going through a logical, rational, reasoning process.

Within this definition there are at least two different kinds of intuition, namely:

- Intuition as intelligence of the unconscious, drawing on our five senses: vision, hearing, smell, taste and touch, and on our memory and experience. Within this, intuition may manifest itself in different ways, which may be very relevant to us as professionals as well as sentient beings.
- Intuition drawing on some "sixth sense", which may range from a form of psychic intuition to a creative process informing artists and scientists alike.

Everyday and expert intuition

Intuition is a cognitive process supported by the right side of the brain. It is perhaps ironic that the subject of intuition is considered by left-brain processing – in a rational, logical way.

It is not uncommon for people to regard intuition as somehow less trustworthy or important than rational decision-making – a sort of flighty sibling who doesn't really take life seriously. Yet intuitions affect so many aspects of our lives. Is a relationship well founded? What direction should one take in one's career? Will a proposed course of action prove to be right or wrong? Whom do you employ after interviewing a range of applicants?

More prosaically, intuition plays a role in deciding whether or not to buy a product, whether to return a phone call now or later, what to wear for any occasion and an unlimited range of daily decisions that we may not even perceive as being decisions.

For professionals, there are some particular aspects that are relevant to our expertise: what we might term "expert intuition". The ability of an experienced engineer to identify the cause of a malfunction in a machine, or of a physician to diagnose the cause of an illness, or a lawyer to spot potential problems in a draft contract – all are using insight that is the product of experience. Experience can develop in us an ability to read patterns of behaviour, to spot irregularities, to extrapolate from past events and predict how events are likely to unfold.

Most professionals are also likely to have experienced a crossover between expert and everyday intuition. How many professionals have written or said something one day, and then later, perhaps in the early hours of the next morning, have suddenly woken up to a realisation that there was something else that might have been said? Perhaps one might become aware in a flash of insight that what one said could be viewed or heard differently by the recipient, or might be misconstrued. The unconscious plays a huge part in guiding us.

It is this ability to draw unconsciously on the experience of one's senses and on all the data stored in one's mind that allows a professional to make spontaneous judgements coherently and effectively. This is not an analytical process. An experienced courtroom lawyer does not make a conscious analysis of all the evidence and the history of the witness when deciding spontaneously whether one tone, strategy or way of questioning will be better than another.

> Intuition will tell the thinking mind where to look next.
>
> (Jonas Salk)

In *Blink: The Power of Thinking without Thinking* Malcolm Gladwell writes about the value of the first two seconds of intuitive response to any situation. He gives an example of expert intuition. The J. Paul Getty Museum wanted to buy a sixth-century BC Greek statue but weren't sure of its authenticity so had technical tests done to check this before deciding that it was genuinely old, and buying it. A year or so after the purchase, an expert in this field took one look at the statue, went cold and decided that it was a fake. He based this on an "intuitive repulsion". Further investigation proved him and his intuition correct: it was a fake.

This example distinguishes expert intuition from everyday intuition. The intuition of the expert who intuitively identified the fake was dependent on his specialist knowledge and experience. Someone who didn't have that expertise would not have had that intuition. So our expert intuitions are broadly reliant on the level of our expertise as well as the acuity of our intuition.

This does introduce some concerns about expert intuition, since it depends in large part on the subjective experience of the professional. Gladwell points out how powerful our unconscious is, but also how fallible it is and how it can be distracted. Intuitive responses may be influenced by competing interests, emotions and sentiments and may be fragile and sometimes biased. Hence this chapter will also address the perils of intuition.

A sixth sense?

As the name indicates, a sixth sense is the taking in of information from the environment that doesn't come through smell, taste, touch, sight or hearing. One's perceptions may have come from other sources, hence this is also called extra-sensory perception or ESP.

This may be understood in different ways. There are those who believe in some form of psychic or paranormal intuition, including telepathy and clairvoyance. On this view, intuition is synonymous with subtle perception ability – beyond the understanding of the intellect but understood through the development of spiritual practice.

Others are sceptical and dismissive of this form of sixth-sense intuition, which they consider to be simply a trick of the mind. ESP is explained as taking something in through the senses without having had time to process it, or picking up subtle clues that are not noticed. Clearly there are very different belief systems at work between these two views.

Creative and predictive intuition

Another kind of intuition that doesn't rely directly on the five senses is one that creative people and even scientists recognise, which has been described as "creative intuition", arising in different fields as varied as the arts and problem-solving. Alongside this sits "predictive intuition" which uses known information, often only partial, to form new ideas: from this arises hunches and hypotheses. Intuition and creativity may be regarded as integral components of much research, working in tandem with one another.

Physicist Albert Einstein, who was also a fine amateur violinist and pianist, pointed out that the greatest scientists "are artists as well". His insights are reported to have come, as they do for artists, from intuition and inspiration. He attributed his scientific insight and intuition largely to music. Many people involved in research will agree that new ideas are the result of hunches developed and revisited over time – supplemented by a great deal of solid painstaking work.

Complementary thinking

Intuition alone is not a substitute for reasoning and logic. Effective cognitive functioning is a combination of (right-brain) intuitive and (left-brain) rational-analytical thinking. The *corpus callosum* connects the two halves of the brain and facilitates communication between them – essential for effective brain function.

These "two ways of knowing" need to work in concert, though there are times when each may have precedence. Most commonly, intuitive responses come first, but when addressing complex and uncertain tasks, when working with computational complexity, when addressing competing claims in an adjudicative way, or when researching and recording factual data, the prevailing need is likely to be for analysis.

> The two operations of our understanding, intuition and deduction, on which alone we have said we must rely in the acquisition of knowledge.
>
> (René Descartes)

Heuristics

There are many situations in which we need to make an instant decision without going through a reflective process. This is assisted by the use of heuristics – mental shortcuts made without conscious awareness, or "rules of thumb", which enable us to jump to very quick conclusions. In *Gut Feelings*, Gerd Gigerenzer describes a heuristic as "fast and frugal" because it needs only minimal information to solve a problem.

So, for example, a person may use a "familiarity heuristic" by acting in the same way as he or she did when dealing with something similar previously; or may follow an "authority heuristic" when simply accepting the opinion of a person who is an authority on a subject.

We use countless heuristics in everyday life. We may form a view about the way a person is reacting based on their body language, for example, taking them to be defensive and guarded if their arms are firmly crossed. We may accept terms and conditions without reading them because we believe that they must be reasonable. If we see a large number of members of an ethnic community eating at an ethnic restaurant, we may decide to eat there on the assumption that the food must be good.

These heuristics may work well in most circumstances generally and facilitate snap judgements, but they are also vulnerable to bias and error.

Intuition cautions

If intuitive responses are influenced by one's experience and expertise, then they can correspondingly be influenced by innate and often unconscious biases, prejudices and emotions, by errors, misperceptions and misremembered data. The advice to "trust your intuition" is generally well founded, but on its own is potentially dangerous. Perhaps it should be: "Trust your intuition as a starting point, but check it out against objective data and verifiable criteria"; less snappy but more reliable.

David G. Myers encapsulated this dichotomy in the title of his book *Intuition: Its Powers and Perils*. A number of psychologists and other writers have identified these biases and perceptual errors, some of which are outlined below.

Availability error

The "availability heuristic" is a mental shortcut in which one relies on knowledge that comes to mind readily and is easily available and able to be recalled. The problem, however, is that one is likely to give greater credence to this knowledge and may overestimate its relevance.

So, for example, if there are a few media reports about someone drowning on a particular stretch of coast, you may have a perception that drowning is a high risk when visiting that area, which may not be the case at all. Or if a friend mentions how well his bread-making machine works, you may be tempted to buy the same make when viewing machines in a shop, without having checked reviews or established whether he may just have been lucky.

Stories that may be atypical and narratives that are dramatic tend to become embedded in our minds and may assume a disproportionate power when drawn on. First impressions and existing beliefs can be hard to shake off. This is notable among professionals who may have been trained in any aspect according to one of a number of competing models or belief systems: there is a greater tendency for them to believe that the model or way of practising that they were taught is better than the competing ways.

The halo (and devil) effect

This is a tendency to develop a bias in favour of a person based on one particular good trait or characteristic, and to assume that he or she is likely to have other good traits or characteristics.

So a person who appears to be generally likeable and who creates a good impression is likely to create an unconscious bias that he or she has other good characteristics, for example is likely to be honourable and perhaps smart. There is also research indicating that people who are attractive are favourably viewed and endowed with a halo effect, an assumption that they also have positive attributes. There may be an assumption that celebrities are likely to be good people because they are famous.

The halo effect has application in many fields of activity and life. We may place more value on what a verbally fluent person says than may be warranted by the content of what is said. In marketing, if a product establishes a good name, people are more likely to trust other products from the same company. In business, people may wrongly assume that the success of one aspect of a business or professional practice indicates that it is successful as a whole.

The corollary of the halo effect is the reverse halo effect, also called the "devil effect", whereby we may form a negative impression of a person generally on one negative trait or characteristic.

Framing effect

In this heuristic, decisions are made on the basis of the framework in which they are presented. For example, people tend to respond more positively to a proposed procedure that is said to have a 50 per cent success rate than if told that it has a 50 per cent failure rate. This phenomenon has application in most fields of professional activity.

The way in which any facts or issues are framed can change the way the information is perceived. The same facts may be presented neutrally or with a sense of moral outrage; and each will have a different impact on the person hearing them. The way words are used will have a different effect. There are countless examples: people may either be "freedom fighters" or "terrorists"; or reference to a car "colliding with" people will have a different effect to being told that the car "smashed into" them.

In counselling and other activities involving decision-making, one of the skills that may be taught is reframing. This is a communication skill in which a statement with a negative connotation is reworded to place it in a more acceptable frame of reference. So, for example, a reference to someone being "obstinate" or "stubborn" may be reframed as their being "strong-minded".

Fundamental attribution error

This is a tendency to interpret another's actions as resulting from an internal disposition or trait, while giving inadequate regard to the circumstances in which that person is acting. People are categorised because of a belief that they have the innate traits resulting in those actions.

So, for example, there is a common tendency in some families to typecast individual members: "That is typical of him, he always acts immaturely." Similarly, professionals may acquire, and give others, reputations for certain kinds of behaviour, and then their subsequent actions are attributed to that behaviour.

A branch of the fundamental attribution error is the "group attribution error", in which a person's behaviour is attributed to his or her belonging to a group with those perceived characteristics, which may be defined by nationality, race, ethnicity, religion, culture, gender or indeed any other kind of group. It seems that this attribution is stronger the more dissimilar the group is perceived to be from one's own group.

Closely related to these errors is the "correspondence bias"; that is, a tendency to attribute a correspondence between a person's actions and his personality. So, for example, seeing someone shout at someone else may lead to a conclusion that he or she is an angry person.

The representativeness heuristic

This heuristic may apply when we have to make a judgement with inadequate data and we assess its likelihood by comparing it to an existing prototype that we have in our mind.

David G. Myers cites an example. You are told about someone – in the US – who is short, slim and likes to read poetry. Is the latter more likely to be an Ivy League classics professor or a truck driver? For many, the answer would be a classics professor because this fits their image of a prototypical classics professor rather than a truck driver. However, an analysis would show that there are only about 40 Ivy League classics professors in the US and that perhaps a half of them are short and slim, reducing the available number to 20. Assuming that half of them might like to read poetry, there are only ten people likely to fit the description. On the other hand, there are about 400,000 truck drivers in the US. Even assuming that only one in eight are short and slim and that only 1 per cent would read poetry, that still leaves 500 short, slim truck drivers who like to read poetry. So it is 50 times more likely that the person described would be a truck driver.

The overconfidence effect

This applies when a person's subjective confidence in their judgement or beliefs is not justified by the objective facts. It seems that we overestimate our knowledge and our ability to predict.

Interestingly, this applies to professionals and experts as much as to laypeople. Indeed, experts may sometimes be even more overconfident than laypeople – whether in economics, politics, business, medicine or law.

Two research projects are interesting. In one, the American Psychological Society published research findings in 2010 by Jane Goodman-Delahunty and her colleagues, *Insightful or Wishful: Lawyers' Ability to Predict Case Outcomes*, in which they investigated US lawyers' realism in predictions. Their overall findings were that lawyers were overconfident in their predictions, irrespective of the extent of their legal experience. Female lawyers showed evidence of slightly less overconfidence.

In the other, Professor Jeffrey J. Rachlinski and Magistrate Judge Andrew W. Wistrich published a research paper in the *South California Law Review* (2013: 101) – "How Lawyers' Intuitions Prolong Litigation". They suggest that several cognitive illusions produce intuitions in lawyers that can induce them to postpone negotiations or to reject settlement proposals that should be accepted.

This is not peculiar to lawyers. Overconfidence arises in a wide range of professions. Other research indicates that while the great majority of medical diagnoses are correct, there are exceptions when ordinarily effective cognitive processes fail and overconfidence results in an incorrect diagnosis. Financial professionals are notoriously prone to overconfidence, both individually and corporately. Indeed, arguably the international financial crises in the first decade of the twenty-first century could be said to be significantly attributable to the overconfidence of those responsible for managing major financial institutions.

Our extraordinary facility at forming explanations to support our beliefs results in our placing too much faith in them instead of carefully examining alternatives.

(Stuart Sutherland, *Irrationality*)

Anchoring

This involves relying on initial information provided or an initial offer made, which serves as a cognitive "anchor", when considering a course of action or undertaking negotiations. The anchor establishes an unconscious bias against which other options are measured.

It seems that even where the person receiving the information or offer regards it as wrong and does not accept it, any response may nevertheless be unconsciously influenced by the anchor. Adjustments made in response to it may therefore turn out to be inadequate and closer to the anchor than might be appropriate.

Sunk costs fallacy

"Sunk costs" refer to costs that have already been incurred and cannot be recovered. The fallacy is in irrationally persisting in a course of action that is objectively inappropriate simply because one doesn't want to regard those costs as wasted; yet such persistence is actually or potentially unproductive or even prejudicial.

For example, you have prepaid for a theatre ticket but on the night you feel exhausted and unwell and the play has had poor reviews. You push yourself to go because you have already paid notwithstanding the fact that had you not prepaid you would certainly not have chosen to go. Or you have spent significant time and personal resource on a training course that is clearly increasingly inappropriate for you, but you continue with it so as not to feel that you have wasted the time and energy already put into it.

The sunk costs fallacy translates into a wide range of personal and professional situations where money, time, energy or any other resource has been put into a project, course of action or relationship that clearly needs to be abandoned or varied.

Some other factors and biases affecting intuition

The above list is by no means exhaustive. Many other biases and factors can influence intuition, including:

Belief systems and prejudices: Given that our intuitions draw on our memory, experience and expertise, it follows that our intuitions are likely to be affected by our belief systems, cultural and social backgrounds and our prejudices. If racism, sexism, homophobia, Islamophobia, anti-Semitism, ageism or indeed any other form of discrimination is ingrained in one, it is inevitable that this will be reflected in one's intuitive responses. Similarly, our cultural and social experience and memory will impact on our intuition.

Risk biases: Individuals' intuitive responses to risk will vary, depending on how they value certainty relative to risk. This is further addressed in Chapter 14.

The confirmation bias: This is a tendency to select and interpret information in a way that confirms one's beliefs and to ignore or minimise the relevance of information that undermines or contradicts one's beliefs. This bias reinforces the overconfidence effect outlined above. The reasons proposed for this bias include wishful thinking, and also a limited cognitive capacity to process information effectively.

Triggers of influence: These include, for example, *perceptual contrast*, where bad news or a low offer is preceded by even worse news or an even lower offer, to make the eventual one more palatable; or *reciprocation*, a tendency to recognise obligations and to reciprocate them in some way, including reciprocating concessions, as where one may accept a less bad option where the other party agrees to reduce his claim or request and the reciprocation takes the form of accepting the concession.

Further reading

Gary Klein's *The Power of Intuition* provides a practical guide to developing and using intuition: how to build it, apply it and safeguard it, with examples and decision-making exercises.

David G. Myers' *Intuition: Its Powers and Perils* addresses the value of developing intuition and the dangers of relying on it.

The Tipping Point author Malcolm Gladwell's readable *Blink: The Power of Thinking without Thinking* is described as being "all about those moments when we 'know' something without knowing why".

Gerd Gigerenzer's *Gut Feelings: The Intelligence of the Unconscious* explains heuristics – shortcuts to decision-making, and "gut feelings in action".

Robert B. Cialdini's *Influence: Science and Practice* questions why and how we are influenced or influence others.

Irrationality by Stuart Sutherland in an updated edition deals with the prevalence of irrationality in everyday life and among professionals and how the mind can make errors.

Many books are available dealing with specialist aspects of intuition, for example Dr Judith Orloff's *Guide to Intuitive Healing: Five Steps to Physical, Emotional, and Sexual Wellness* or Dean Nimmer's *Art from Intuition: Overcoming Your Fears and Obstacles to Making Art*.

There are many books on intuition written on a sixth sense or psychic basis including, for example, Shakti Gawain's *Developing Intuition: Practical Guidance for Daily Life* or *The Time Has Come ... to Accept Your Intuitive Gifts!* by Sonia Choquette.

Chapter 5

The hidden power of the unconscious

Doctor, last night I made a Freudian slip.
I was having dinner with my mother and wanted to say:
"Could you please pass the butter."
But instead I said: "I hate you... You rotten pig!"

Credit: Blifaloo.com

Don't mention the war

Dagwood Bumstead and Basil Fawlty

In an American cartoon strip, Blondie asks her husband Dagwood to answer the doorbell and let in a rather large neighbour, telling him that it's Mrs Jones, and that she's rather sensitive about being fat, he shouldn't say anything about it. As he goes to the door, Blondie again emphasises that he should not say anything about her being fat. As Dagwood opens the door, he welcomes his neighbour with the words: "Come in, Mrs Jones. Would you like a cup of fat?"

In a 1975 episode of the classic British comedy television series *Fawlty Towers*, German visitors are staying at the hotel and manager Basil Fawlty (John Cleese) is required to avoid mentioning the war. However, after doing so by mistake, he seems unable to stop himself blurting out repeated references to the war, with rather excruciating embarrassment.

Fawlty Towers has turned the phrase "Don't mention the war" into a reminder about things that we shouldn't talk about in certain circumstances. But as both Basil Fawlty and Dagwood Bumstead discovered the unconscious mind has other ideas and can play tricks on us, bringing things to the surface that we might have wanted to keep suppressed.

These are examples of *Freudian slips* (or *parapraxes*), which are verbal errors such as slips of the tongue or misreading, caused by the unconscious mind.

Fundamental relevance of the unconscious

The unconscious is not just some interesting abstract concept, but has fundamental importance to every human being, and direct relevance to professionals and their clients and patients. It is the part of our functioning that, by definition, we cannot access through conscious thought. And yet it profoundly influences our thinking, our actions, our personalities, our decision-making and our lives.

There are different views about the nature of the unconscious, whether indeed it exists, and how it functions. There is also an overlap between the unconscious automaticity of the brain, with its support for the basic workings of the body and the carrying out of tasks embedded in the memory such as driving, and its under-lying role and effect in the way we live, establish our belief systems, make our decisions, form our intuitions and send unintentional messages to others by our words, expressions or actions.

As professionals and as human beings we need to be aware of the power and function of the unconscious, which will help us to understand, and perhaps to regulate, the forces underlying and powerfully influencing the decisions and actions that we and our clients and patients take.

Freud's unconscious

Sigmund Freud (1856–1939) revolutionised ideas about the mind and the extent of control that an individual has over it. He distinguished between the conscious mind (the rational part of our mental process) and the unconscious mind (with feelings, thoughts, urges and memories outside our conscious awareness). He considered that unacceptable impulses and desires and painful emotions were repressed and thrust out of consciousness into the unconscious where they influenced our behaviour, even though we were unaware of this.

Freud considered that the process of psychoanalysis could help shift content from the unconscious mind into consciousness.

Anthony Storr, in his biography of Freud, points out that the concept of the unconscious was not invented by Freud, but that he gave it clinical application and made it operational.

In fact, the roots of the unconscious and indeed of present-day psychotherapy can be traced back to various forms of primitive healing, for example by medicine men, witch doctors and shamans. Healing might involve a ritualistic ceremony of searching for and retrieving part of a lost soul or demonstrating the apparent extraction and disposal of a disease-object, which helped recovery. Belief in this treatment had a healing quality: clearly recovery was assisted by the unconscious mind. This was an early form of psychology.

Nineteenth-century discoveries about hypnotism, hysteria and multiple personalities were forerunners to the development of concepts of the unconscious. The social and political climate, with Darwin's Theory of Evolution, Marx's dialectics and Nietzsche's attacks against prevailing ideologies, provided its backdrop. By the end of the nineteenth century, the concept of the unconscious was accepted.

> The concept of the unconscious has long been knocking at the gates of psychology and asking to be let in. Philosophy and literature have often toyed with it, but science could find no use for it. Psychoanalysis has seized upon the concept, has taken it seriously and has given it a fresh content ... But ... being conscious ... remains the one light which illuminates our path and leads us through the darkness of mental life ... our scientific work in psychology will consist in translating unconscious processes into conscious ones, and thus filling in the gaps in conscious perception.
> (Sigmund Freud, "Some Elementary Lessons in Psychoanalysis" in *The Standard Edition of the Complete Psychological Works of Sigmund Freud*, Volume XXIII)

Jung's collective unconscious and "shadow"

Carl Gustav Jung supported various of Freud's ideas, but diverged from others and broke from Freud and psychoanalysis, developing a system which he called *analytical psychology*.

Jung believed that apart from the individual's personal unconscious, everyone also had a *collective unconscious* (or *objective psyche*), the inherited deposit of the past experience of the human race: "the seat of universal primordial images, the *archetypes*". Archetypes are universal ideas, images or themes that appear in the form of myths or symbols.

One of Jung's archetypes is the *shadow*: unacceptable aspects of one's own personality that one prefers not to look at too closely, and that one may project onto other people. In *Jung and the Story of Our Time*, Laurens van der Post referred to Jung's *projection* as "a primordial mechanism in the spirit of man" compelling people to blame on others what they unconsciously disliked most in themselves.

The cognitive approach

Cognitive science is an interdisciplinary field, seeking to understand the human mind from the viewpoint of different disciplines including psychology, neuroscience, philosophy, linguistics, artificial intelligence and anthropology.

The cognitive approach does not accept Freud's concept of a repressed unconscious. It is instead based on a concept of *automatic thinking*, described by cognitive psychologist Aaron Beck as "brief bursts at the fringe of consciousness". This view of the unconscious (or "non-conscious") is a bit like the software of a computer or satellite navigation instrument, whirring away underneath the surface with a huge store of programmes and data, helping to get one to a destination or outcome, while the user operates the hardware.

This automatic *cognitive unconscious* does not require intention or conscious awareness. Its *automaticity* is "friendlier, more cooperative and more speedily efficient" than "Freud's unconscious mind, filled with rebellious repressed workers in conflict with management" (David G. Myers, *Intuition: Its Powers and Perils*).

This cognitive concept is sometimes also called the *adaptive unconscious* – a term adopted by psychology professor Timothy Wilson in his book *Strangers to Ourselves: Discovering the Adaptive Unconscious*. Wilson acknowledges "Freud's genius" and that the unconscious influences judgements, feelings and behaviour. He believes that Freud's view of the unconscious was too limited and that it plays a far more major part in all aspects of our lives.

Wilson questions whether one can, as Freud aspired, bring everything from the unconscious into consciousness. He believes that much of what people may want to see is unseeable: there is no direct access to the adaptive unconscious, no matter how hard people may try.

Freudian, Jungian or cognitive? What is this elusive unconscious? Does it even exist?

Because the unconscious cannot be observed, questions as to its existence have been raised by various people, including the philosopher Karl Popper, who queried its scientific verifiability, and the psychologist Hans Eysenck. There is, indeed, a materialist view among some scientists, neuroscientists and philosophers that all that exists is matter; views about the mind and unconscious fall into the realm of "folk psychology".

The predominant and compelling view, however, is that not only does the unconscious exist, but it plays a fundamental and powerful role in our lives. Whatever it may be called, and however it may function, there is clearly a powerful hidden influence in human behaviour that emerges in all our actions, as well as in dreams and in unintentional and unconscious ways, which has a profound effect on the way we think and act.

Shakespeare observed the working of the unconscious with huge insight in many of his plays, such as *Hamlet* and *Macbeth*. Lady Macbeth, for example, betrays herself through her unconscious while sleepwalking. J. P. Brockbank, erstwhile Director of the Shakespeare Institute, wrote about the insight that Shakespeare shared with Freud. A number of writers have commented on the inspiration that Shakespeare provided for Freud and a psychoanalytical perspective that can be found in Shakespeare's writing.

Some practical implications

Making decisions and choices: free will?

The role of the unconscious in relation to decision-making is, of course, fundamental, touching every aspect of our lives, from deciding what brand of beer to drink to choosing one's life partner or profession. As professionals, we need to understand the factors that influence us, our clients, colleagues and others in the way choices are made. Appreciating the effect of the unconscious is the first step in that direction.

In their classic work *Families and How to Survive Them*, psychotherapist Robin Skynner and actor John Cleese discuss the reasons why couples get together. In addition to social factors and conscious personal reasons like good looks and shared interests, Skynner identifies unconscious attraction or "chemistry". Cleese observes that while Skynner is familiar with the impact of the unconscious on behaviour "it's a bit of a shock for a layman like me to realise ... how much we're doing for reasons we're not aware of".

Skynner and Cleese employ the metaphor of keeping emotions that we find uncomfortable and haven't learned to handle "behind the screen". When initially establishing relationships, couples unconsciously accept elements that one another keep behind the screen.

> Jung's analogy is that being out of consciousness is like a car going round a corner and out of sight. It has not ceased to exist even though it cannot be seen (Carl Jung, "Approaching the Unconscious", in *Man and His Symbols*).

It seems that whereas we may have freedom of choice, psychologically speaking, we are all to some extent circumscribed in our decision-making by the bounds of our unconscious. This in turn is shaped by anxieties and neuroses, suppressed emotions and attitudes, family belief systems, hidden prejudices and biases and erroneous internalised information (as well as the DNA of our human history if Jung's collective unconscious is considered).

While referring to DNA, what has been emerging of late is epigenetics – changes within a generation of direct and indirect chemical modifications of our DNA which, to an extent, imprints our current experiences and environment. These modifications (or "learning") can be passed on from parent to offspring, sometimes down two or three generations, albeit in a more complex and somewhat random fashion compared with the strict inheritance of the very conserved genetic code. In other words, it's not all genetics.

Advances in neuroscience are providing information about how the brain functions and how this relates to the conscious and unconscious mind and to behaviour. They raise huge issues about the nature of free will: if we are prescribed in our choices by the way the brain functions (and by the nature of the unconscious), to what extent is free will an illusion?

In *The Ethical Brain*, Professor Michael Gazzaniga, a distinguished cognitive neuroscientist, addresses practical and ethical questions raised by neuroscientific developments. "Neuroscience tells us that by the time any of us consciously experience something, the brain has already done its work. When we become consciously aware of making a decision, the brain has already made it happen."

Neuroscience is divided about some of the more profound implications of the functions of the brain and nervous system. If the brain, acting as a sort of computer, predisposes us to certain courses of action, do we really have free will? In a far-reaching exploration of these and other related questions, neuroscientist Mario Beauregard and Denyse O'Leary conclude in their work *The Spiritual Brain* that materialism is mistaken and that what we fundamentally know is actually true: free will is real.

Intuition and "gut feelings"

Intuition, addressed in Chapter 4, is defined in the *Oxford English Dictionary* as "the immediate apprehension of an object by the mind without the intervention of any reasoning process". We all understand intuition as the sense of feeling spontaneously that we know something without going through a logical, rational process – "gut feelings". These intuitive and instinctive feelings come from our unconscious; and it does seem that by developing our conscious understandings and awareness we can help to make our unconscious more effective in the way it arrives at its "gut reactions".

Slips of the tongue and other errors

A *parapraxis* is an unconscious error of speech or action that indicates what a person is really thinking. Commonly it is a slip of the tongue, but it may also take the form of erroneous action, such as forgetting to sign a cheque especially if the payment is for something that unconsciously one may resent or is troubled about paying for, or misreading a word. Clearly, there may also be other possible explanations, but in many cases there may well be an unconscious "give-away".

Body language (non-verbal communication)

Non-verbal signs can give strong clues to a person's underlying thoughts or feelings. It is easier to mislead with words than with the body. If there is no congruence between the words and the accompanying non-verbal signals, it may be better to trust the body than the words. Allan Pease, who has written extensively about this, explains that when a person tells a lie the unconscious acts independently of the words, so that his body language gives him away.

An appreciation of non-verbal communication can help lead to a better understanding of underlying thoughts and feelings, and hence improve communication and relationships.

> Although body language can be very informative, there is a widely misused statistic about it. In laboratory experiments Professor Albert Mehrabian measured listeners' attitudes towards speakers who gave deliberately inconsistent messages. Focusing on words, vocal qualities and facial expressions, he found 7 per cent verbal liking, 38 per cent vocal liking and 55 per cent facial liking. This limited experiment has been widely and wrongly misquoted to suggest that "only 7 per cent of all communications are verbal". As Mehrabian's website warns, this distortion of a limited test creates a nonsensical proposition.

Placebos and nocebos, Pygmalion and Rosenthal

The placebo effect originates in the medical field, but its principles and the lessons that we can draw from it are applicable to all other professions and activities in which people's beliefs actually or potentially affect their physical or mental capacities.

A placebo is a fake medical intervention – medication or process – that is entirely inactive but which creates a belief in the recipient's mind that it is real and effective. It is commonly used in the testing of active medication, by splitting people into two groups, the one taking the real drug and the other – a control group – taking the ineffective placebo (but not knowing that it is sham and inert), in order to compare outcomes.

Patients with real medical conditions taking a placebo in the belief that it is effective have commonly been known to have had beneficial therapeutic effects: this is known as the placebo effect. Real (and not imaginary) physical changes in the body are brought about by the person's belief that a healing process is taking place. For example, the placebo effect can cause the brain to trigger the release of chemicals in the body such as dopamine which eases the tremors of Parkinson's disease.

The corollary of the placebo effect is "the nocebo effect", which is a belief that some medication or process will cause harm, with a negative result on the body, notwithstanding its neutral content. A person, for example, reading the contra-indications of a medicine might exhibit symptoms that he or she had read, and believed, would have that effect. Voodoo curses have been known to have an effect on people who believe in them.

The placebo effect has created something of an ethical paradox for practitioners. Providing an intervention that has no clinical effect in the expectation that it will generate a healing process in the mind may be regarded as deceiving the patient; but explaining the practice will negate the belief system on which the effect depends. The use of a placebo function to help the healing process does seem to be widely accepted as ethically proper.

Beauregard and O'Leary point out that doctors are taught to behave in a way that invokes the placebo effect, for example speaking with authority, displaying their qualifications, wearing a white coat and stethoscope and generally behaving in a way that generates confidence. If they did not do so, they might evoke a nocebo effect. How, then, do other professionals create a placebo effect, wittingly or unwittingly, and avoid their clients slipping into a nocebo effect?

It is a pity that the expression "placebo effect" has acquired a "fake" connotation, since the physical changes that it induces can be very real, based on activation of the body's healing mechanisms. Perhaps the placebo effect should have another name, such as "the transformative belief effect" to distinguish it from the concept of a fake pill. Indeed, there is a book, the title of which uses a similar term: *Placebo: the Belief Effect* by Dylan Evans.

The capacity of the body to respond to the mind's belief system carries important lessons for all professionals, not just in the medical field. The "Pygmalion" or Rosenthal effect, further developed in Chapter 9, refers to the phenomenon that the greater the (conscious or unconscious) expectation placed on people, the better they are likely to perform.

Perhaps this helps to explain why authoritative and empathetic experts gain clients' confidence more readily than those who may have equal process ability, or why parties to a dispute who believe that there is a mutual commitment to resolve the issues have a greater prospect of settlement than where there mistrust and scepticism.

Powerful and suppressed emotions distort effective functioning

When people behave in a way that is not congruent with their real feelings and emotions, there is likely to be a consequence somewhere, because the unconscious has a way of showing this up.

For example, if a person feels angry but resolves to ignore and suppress the anger, there is a strong likelihood that the unconscious will bring the anger out in some other way, for example through destructive comments or behaviour.

The unconscious mind can also divert suppressed anger into physical ill health, as it diverts other suppressed emotions. There is considerable evidence of links between suppressed anger and illness, depression, sleep deprivation and other ill effects.

Powerful emotions can undoubtedly affect cognitive functions. "Passions over-whelm reason time and time again" writes Daniel Goleman in *Emotional Intelligence*. Anger, fear, happiness and love all affect rational decision-making. Anxiety, stress and panic inhibit the effective working of the rational mind. There are neuro-biological reasons for this. Understanding why and how emotions and their suppression can affect one's work is critical to effective relationships; strategies for helping clients and patients to function better when assailed by stress, panic and strong emotions can enhance professional relationships.

Unconscious competence

In any activity, whether speaking a foreign language, playing the piano or practising one's profession, there tends to be a progression of competence from being a beginner through to becoming skilled and proficient. There is a four-stage model, attributed to psychologist Thomas Gordon, which is widely accepted, namely:

Stage 1:   Unconscious incompetence, in which you don't know what you don't know – you don't even realise that you can't perform a function.

Stage 2:   Conscious incompetence, in which you come to realise what you don't know – you know what you need to do but you don't have the skills to do it.

Stage 3:   Conscious competence, in which you know what you should know, but it takes conscious effort to do it.

Stage 4:   Unconscious competence, in which you know what to do and can do it easily and well without conscious thought.

At Stage 4, the process has entered the unconscious and can be performed automatically.

Higher intuitions and inspiration

The unconscious should not be thought as limited only to repressed feelings, anxieties and neuroses, or to a collective history of humanity, or to automatic cognitive functioning. There is also a view that it includes a "higher uncons-cious" from which we have access to artistic, philosophical and scientific inspiration and indeed even to genius. Roberto Assaglioli, the founder of the therapeutic process called *psychosynthesis*, saw this higher unconscious as an available force of the human spirit and the source of higher feelings such as altruistic love.

A springboard to other aspects

This brief introductory outline of the unconscious is intended to serve both as a source of understanding and awareness in its own right, and as a springboard to the further aspects that this book will address.

Further reading

There is a vast amount of available reading on the subject of the unconscious. Henri Ellenberger's monumental work *The Discovery of the Unconscious: The History and Evolution of Dynamic Psychiatry* traces the history of the unconscious from primitive belief systems through to 1970.

There are very many books about Sigmund Freud and his work, in addition to his own writing. A brief outline may be found in Anthony Storr's *Freud: A Very Short Introduction* and David Stafford-Clark's *What Freud Really Said*. Freud's own works are available individually, or the whole set can be acquired as *The Standard Edition of the Complete Psychological Works of Sigmund Freud* (Vintage edition in paperback).

Similarly, there are innumerable books by and about Jung. Jung's personal revelations are contained in his *Memories, Dreams, Reflections*. Biographies include Gerhard Wehr's *Jung*, which has been described as creating "an interesting counterpoint" to *Memories, Dreams, Reflections*. Laurens van der Post has written an influential, densely packed portrait of Jung – *Jung and the Story of Our Time*. The richly illustrated *Man and His Symbols* edited by Jung and after his death by M.-L. von Franz is a fascinating read.

For the cognitive approach, see Timothy Wilson's *Strangers to Ourselves: Discovering the Adaptive Unconscious* and David G. Myers' *Intuition: Its Powers and Perils*; also *The New Unconscious*, edited by Ran R. Hassin, James S. Uleman and John A. Bargh.

Because the unconscious underpins many aspects of life and work, books that refer to it in a more specialised context, such as neuroscience and body language, will be mentioned in the chapters dealing with those aspects.

And finally, although not strictly about the unconscious, but covering it inherently throughout, *Families and How to Survive Them* by Robin Skynner and John Cleese is a wonderful read, with the bonus of brilliant cartoons by Bud Handelsman.

Chapter 6

The amygdala hijack

Triggers and strategies

Credit: Peretz Partensky from San Francisco, USA

The multiple roles of the amygdala

The amygdala seems to be known for its role in protecting us from perceived threats by responding instantaneously and intensely to emotions such as fear and anger.

Yet in fairness to the poor overworked amygdala, reference should also be made to its other roles including positive reinforcement, by effectively providing positive (or negative) emotional values to data, including words and images, received by the senses. It also has a role, for example, in relation to trust and in guiding social interactions. It does this by integrating emotional associations into cognitive thinking, bringing emotional issues into the decision-making process by releasing neurotransmitters such as noradrenaline, dopamine and serotonin that influence cognitive processing.

While these aspects of the amygdala will be of interest to neuroscientists and those wishing to develop a greater understanding of its processes, our attention will be focused on its profound potential effects on our functioning in general and decision-making in particular.

The amygdala hijack

We have touched on the amygdala's functions in dealing with fear, arousal and other strong emotions including the generation of the fight, flight or dissociate (freeze) response.

In essence, when faced with a situation engendering fear or other strong emotions, the amygdala identifies this in milliseconds and activates the sympathetic section of the autonomic nervous system, which in turn generates a chemical neurotransmitter noradrenaline (norepinephrine). This instantly affects the body by increasing the heart rate, preparing the muscles for action by increasing blood flow to them, increasing blood pressure, dilating the pupils and inhibiting bladder contraction. In addition, the stress hormones adrenaline and cortisol are released. The body is immediately primed for action.

But from the professional's perspective, something even more significant happens when the body is prepared for action in this way: alert, tense and stressed, rational and logical thought has to go on hold. The rational part of the brain – the pre-frontal cortex, a mere one million or so years old – is temporarily bypassed by the 200-plus-million-year-old amygdala during this crisis period. This is the amygdala hijack.

The implications of this for someone who is in this mode or who is highly stressed and who has to make a decision based on rational and logical thought will immediately be obvious: this is not the time to make, or to be asked to make, any such decisions.

The term "amygdala hijack" refers to an immediate and often inappropriate and excessive response to a stimulus such as a perceived threat or anger. It is attributed to Daniel Goleman, author of the seminal work *Emotional Intelligence: Why It Can Matter More Than IQ* in which he acknowledges Joseph LeDoux, author of *The Emotional Brain*, as revealing the role of the amygdala as "an emotional sentinel, able to hijack the brain" while the neocortex reacts more slowly, but in a more refined and better informed way.

Triggering the amygdala hijack

In his paper "The Neurobiological Foundations of Being Human" Professor Mark Solms refers to seven instinctive systems shared by all mammals, namely seeking (closely tied to meaning-making); pleasure (having needs met); anger; fear; panic/ grief; care (linked to attachment); and play (shared by all juvenile mammals).

Three of these instincts are triggers for the amygdala hijack: fear, panic and anger; but there are also other emotional reactions that do the same.

Fear

The effect of fear in triggering the amygdala's response transcends race, gender, ethnicity, nationality or culture. This emotion may be primitive but there are countless situations in everyday modern life when it is activated – a vast array of possible threats to our safety and well-being, and sometimes to our lives.

In addition to the reality of specific threats, we are bombarded with frightening news in the media: crime, terrorism, pandemics, accidental death, the stranger in our midst – what has been described as a "culture of fear". These are supplemented by very real fears and concerns: damage to the environment from climate change; global or regional economic crisis; religious and cultural intolerance; mass displacement of populations. We live in a state of existential insecurity: our brains are becoming primed to expect fearful events.

Fear may arise in a number of professional contexts, at different levels of intensity. In a medical situation, there may be fear of pain, functional disability, uncertainty and, in more serious conditions, death. In a legal context, facing a trial can be frightening or fear may arise on recounting frightening events. People may fear family breakdown, financial problems, bereavement or myriad everyday concerns. Professionals in many fields may encounter clients or patients with different levels of fear.

Panic

Panic represents a period of intense fear and discomfort commonly accompanied by physical symptoms such as dizziness or light-headedness, trembling, accelerated heart rate or palpitations, sweating and shortness of breath. Panic attacks may be spontaneous and without warning, or specific and related to particular situations or places.

Someone experiencing a panic attack generally feels out of control, which itself is very frightening. Anxiety about it recurring in a similar situation in the future can then become self-fulfilling as the stress of the prospective situation causes all the symptoms to reappear.

Panic can be linked to specific fears, such as public speaking or being alone at night. People can develop coping strategies for these, but sometimes the fears are too great and the coping mechanisms do not work, when these fears may become phobias.

Although the immediate cause of the panic symptoms can be linked to the amygdala hijack, various different underlying causes may create the propensity to panic. These may include trauma – an external shock or assault to the system causing physical and/or psychological injury or harm; stress; and post-traumatic stress disorder (PTSD). There are also links with insecure attachment (see Chapter 8) and perfectionism. Other possible causes may include links to genetics, food intolerances and sleep deprivation.

Laurence Olivier dubbed stage fright "the actor's nightmare" … The stricken actor seizes up, both physically and mentally; the mouth goes dry, breathing becomes short and shallow, vision blurs and concentration evaporates … Up to 50 per cent of performers experience stage fright to some extent. "It's the old fight or flight syndrome," says Dr Glenn Wilson, visiting professor of psychology at Gresham College, London, "Today, making a fool of yourself in front of an audience might have consequences that are almost as bad as being chomped by a sabre-toothed tiger."

(Matt Trueman, *Guardian*, 21 September 2012; courtesy Guardian News & Media)

Anger

The evolutionary explanation for anger is that it arises when we face obstacles to getting what we want, supporting our efforts to gain the upper hand in whatever we are confronting or whatever we perceive to be threatening us or violating or transgressing our rights and well-being or those of people we need to protect. We may experience anger when things feel out of our control: it can motivate us to try to establish some control (or some sense of control) and can signal to others that we intend to do so.

At an everyday level, the expression of anger may be healthy and constructive where it is proportionate and appropriate. For the angry person, it may give them a sense of greater control and may be healthier by providing a more effective coping mechanism than suppressing any anger felt. It may also serve to make clear to the other person where lines have to be drawn, where limits need to be set.

On the other hand, anger may be inappropriate and disproportionate; for example where something rekindles underlying anger or where someone has anger-management issues and is unable to control his anger or maintain it proportionately.

Professionals are bound at some time to have to deal with angry clients or patients. The anger may be directed at the professional or towards someone or something else, but the effect is the same: the professional has to be able to cope effectively with the anger. Or it may be the professional who is angry: it would be extraordinary of we didn't find ourselves angry on occasions, whether with people, organisations or just the system.

Shame and humiliation

It may be a sign of the brain's social development that shame has become as profound an amygdala trigger as fear, panic or anger. Like these other triggers, shame operates at a primitive level outside rational cognitive processes.

Shame has to do with negative self-perception, self-evaluation and/or self-image, the painful feeling of having done something wrong or foolish, of looking wrong, of feeling small, of being perceived by others as worthless and unacceptable. Shame researcher Brené Brown sees shame as an intensely painful feeling in which one believes that one is "flawed" with a consequent sense of feeling "unworthy of acceptance and belonging".

Like the other triggers, shame can produce similar autonomic reactions such as sweating and an increased heart rate and generally a state of heightened bodily awareness; and significantly for professionals, a shift away from rational thinking. A person who is in a state of shame is not generally in a fit state to make decisions involving cognitive processing.

Although many of the physical manifestations of the amygdala hijack may arise with shame, one difference from the other triggers is that it may not necessarily be as visible to others. Whereas anger, fear and panic may be observable from their physical signs, shame is more of an internalised process and while it may sometimes manifest – for example if coupled with the blushing of embarrassment – in many cases there will be no outward sign of its presence.

This may be compounded by the fact that since by its very nature shame feels shameful, people are less likely to admit to it than when they feel angry or fearful.

Shame and humiliation: Humiliation is an emotional response to the perception of being unfairly or unjustly debased, disgraced or diminished, with respect and dignity reduced or of being exposed to ridicule, scorn or contempt. Humiliation can be personal, but whole groups or nations can feel a collective humiliation for example as when defeated in war.

Shame and humiliation are concepts that are sometimes used interchangeably, but they are different. Brené Brown explains that whereas the experience of shame is linked to some sense that it is deserved, humiliation does not have this connotation and may feel unfair and underserved. Also, shame tends to be private whereas humiliation tends to be public.

But the effects of shame and humiliation can be equally damaging and sometimes devastating. Severe humiliation can lead to depression, loss of self-esteem, loss of focus, damage to relationships, rage, anxiety and in more extreme cases self-harm or suicide.

Shame and embarrassment: Embarrassment, which can co-exist with shame, involves a state of painful discomfort as a result of having said or done something socially, professionally or personally inappropriate, inept or silly. Embarrassment can also result from self-consciousness, for example (and paradoxically) when being publicly praised. For some people, embarrassment's physical give-away may be blushing, looking down or stammering.

Shame and guilt: Guilt is an emotion that one feels when one knows (or believes) that one has done something wrong, morally or legally. Brené Brown sees guilt as a self-evaluation of our actions or behaviour in the light of our ethics, values and beliefs, which can be distinguished from shame, which is "focusing on who we are rather than what we've done".

Shame and blame: Blame often exists alongside shame, either self-blame or diverting the feeling of shame by blaming others. In politics and the media, there seems to be a tendency to shame and blame people, to demand public apologies, to seek humiliation in an almost triumphant way that borders on abuse. While accountability may be appropriate, the notion of naming, shaming and blaming is likely to be counter-productive and result in hurt, denial, anger and retaliation.

Shame and behaviour: So can and should shame be used to help shape people's behaviour and to bring children into line? The strong consensus is that although this may be a common practice, it does not work and can store problems for the future. Shame creates an inward and negative focus on ourselves and what we perceive to be wrong with ourselves rather than on our actions.

For children, shaming and humiliating them, rather than changing their behaviour positively, has an element of emotional abuse in it and is quite likely to send negative internal messages that may stay with them for life. For adults, the reinforcement of a negative self-image does not have a positive effect but may increase a sense of isolation from the community and a destructive behaviour pattern.

That is not to say that people should not be aware of things that they may have done wrongly and to have a sense of guilt and a need for accountability; but that is different from creating a sense of shame and humiliation.

Twenty-first-century multi-tasking

Most professionals will be familiar with the experience of having to do a number of things at once, to spin and balance a number of figurative plates in the air, hoping that none will come crashing down – with the increase in stress levels that this involves.

Neuroscientist Daniel J. Levitin's book *The Organized Mind: Thinking Straight in the Age of Information Overload* is primarily directed at the professional, the manager, and all who use and store the increasing amount of information with which we are overloaded these days. His view is that our activities in checking e-mail and social media constitute a neural addiction.

In a related article in the *Observer* newspaper, Levitin explains that repeated multi-tasking leads to anxiety and increased production of the stress hormone cortisol as well as the fight-or-flight hormone adrenaline, which in turn can lead to aggressive and impulsive behaviour.

Communications are now instantaneous. Texts, e-mails, social media communications and mobile-phone calls can reach one at any time or place – and, as Levitin points out, many of us feel a need to check these out all the time, for fear of missing something important.

It seems, however, that there is a corresponding "high" every time we deal with electronic communications, social media or online games, a "shot of dopamine"; but there is a price to pay in terms of both the stress caused by its immediacy and the addictive nature of electronic communications and games.

Rekindling amygdala hijack activators

Brain research indicates that talking about traumatic events can unconsciously rekindle the original feelings and replicate the amygdala's reaction, including shutting down cognitive functions and triggering the reactions of fight, flight or dissociation.

This has implications for professionals whose work may involve having clients or patients recount such events. There is a view that telling their stories and expressing emotions may help people to move on emotionally, but this catharsis theory has not been supported by research or by empirical evidence, and on the contrary some tests have shown that reflecting on the emotions and their cause can increase rather than decrease anger: the rekindling effect tends to undermine the concept of "venting". Professionally addressing such experiences requires some greater understandings and counselling skills.

Experience of intense fear can also lead to PTSD. Recalling that traumatic event can re-activate the amygdala, with all the effects of the hijack.

> Any traumatizing event can implant such trigger memories in the amygdala … human cruelties stamp their victims' memories with a template that regards with fear anything vaguely similar to the assault itself … the imprint of horror in memory – and the resulting hypervigilance – can last a lifetime.
>
> (Daniel Goleman, *Emotional Intelligence:*
> *Why It Can Matter More Than IQ*)

Some strategies for dealing with amygdala hijack triggers

Counsellors, psychotherapists and others trained in the mental health field may well have strategies to help their clients and patients – and indeed themselves when appropriate – to cope with these emotional triggers. But most professionals who do not have this training are generally left to their own devices when these triggers arise.

The following are some considerations and strategies that professionals may find helpful:

1   *Empathy and compassion:* Empathy is particularly apposite when dealing with people who are experiencing such intense emotional reactions that they find it difficult to function effectively.

 People going through the experience of fear, panic, anger or shame while trying to work with you as a professional need you to see and understand what they are going through and to communicate with them in a non-judgemental, supportive and authentic way, with compassion but without being patronising. This may be the start of helping them through the crisis.

2   *Move off the topic causing distress*: As soon as is reasonably practicable, move away from the distressing subject, unless it is an essential part of your professional brief, in which event consider moving away from it temporarily to allow time for your client or patient to recover.

It may sometimes be necessary or appropriate to continue discussing the topic despite the distress. This needs to be done with sensitivity and understanding, and if you do not have counselling experience, you need to proceed with particular caution.

3   *Support a shift into cognitive brain mode:* When people are caught up in amygdala hijack mode we can try to help ease them away from that mode and into a more functional, cognitive state.

From a neurological perspective, the amygdala hijack, or indeed most forms of stress, move us primarily into right-brain mode. To return to functional rationality we need to shift to a more left-brain, pre-frontal cortex mode which can inhibit the impulses of our amygdala.

One way to help achieve this is to engage the person in a simple task that involves undemanding cognitive effort, such as asking for and discussing basic factual information, which will not require deep thought but which will necessitate pausing and thinking. For example, if discussing something in a family context, perhaps ask for the names and dates of birth of children and enquire about their schooling and interests – or suchlike. Engaging the person in this way for a while can facilitate recovery.

4   *Take a break:* If necessary, take a short break and allow the person some quiet recovery time. Perhaps he or she may want to take a short walk or just sit in another room and read a magazine. Pausing for "a nice cup of tea" is quite basic but can be really supportive.

If the client or patient feels able to continue after a short break of maybe five or ten minutes, you can move on with your professional role. Most people are pleased to be able to do so. However, for some people recovery takes much longer and a longer adjournment may be necessary, perhaps returning at another time or another day.

5   *Deep breathing:* This may sound somewhat basic and simplistic, but effective slow and deep breathing establishes a pattern of relaxation in the body and mind and helps a person to move out of the amygdala hijack and to re-establish connection with the pre-frontal cortex.

Although any form of relaxed breathing may be effective, diaphragmatic breathing may have some greater benefits in this situation. In this type of breathing, on inhalation the stomach expands rather than the chest and it feels as though one is drawing air into the belly.

6   *Humour:* Employed with empathy, gentle humour can sometimes help to de-escalate stressful, angry and sometimes potentially conflictual situations. This does, however, have to be used with judgement and sensitivity as

misplaced humour can have the opposite effect of being seen as disrespectful and facetious and can inflame a volatile situation.

7   *Longer-term strategies:* Where the triggering emotions are recurrent or severe, the person experiencing them may well benefit from some other approaches in his own time, such as:

Meditation/mindfulness: Various meditative techniques have been found to help with stress reduction, apart from any other benefits that may exist. One approach in particular that has been recommended by many people, including Daniel Goleman, the author of the classic *Emotional Intelligence: Why It Can Matter More Than IQ*, and psychiatrist Daniel J. Siegel, is the practice of mindfulness meditation. Associated with this is Professor Jon Kabat-Zinn's mindfulness-based stress reduction. The Mindful Living Programs' website reflects that "The mind is known to be a factor in stress and stress-related disorders, and meditation has been shown to positively effect a range of autonomic physiological processes, such as lowering blood pressure and reducing overall arousal and emotional reactivity."

Counselling or psychotherapy: Neuroscientist Joseph LeDoux, whose work was critical in developing knowledge about the functions of the amygdala in relation to the emotional brain, has expressed a clear view that, despite the brain's emotional system's propensity to cling to traumas that have affected it, there is scope for psychotherapy to teach the neocortex how to inhibit the amygdala.

Different kinds of therapy are available, including in particular cognitive behavioural therapy (CBT), which helps people manage their problems by changing the way they think and behave. Within CBT, exposure therapy encourages people to expose themselves gradually and become habituated to situations that may trouble them, allowing the amygdala to adapt to these and its power over them to subside.

Anger management: Where recurrent anger is a problem, anger-management courses or programmes can be helpful. These may involve individual counselling and/or working in a small group, on a one-day or weekend course, or in some cases spread over months.

Medication: In some more severe cases, medication may be prescribed, generally but not necessarily alongside some form of therapy. Beta-blockers such as propranolol, for example, can control the physical symptoms of panic attacks but do not prevent the fear or panic itself. Where people suffer from uncontrollable rage or other severe conditions, medication such as antidepressants, mood stabilizers or antipsychotic drugs may be prescribed.

Countering information overload: Levitin suggests strategies for coping with the challenges of modern multi-tasking including, for example, creating and maintaining a prioritised task list, which paradoxically provides more time for creativity and spontaneity; taking short breaks from intensive work; and pressing a "neural reset button" by, for example, meditating, reading, viewing art, or taking a walk or a nap.

Further reading

Daniel Goleman's *Emotional Intelligence: Why It Can Matter More Than IQ* may be regarded as essential primary reading.

Professor Joseph LeDoux, who originated work on the function of the amygdala, has joined with others in editing an update on his earlier work, now comprised in a set of essays entitled *The Emotional Brain Revisited.*

Brené Brown's *I Thought It Was Just Me (But It Isn't)* addresses issues around shame and how to deal with our vulnerabilities (focused on her work with women's shame, but more generally applicable). Her later work *The Gifts of Imperfection: Let Go of Who You Think You're Supposed to Be and Embrace Who You Are* develops the concepts of shame and imperfection.

Neuroscientist Daniel J. Levitin's book *The Organized Mind: Thinking Straight in the Age of Information Overload* has been very well reviewed.

Some excellent books on mindfulness are listed in Chapter 17.

The Human Amygdala edited by Paul J. Whalen and Elizabeth A. Phelps provides detailed coverage of amygdala function and dysfunction and its principles helped to inform the outline introduction to this chapter. It is highly technical and may be more relevant to those wishing to undertake research into this subject.

Chapter 7

Understanding personality

Credit: CartoonStock.com

The uniqueness of personality

Lord Scrutton's elephant

Each of us has at least two things that are so rare as to be virtually unique to ourselves: our fingerprints and our personality. Even identical twins do not share either of these attributes.

Professionals are ordinarily unlikely to need an understanding of fingerprints. But where an inherent part of our daily work involves dealing with people, it must be helpful to be aware as to how each person functions differently.

English judge Lord Scrutton referred in a case to someone who could not define an elephant, but said he knew one when he saw it. Personality is rather like that, because although we may know what we mean by the term, the individual components of personality do not necessarily tell the full story.

The Royal College of Psychiatrists defines personality as referring to the collection of characteristics or traits that makes each of us an individual, including the ways that we think, feel and behave. Perhaps a fuller description would be that personality is the distinctive manifestation of an accumulation of individualistic qualities, traits, beliefs, attitudes and characteristics that each one of us has, and which together help to define who we are and how we relate to others and to our environment.

> Man's main task in life is to give birth to himself, to become what he potentially is. The most important product of his effort is his own personality.
> (Erich Fromm, *Man for Himself: An Enquiry into the Psychology of Ethics*)

The relevance of personality

Despite our distinctive and individual characteristics, a number of permutations of traits and characteristics exist, which allow some broad type groupings to be identified and assessed. Assessing these personality types is used by some employers to help decide whether a job applicant has the aptitude and is suitable for a particular kind of work; and conversely it may help individuals to decide what kind of work or career they are best suited to.

But understanding personality has a wider function. Where people operate in partnerships or teams, personality differences can create clashes and understanding the underlying personality issues can help address these and develop greater cohesion. And where the professional and the client or patient have different personalities and find it difficult to relate to one another's ways of functioning, appreciating and accommodating these differences can transform a potential clash of personalities into a mutually stronger relationship.

Significantly too, self-awareness of your own personality can be personally liberating and can enhance your ability to function maximally as a professional and in your personal life.

Personality types and traits

In popular culture, personality represents the way we come across to others, largely distinguished between extrovert and gregarious or shy and reserved. While these are part of the picture, a much larger canvas is needed to accommodate personality.

Psychometric tests have been developed to help in assessing personality. Two well-known assessment tests are the *Big Five* and the *Myers–Briggs Type Indicator*.

Big Five

This test identifies the following five sets of personality traits and, using multiple questions, creates a personality type based on a permutation of the responses.

Extraversion v. introversion

As the names indicate, extraverts tend to direct their energies outwards and to be lively, sociable, talkative, gregarious and have their attention on other people and the outside world. Introverts on the other hand tend to direct their energies inwards, to process information and emotions internally and privately, to be reserved and to enjoy their own inner world.

Agreeableness v. antagonism

At the one end, people who are high on agreeableness tend to be kind, altruistic, trusting, considerate and helpful. At the other end, people low on agreeableness tend to be more antagonistic, competitive, suspicious and untrusting. At the extremely low end they may be socially manipulative.

Conscientiousness v. undirectedness or disinhibition

The conscientious person is well organised, reliable, hardworking, efficient and practical, and is also likely to be careful and thorough. At the extreme high end of this he or she may be compulsive and obsessive, a bit of a perfectionist. Someone at the other end is likely to be undirected and disorganised, unreliable and impractical and is likely to be less goal-oriented. At the extreme opposite end of conscientiousness, a person could be severely disinhibited; that is, disregards social conventions and may be perceived as rude and offensive.

Neuroticism v. emotional stability

The neurotic personality tends to feel anxious, insecure and may have periods of self-doubt and negativity, is easily upset or angry and has a bad emotional reaction to stress. Neuroticism can manifest as suppressed (and potentially depressive) or overt and over-sensitive to the slightest stimuli. People with high neuroticism may well be very sensitive, and thus experience all kinds of emotions more keenly. The opposite personality is emotionally stable, calm and even-tempered, less likely to get flustered or agitated.

Openness v. closedness

In this context, openness identifies a person who is imaginative, independent minded, receptive to new ideas and experiences, and tends to be non-conformist and tolerant of ambiguity. Closedness refers to someone who tends to have a conservative approach to life, who prefers the conventional and familiar, who is more likely to resist change.

Myers–Briggs Type Indicator (MBTI)

Based on Carl Jung's theories of personality types, this identifies four sets of individual preferences, and by correlating these to one another creates a table of 16 distinctive personality types. The four sets of competing preferences are:

extraverted or *introverted* as outlined above;
sensing (relying on information received through one's five senses) or *intuitive*;
thinking and analytical or *feeling*;
judging (planned and organised) or *flexible and spontaneous*.

MBTI does not measure traits, ability, or character and is non-judgemental as between the different types, all of which are considered to be equal. For professionals, it can be a useful tool and can support various functions such as management and training, organisational tasks and change management though the process does have its critics.

Contradictions in traits and preferences

Although traits and preferences are reflected at opposite ends of the spectrum, most people have some elements of both characteristics, though one is likely to predominate. As a professor observed: "When my students see me in lectures, they would assume that I am clearly an extrovert; but if they saw me at a party, standing at the edge of the room, they would take me for an introvert."

Traits and preferences are complex, and tensions can occur in all kinds of personal and work situations and relationships. People can be open in some circumstances and protective and closed in others. Someone might generally be very law-abiding, but at moments might feel an anarchic streak. Having an innovative tendency and a willingness to embrace change does not necessarily mean that one will necessarily adopt organisational change without being wholly satisfied that it does not involve unnecessary risk and disadvantage.

Of course, in the context of personality testing, one's traits relate to those at one's core and not necessarily situation-specific, but inevitably this is a complex exercise and identification cannot be completely accurate, though MBTI and the Big Five are reputedly reliable.

Other personality tests

There are other tests available, not all of which can necessarily be taken too seriously. A brief web trawl discloses tests to identify anger and anger management, attention span, social anxiety, optimism/pessimism, self-esteem, stress triggers, risk-taking and sensuality.

For those familiar with J. K. Rowling's boy wizard Harry Potter, personality tests have even been established on the web to consider into which house the Hogwarts School hat would place participants: Gryffindor, Hufflepuff, Ravenclaw or Slytherin. (Harry Potter readers will know that student wizards are directed by the "sorting hat" into one or other of these houses, depending on their dispositions and personalities.)

Personality disorders and traits

We all have a collection of personality traits, each of which may be somewhere on a spectrum from one extreme to another. Where any of these traits is outside what may be regarded as the norm, a person may perhaps be regarded as odd, eccentric or difficult.

Personality issues arise where any of a person's traits are so far from the norm and so maladaptive that they significantly impair the way he or she functions. Where anyone finds it so difficult to live with themselves and/or with other people and to change those ways of thinking, feeling and behaving, resulting in unwanted consequences such as difficulty in making or keeping relationships, getting on with people and/or controlling feelings or behaviour, the person may have a personality disorder.

Personality disorders are deep-rooted and people who have them tend to have a narrow and inflexible range of attitudes, behaviours and coping mechanisms. They may not regard themselves as having a problem but may rather see others as responsible for their difficulties.

DSM-5 and other classifications

The American Psychiatric Association (APA) has taken an international lead in identifying and classifying personality disorders, which it defines as "an enduring pattern of inner experience and behavior that deviates markedly from the expectations of the culture of the individual who exhibits it".

The APA has been publishing its *Diagnostic and Statistical Manual of Mental Disorders* (DSM) since 1952. Its latest edition DSM-5 was published in 2013. It assists mental health clinicians and those in more general practice to diagnose disorders. It also affects the legal system, inasmuch as mental functioning can be relevant to a range of legal matters, not least in the criminal and family sectors.

Broadly equivalent classifications have been published by the World Health Organization (WHO) in Chapter V of the International Classification of Diseases (ICD). In China, classification is undertaken through the Chinese Classification of Mental Disorders.

DSM-5 lists six distinct types of personality disorders:

- *Borderline personality disorder* (typified by impulsive behaviour and risk-taking, erratic and unstable moods, reality distortion, rigid world views, excessive behaviour such as gambling or sexual promiscuity, and proneness to depression – all making it difficult to maintain relationships, which may be conflictual and clingy).
- *Obsessive compulsive personality disorder* (typified by rigid perfectionism, a need to control one's environment and negative affectivity).
- *Avoidant personality disorder* (typified by a pervasive pattern of social inhibition, feelings of inadequacy and anxiety, and hypersensitivity to negative evaluation).
- *Schizotypal personality disorder* (typified by eccentric behaviour and thinking resembling those seen in schizophrenia including cognitive or perceptual distortions, paranoid or bizarre ideas, difficulty in establishing or maintaining close relationships and a tendency to social withdrawal, an inability to get pleasure from enjoyable activities, occasional episodes with intense illusions, auditory or other hallucinations, and delusion-like ideas).
- *Anti-social personality disorder* (typified by a pervasive pattern of disregard for the rights of others, hostility, aggression, lying and deceit, manipulation, impulsiveness, irresponsibility and risk-taking. There is typically no genuine remorse for any harm they cause but they can feign remorse when they need to.)
- *Narcissistic personality disorder* (typified by an exaggerated sense of their own importance, an excessive need for approval, an expectation that they will be admired and a limited capacity for empathy and intimacy or for appreciating others' perspectives).

Maladaptive personality traits

It can be difficult and controversial even for mental health professionals to categorise any individual as having a personality disorder and certainly for professionals generally, other than mental health specialists, one would not dream of making any diagnosis or "labelling" anyone. It is preferable to think about relevant personality traits, rather than disorders. Hence an understanding of the different traits comprising personality disorders is useful. This will also be relevant when considering high-conflict personalities.

Personality development

Theories of personality development mirror psychology's wide range of theoretical perspectives. Valerie Simanowitz and Peter Pearce in their book *Personality Development* refer to a "wide and somewhat bewildering array of models of the development of personality". The following will briefly outline some of the main theories:

- *Freud's psychoanalytical approach* views development as a series of stages, especially in childhood and adolescence. So, for example, an "anal" character refers to Freud's anal stage (1–3 years old) when the child is learning bowel control: in an adult this may refer to their being obstinate, orderly and miserly.
- The *attachment theory* of John Bowlby places prominence on the nature and level of the attunement between carer and child during infancy. Styles of adult attachment, resulting from childhood experience, may be secure, insecure or disorganised.
- *The behaviourist approach* going back to Pavlov's research on conditioned responses was advanced by B. F. Skinner, who developed ideas about behaviour based on positive and negative reinforcements (rewards and punishments).
- *The type theory* of Carl Jung is the basis of the Myers–Briggs testing outlined above. Trait theories are similar: these consider people's individual traits or characteristics.
- *The humanistic approach* of Abraham Maslow, Erich Fromm, Rollo May and Carl Rogers informs many therapists and counsellors. This tends to be subjective and holistic (emotionally and spiritually) and to accept each person's capacity for self-healing. Rogers' person-centred theory assumes that individuals have a potential to be integrated and self-fulfilling, living in a congruent way. Positive or negative childhood experiences influence self-concepts and self-esteem, creating "conditions of worth", which affect one's inner guiding sense or wisdom.
- *Existentialism* follows its philosophical equivalent (broadly, that there is no intrinsic meaning in life and that we must just be uniquely who we are).

Cultural influence on behaviour patterns

Richard D. Lewis, author of *When Cultures Collide*, has devised a classification of behaviour based on cultural differences, comprising three groups: *linear-active*, *multi-active* and *reactive*. It may be helpful to outline some of the differences between the linear-active and multi-active groups:

Linear-active	*Multi-active*
Tends towards logic	Tends towards emotion
Detailed planning and work	Prefers broad outline planning and work
Purposeful with one thing at a time	Multi-tasks with several things at once
Patient	Impatient
Follows procedures and timetable	Casual about procedures and timetables
Focuses on the job in hand	More concerned about relationships
Principle important	Adapts principle to context

This categorisation explains the way in which different individuals may behave. So, if a professional can self-identify as being within either of these groups, and is dealing with someone who corresponds to the other group, there should be a clear awareness of the different personality styles that each will have and according to which each will function.

It should be emphasised that neither group represents a better way of being, but rather that people will vary in the way that they feel comfortable in functioning, and this needs to be accommodated by the sensitive professional.

Anthropologist Edward T. Hall coined the terms *polychronic* and *monochronic* in relation to the time frames that people employ in dealing with their affairs. Monochronic people tend to take time seriously, do one thing at a time, have detailed plans and schedules and adhere closely to these. Polychronic people, on the other hand, tend to do several things at once, are relatively unstructured and change plans readily.

Both Lewis' and Hall's categorisations identify different ways of functioning and of seeing life, bearing resemblances to the distinctions between people who function primarily from a rational perspective and those who tend to be emotional-intuitive.

Cultural norms

As indicated by both Lewis and Hall, and as our own experience tells us, personality is also likely to be affected by the norms of the culture within which individuals develop and function.

Culture may be seen in different contexts. There is the national culture in which one lives, then there are regional, community, group or ethnic/religious culture; attitudes are, for example, likely to be different within a community in the Hebrides from those of a community in the East End of London.

Culture also applies to families, in that each individual family will have its own culture, beliefs and norms, which will affect those growing up within them. And ultimately, there is an individual culture, covering the way of life, belief system, values and norms, customs and understandings of each individual person (their "world view").

Nature or nurture?

There has been much debate as to which has a greater influence on personal development: nature (innate genetic characteristics) or nurture (social and environmental influences during the course of development). Clearly nature and genetic make-up may have a significant physical role, but the position is less clear in relation to personality development.

While both sides of this argument have found support for their positions, for example through developments in DNA research and tests done with identical twins, there is a growing consensus that both elements have a significant role in relation to personality development.

> Matt Ridley considers in his work on nature and nurture that this debate raises a false dichotomy and that the environment affects the way in which genes express themselves. These two elements need to be integrated (Matt Ridley, *Nature via Nurture: Genes, Experience and What Makes Us Human*).

Whatever the relevance of genetic hereditability, there seems little doubt that social and environmental factors play a large part in a person's development. The subjects of nurture, affectional bonds and parental attunement are addressed in Chapter 8.

Some practical implications

Self-awareness

Understanding your own personality means that you have an appreciation of your strengths and weaknesses, your motivation and your emotions. It is a precursor – some would say essential – to understanding and relating to others and how they perceive and relate to you. It is one of the attributes of emotional intelligence.

This understanding can help one to live and work in an environment that is more compatible with one's fundamental needs and to avoid situations that are uncomfortable and stressful. Recognising and understanding one's own personality can help the professional to work in a way and in an environment that is more congruent with it, rather than struggling to "fit a square peg into a round hole".

> John Holland has a theory that people fall into six vocational personality types: realistic, investigative, artistic, social, enterprising and conventional. His fundamental hypothesis is that satisfaction and success are most likely when people follow occupations that are congruent with (i.e. match) their personality (J. L. Holland, *Making Vocational Choices: A Theory of Vocational Personalities and Work Environment*, quoted in *Work Psychology: Understanding Human Behaviour in the Workplace*).

Relating to clients, patients, co-workers and others

Potential personality clashes can be avoided if they are better understood. So, for example, if a professional works in a conscientious and organised way and the client operates in a disorganised manner, apparently unplanned, unreliable and chaotic, it can be enormously helpful to understand this distinction and to accommodate it.

Similarly, professionals will benefit from understanding and respecting the differences between multi-active and linear-active functioning, introverted or extraverted personalities, openness and a willingness to embrace independent thought and change or closedness and resistance to change, and the range of sensitivities between neurotic and stable behaviour.

These principles apply with equal force to relationships with partners, colleagues and other co-workers, teams and groups.

Identifying and working with troubled personalities

Without labelling clients, having some understanding of personality disorders and the traits that are linked to them can assist the professional in identifying troubled personalities who might need to be handled with some special care and strategies.

The well-rounded professional

There is a thread that runs through this whole book, namely that the well-rounded, thoughtful and competent professional needs to have an understanding not only of his or her own field, but also of the broad principles of human behaviour inherent in their work and relationships. An understanding of human personality falls squarely within that broad ambit.

Further reading

Psychiatrist and neuroscientist Samuel Barondes' book *Making Sense of People: Decoding the Mysteries of Personality* addresses the question of personality, drawing on genetics and neuroscience, with particular reference to the Big Five and patterns of disordered behaviour.

The Intelligent Clinician's Guide to the DSM-5 by psychiatrist Joel Paris takes a balanced and critical look at the DSM manual, recognising its value but unafraid to challenge aspects that he found wanting.

Valerie Simanowitz and Peter Pearce's book *Personality Development* clearly and effectively examines and critiques the different models and theories relevant to personality.

Snakes in Suits: When Psychopaths Go to Work by Paul Babiak and Robert D. Hare is a fascinating and informative study of psychopaths in the workplace written by two psychologists.

Chapter 8

Empathy, attunement and professional boundaries

"Of course I'm listening to your expression of spiritual suffering.
Don't you see me making eye contact, striking an open posture,
leaning towards you and nodding empathetically?"

Credit: CartoonStock.com

Empathy: the essence of professional and personal relationships

The *Penguin Dictionary of Psychology* provides four different definitions of empathy, reflecting perhaps some essential differences between psychologists and others as to what it means and involves. For some, it entails experiencing the emotional world as someone else does, effectively mirroring those emotions (sometimes called "emotional empathy"). For others, empathy is the ability to sense and understand another person's emotions and to imagine what he or she might be thinking or feeling. One does not lose oneself in the other's world, but rather one retains a sense of self and objectivity while recognising their experience. You place yourself in their shoes, but you are not them. This is known as "cognitive empathy" and is the kind of empathy that this book refers to – though of course emotional empathy may sometimes be felt – and be entirely appropriate.

Empathy involves a cognitive state of awareness of the feelings behind what is being said. The key to effective empathy lies in the ability to read the non-verbal messages that a person is giving, including body language, tone of voice, facial expressions and the cues and clues that they give in the way that they communicate. This in turn involves intuition and an ability to attune to oneself and to others.

In personal life, an ability to feel empathy towards another can sustain and enhance a relationship and its absence, especially over time, can sometimes be fatally damaging to it.

In professional life, empathy lies at the core of a counselling or therapeutic relationship, and is central to other professions that involve trust, interpersonal communications and mutual understanding. It is the cornerstone of building rapport, whether with clients, staff or colleagues, so there is barely any field of activity in which it is not needed.

Empathy and evolution

Charles Darwin's theory of natural selection gave rise to the concept of "survival of the fittest", which has been largely interpreted to justify fierce competition in many fields.

There is, however, also a view that cooperation, social connectedness and empathy played a great part in mankind's evolutionary development. This view goes back more than a century, and has been reinforced by the psychologist and biologist Frans de Waal, who has pointed out that many animals survive not by competition and killing, but by cooperating and sharing. De Waal believes that although we as a species are incentive-driven and have both a selfish and social side to our natures, our development is primarily based on our capacity for empathy and our ability to understand the other.

> In his book *The Age of Empathy: Nature's Lessons for a Kinder Society* Frans de Waal reminds us that we are a group of animals who may at times be belligerent and aggressive, but mostly we are peace loving, cooperative and responsive to injustice; and that when we are in danger we overlook our divisions. He points out that we share these reflexes not just with other mammals but also with many animals: they are reflexes that "go back to the deepest most ancient layers of our brain".

Empathy and sympathy

Although the terms empathy and sympathy are often used interchangeably, they embrace different ways of responding, though not always consistently.

Empathy involves sensing and identifying with what the other person is feeling while maintaining objectivity, whereas sympathy can have different meanings including support for a cause or sharing another's feelings, but is primarily understood to mean a state of support or concern for another's sorrow without necessarily sharing the feelings.

Empathy and rapport

Rapport is a comfortable, relaxed and mutually accepting interaction between people who relate well to each other and who may be said to be "on the same wavelength". When people have established rapport with one another, communications are easier and understandings can more readily be arrived at.

Establishing rapport can be fundamental to gaining mutual trust and confidence. There are various ways to develop rapport, but empathy is undoubtedly a key factor in doing so.

Empathy in a professional context

Empathy and rapport can play a considerable part in a professional, business or any other working relationship, establishing trust and better communication and understanding, an enhanced sense of confidence and goodwill and inevitably also an enhanced professional reputation. The professional "gets" what the client or patient is saying and feeling.

Although the principles relating to empathy apply universally to all fields of activity, some specific professions will be briefly considered by way of example:

Counselling and psychotherapy: The therapist's ability to understand the client's feelings with sensitivity and accuracy is critical to the counselling or therapeutic relationship. The psychologist Carl Rogers, one of the founders of the humanistic approach to psychotherapy, observed in his classic work *On Becoming a Person: A Therapist's View of Psychotherapy* that change was most likely to occur when the therapist empathetically grasped the immediate experience of the client's inner world, without losing the separateness of his own identity.

Social work: Empathy is similarly integral to an effective social worker–client relationship: To assist people effectively, social workers need to understand their clients and enter their situations and their worlds.

Medicine: Patients are likely to respond better to empathetic practitioners. Taking care not to over-identify with the patient's emotions does not preclude attuning to the patient, which may help to identify underlying needs. Despite time constraints, rapport and attunement can be established in a few minutes if genuinely felt.

Law: Working with facts, laws and opinions and exercising intuitive judgement is not mutually exclusive with empathy. On the contrary, many (perhaps most) clients will want and expect their lawyers to have a sensitive understanding of them and their issues and needs.

Education: In order to enhance learning, educators need to understand their students and their individual needs. Furthermore, students may model their behaviour and relationships on what they experience from others, including family, friends and teachers. An empathetic teacher will not only teach the curriculum more effectively but will be teaching life skills.

Banking and financial services: As reported in the UK's *Financial Times* in 2013, crises in this sector have moved the profession towards placing greater value on the "softer" skills of empathy and social responsibility. One leading banker observed that "client-centricity is the key". There is a need to build and maintain relationships and to enhance trust within society.

Marketing, advertising, design and creative arts: These activities demand an understanding of the people one is working with and for, their needs, thinking and feelings. Correspondingly, the arts may be used as a way of developing empathy, particularly in collaborative projects.

These examples all overlap: what has been said for any profession may have a resonance and relevance in almost any other.

Empathy, compassion and humanity

Compassion for those who are troubled, suffering or experiencing illness, poverty or misfortune is an integral part of our common humanity, revered by all the world's major religions. It is founded on empathy, in the sense of feeling for another, but adds to it a wish and motivation to do something to help those with whom we feel empathy.

Should judges, politicians, administrators and others in public office have and exhibit empathy and compassion? On the basis that compassion is integral to our humanity, arguably this is not optional but essential.

President Barack Obama referred to an "empathy deficit" in the US and said that: "We need somebody who's got the heart, the empathy, to recognize what it's like to be a young teenage mom, the empathy to understand what it's like to be poor or African-American or gay or disabled or old – and that's the criterion by which I'll be selecting my judges."

Empathy and reflective function (mentalisation or "theory of mind")

Empathy is closely related to the reflective function (or "mentalisation") which Professor Peter Fonagy refers to as the way in which people "try to understand each other's mental states: their thoughts and feelings, beliefs and desires in order to make sense of and, even more important, to anticipate each other's actions". Also known as "theory of mind", this is what enables people to understand their own and others' behaviour.

Reflective function embodies two components, self-reflection and interpersonal reflection. These fundamental components apply to all people, irrespective of gender, race, ethnicity or culture. However, there are likely to be significant differences between individuals as to how in practice they are able to function reflectively, depending primarily upon their own personal experience of having their caregivers and others attuning to them.

The reflective function does not operate effectively in certain conditions. For example, some people on the autism spectrum may have difficulty in understanding the inner states of others. Similarly, people with certain personality disorders may lack capacity for emotional empathy; there would appear to be a neurological basis for this shortcoming.

"Against empathy"?

Notwithstanding the importance of empathy, there are also concerns about it in some circumstances including, for example, its potential to create an inappropriate bias in favour of those for whom one might feel emotional empathy when that is not combined with cognitive awareness and rational thought. This is an aspect developed in the work *Against Empathy: The Case for Rational Compassion* by Professor Paul Bloom.

The argument against emotional empathy is also illustrated by a report that English barristers questioned regulatory guidance for youth court advocacy that they should have the ability to "empathise and build trust with young people". One barrister's response to this was that she would have trouble empathising with someone who had daubed a swastika over a building – though she would nevertheless do her best to do her job of representing such a person.

These are legitimate concerns that demand reflection on what empathy embodies in a professional context. It certainly does not mean sharing the feelings (with emotional empathy) of anyone engaged in a hate campaign. It might rather involve understanding those feelings while providing professional support, even while also fundamentally disagreeing with them and expressing that disagreement. The professional is not neutral in the face of unacceptable behaviour or beliefs, and can make his or her views perfectly clear, but can still maintain empathy and compassion for the client at a personal, human level.

Professor Bloom might perhaps contend that this is not empathy but kindness. He is not in fact against all empathy, but primarily where it is said to arise in a moral context and where it is misapplied. He supports the concept of empathy combined with reason (and ideally with a cost–benefit analysis), drawing on a "more distanced" compassion and kindness. This may resonate to some extent with the concept of "boundaried empathy" that this work espouses.

But being professionals does not mean that we lose our humanity or our ability to feel emotional empathy – to respond with emotional resonance to a parent experiencing or recounting the death of a child, a couple having a moment of deep sadness and tenderness when recognising the ending of their marriage or the sense of relief and joy felt by someone anxiously awaiting an outcome and receiving positive news. We do not need to over-intellectualise empathy.

There is undoubtedly scope for debate about the distinctions between empathy, kindness and compassion and the extent to which this may be a semantic distinction. However, the underlying thesis of this work is that the combination of head, heart and gut supports good professionalism – which can support the beliefs of both Frans de Waal and Paul Bloom.

Attunement

In its broadest and simplest sense, attunement means reaching harmony and accord.

In the musical sense, this involves being in tune and at the right pitch. In the personal relational sense, it involves being in harmony with another person – or with oneself.

Attunement is an integral component of empathy and as such warrants consideration. Three aspects of attunement will be considered.

Attunement between parent and child: attachment theory

Attachment theory is a concept formulated by psychoanalyst John Bowlby that the infant is in effect programmed to seek closeness to a parent or carer who provides comfort and protection. His thesis was that humans need to form close affectional bonds and that the carer, by offering that closeness, allows the infant the secure base from which to develop. With well-attuned bonds, the infant is likely to develop greater emotional security as a child and adult. If, however, there is no carer or the carer cannot attune effectively to the infant, then the infant is likely to have later insecurity problems manifesting in different ways.

For an infant to develop a secure sense of self, the primary caregiver (generally the mother) must not just demonstrate that she understands the child's feelings, of distress for example, but she must respond in a way that communicates her understanding effectively and in a way that sensitively contains such distress or other feelings.

If the infant does not have a well-attuned relationship with an adult caregiver during the early critical years, the later insecure attachment may take different forms including avoidance of emotional connection, ambivalence or attention-seeking. In extreme cases, the level of attachment may be so poor as to be regarded as *disorganised*, which in turn can result in other issues as set out in Chapter 12 relating to high conflict personalities.

Peter Fonagy has observed that there is a circular nature in relation to reflective function and secure attachment in that "a reflective caregiver increases the likelihood of the child's secure attachment which, in turn, facilitates the development of mentalisation". This mirroring enables the child to develop a proper understanding of his or her own mental states (and feelings) and those of others.

Interpersonal adult attunement

Effective attunement enables us to pick up non-verbal signals from another – body language, facial expressions, tone of voice, eye contact – and responding appropriately and authentically in a way that acknowledges that he has been truly heard and understood.

Authenticity is critical to attunement. This cannot be simulated: we can't adopt Groucho Marx's (slightly adapted) quip: "Authenticity is everything in life. If you can fake that, you've got it made." People can lie with words, but our bodies do not lie.

In *The Mindful Brain: Reflection and Attunement in the Cultivation of Well-being*, Daniel J. Siegel refers to the focus that one person can have on the mind of another, which he considers to be crucial "if people in relationships are to feel vibrant and alive, understood, and at peace". His work explores the relevance and value of *mindfulness* in helping people to move towards a state of attunement and well-being.

> In an article on the www.scholastic.com website entitled "Attunement: Reading the Rhythms of the Child", Bruce D. Perry has written about the importance of attunement in working with children. He sees it as central to good teaching. The teacher is aware of the child's feelings and whether she is interested and engaged, and considers individually and in the immediate circumstances what the best way is to communicate ideas and facts to her and to "engage, encourage and excite her about this subject". How the child hears, perceives, feels and learns will depend on the child's receptivity, which the teacher needs to be able to pick up and communicate non-verbally.

Intrapersonal attunement

Being attuned to oneself is arguably essential to optimal professional functioning, having readier access to one's intuitive faculties, attuning to others and coping better with the demands of professional and personal life. We become more aware of our immediate experiences and intentions. Daniel Siegel refers to the ability to attune to our own state by attending to our intentions, creating "a kind of internal emotional closeness or 'becoming our own best friend'". This self-awareness and harmony with ourselves enables us to be more flexible and resilient as well as receptive, connected, compassionate and empathetic.

For many of us, achieving self-acceptance, letting go of self-criticism, judgements and thoughts, living "in the moment", functioning with a sense of inner harmony may not be easy. People have different ways of seeking to do this. For some it may be meditation or prayer, for others it may be losing themselves in music, physical activities or other forms of relaxation. Some seek support in counselling, others in spiritual practice.

The basic neuroscience of empathy, attunement and attachment

Mirror neurons

Observation of the way in which monkeys mimic the actions of those they are watching contributed to the awareness that we share with them brain functions that notice others and resonate with them and their actions, producing a reflexive response ("resonance behaviours"). The parts of the brain activated in this way are the *mirror neurons*, which help us to attune to the emotional states of others.

Research incorporating scanning technology has lent support to the view that the mirror neuron system is involved in empathy. Regions of the brain shown to be operative when one experiences certain emotions are similarly operative when observing someone else experiencing those emotions.

Other parts of the brain affecting empathy and attunement

Louis Cozolino in *The Neuroscience of Human Relationships: Attachment and the Developing Social Brain* postulates that mirror circuitry may be expanded to include other brain systems with a fundamental network that links imitation, resonance and empathy.

Research has shown that our right-side *supramarginal gyrus* (part of the parietal lobe) has a role in controlling the projection of our own emotions onto others, and enables us to be empathetic and compassionate towards others. The *insula cortex* too has a role, by enabling us to distinguish between ourselves and others. It bridges our bodily experience and our conscious awareness, and becomes activated both when we experience pain ourselves and when we observe someone else for whom we care experiencing pain.

Daniel Siegel observes that our internal attunement creates a state of internal resonance within the brain. He considers that repeated activation of attuned intrapersonal states results in neuroplastic changes and integration within our neural structure. If intrapersonal attunement produces integration in the brain, then interpersonal attunement can occur.

Neural development and attachment

At birth, the neural circuits of the brain responsible for vital functions are fully viable but the higher regions (the limbic system and cerebral cortex) are undeveloped. The infant brain has its most rapid growth during the first 12 months of life, continuing to 24 months. During this early period, the orbitofrontal part of the pre-frontal cortex develops and matures. This has a critical function in relation to emotions, to social facility and to the ability to empathise with others. It also has the capacity to suppress impulses that are not socially acceptable.

The way in which the orbitofrontal cortex develops is directly linked to the infant's experience with caring adults. If the carer's reactions are positive and pleasurable, the infant's body produces a biochemical response that helps the brain's connections to grow more effectively. If, however, the infant experiences the carer's reactions as negative and fearful, both the biochemical response and the memory are different, with consequent negative effects on the development of the orbitofrontal cortex.

One of the chemicals that has a significant effect on the body is the stress hormone *cortisol*. Excesses or deficiencies can lead to various physical symptoms and disease states. The body has an elaborate system for regulating the amount of cortisol in the bloodstream. When infants become stressed, their bodies produce higher levels of cortisol. This is dangerous for them because their immature systems do not cope well with high levels of cortisol which affect the development of neurotransmitter systems whose pathways are still being established. Too much cortisol in infancy can reduce the number of cortisol receptors in the hippocampus, and result in there being fewer of these to cope with stress in adulthood.

Cortisol generation in infants can be triggered by various interactions with their caregivers. Being consistently ignored when crying or even negative facial responses can create stress. Infants responded to by sensitively attuned adults are likely to have lower stress and cortisol levels in infancy. As adults they can cope more easily with stress-induced cortisol.

Alan Schore believes that positive caregiving and consequent secure attachment promote brain growth and the development of complex internal regulatory systems and produce individuals who can respond with greater flexibility to emotional stimuli. Negative caregiving has a correspondingly negative impact on neurological development. Schore correlates caregiver–infant attunement with its accompanying neurobiological states and considers that these states may promote the wiring of healthy brain circuitry.

Neurobiology

There is also a chemical component to empathy. The body produces neurochemicals that affect reward, pain reduction and well-being and have a function in regulating bonding, empathy and altruism.

One of these most relevant to empathy is understood to be *oxytocin*. This is a hormone that facilitates childbirth and lactation, and which also has a role in maternal behaviour and bonding: between couples, between parent and child and between friends. It lowers the heart rate and blood pressure, counteracting the effects of stress hormones like cortisol.

Research has indicated that oxytocin in the body increases trust and generosity; and oxytocin levels have been shown to increase in response to the generosity of others – which in turn counteracts and reduces stress. Continuing research, not surprisingly, also indicates that hormonal effects are complex; there are, for example, situations in which being too trusting can have its own problems, and while oxytocin may facilitate bonding between those with similar characteristics, it could have an opposite effect in relation to those who do not share those characteristics. The overriding point, however, seems to be that oxytocin is associated with our ability to empathise and has been shown to play a major role in mediating social behaviours.

> In their book *Born for Love: Why Empathy Is Essential – and Endangered* Maia Szalavitz and Bruce D. Perry employ the metaphor of oxytocin as the oil that keeps social machinery running smoothly – eliminating friction and making people comfortable with one another.

Professional boundaries

Just as an absence of empathy may be damaging to a professional relationship, so may empathy and attunement with a complete lack of professional boundaries.

Boundaried empathy

Some professionals have difficulty in knowing how to balance empathy and boundaries. The concern is that if you get too close to your client or patient and "over-identify", you are likely to lose objectivity and as a result be less effective professionally. Perhaps this is a particular issue for those who are helping to take their patients or clients through difficult times which may not necessarily end in the way that may be desired.

Yet it is a misconception that a professional cannot combine empathy with boundaries. An empathetic relationship with genuine concern for the client or patient does not necessarily require informality. A formal professional demeanour can be combined with empathy – though excessive formality can make it more difficult to establish empathy and attunement.

By the same token, excessive informality may be inappropriate and may feel uncomfortable, unless one has a genuinely informal relationship with the client or patient. Empathy with a client does not require you to become his or her "buddy".

You can be friendly without becoming a friend. You are still the professional and need to have a clear boundary as such.

The concept of "boundaried empathy" is outlined in Chapter 12 in the context of high conflict situations, but it is in fact relevant to all professional relationships. The guiding rule in all cases may be: "Be fully and genuinely empathetic but also remember your boundaries."

Other professional boundaries

Professionals of course have other boundaries to observe. The professional relationship may commonly involve some power imbalance, an element of authority on the part of the professional, and trust and sometimes vulnerability on the part of the client or patient.

Consequently, the professional has a responsibility not to exploit that relationship. This may be part of the professional's prescribed code of ethical behaviour, but even if it isn't specified, it should be an implicit and normal expectation of professional conduct.

The boundaries may relate to different aspects. For example, there need to be clear sexual boundaries between healthcare professionals and their patients. In the UK, the Council for Healthcare Regulatory Excellence has an information booklet, which includes warnings against sexualised behaviour and how to avoid this. Similar prohibitions apply in the counselling and therapeutic and social work fields. The British Association for Counselling and Psychotherapy has an ethical requirement that practitioners must not abuse their client's trust in order to gain sexual, emotional, financial or any other kind of personal advantage.

Financial professionals would be breaching ethical boundary rules – and in many jurisdictions also the law – by using information gained through their professional activities in order to achieve a personal gain, for example by trading in a public company's shares or stock based on insider information not available to the general public. A financial adviser should not receive an undisclosed commission on funds that he is investing for his client.

The message is quite simple: the professional must respect professional boundaries and must not do anything that may be, or may be perceived to be, an exploitation or abuse of that relationship.

Personal–professional boundaries

How do we each choose to balance and maintain boundaries between our work and private lives? A doctor who may be on call at any time, a lawyer who has a genuine deadline, a journalist who has to follow up on an important story: there will be real difficulties in trying to separate work and private time. But these may at times indeed be choices: sometimes one can choose not to bring work home or to contact clients after hours. They become patterns of behaviour, ways of life.

There is an anecdote about the artist René Magritte (which may well be apocryphal). It is said that in the morning he would get up, put on a suit, leave his home, walk round the block, return to his house at a different entrance, enter his studio, change into his artist's smock and paint for the day. At the end of the day he would do the reverse: change back into his suit, walk round the block, and return home. Thus he managed to separate his work and professional life in a very distinct way. Whether or not actually true, the story graphically illustrates the concept of division between professional and personal life.

Especially with ever-increasing communication and networking resources and expectations, it can be really hard for a professional to create and maintain boundaries between work and home life. Nor can these be rigid, since there will inevitably be times and circumstances when breaching these boundaries will be necessary.

These difficulties may be compounded when a client or patient tests one's personal boundaries. What to do if they ask for your home phone number in case they need to contact you urgently over the weekend? Of course, much depends on the circumstances and needs of the situation and the nature of the professional relationship. This may be a genuine need and an inherent part of the professional role; but you may be faced with a choice about how far you are willing to go in allowing the work to cross over into your personal and family life. Might this be "the thin edge of the wedge" in a creeping erosion of boundaries?

Some final thoughts about boundaries

While ethical boundaries need to be strictly observed, there can be no definitive rules about personal boundaries that will apply generally. They will vary for different kinds of work and for different needs.

Each of us will need to reflect on our approach towards personal and professional boundaries and consider our "default" policy – our standard response in the absence of special considerations. We may, for example, decide to preserve our private life and details unless special circumstances necessitate some other approach. Having a thoughtful, considered and appropriate approach may at least save us from slipping unconsciously into boundary breaches.

Where we may have to provide personal details, it can be helpful to maintain a dedicated private landline or mobile-phone number and e-mail address specifically for professional needs, so that without prejudicing our client relationships we can protect our personal details when we need to, and distinguish personal communications from work ones.

Sometimes we need to remind ourselves that empathy and personal boundaries are not mutually exclusive and that supporting our clients effectively can co-exist with preserving the integrity of our personal and family life. We need to keep these thoughts in our consciousness.

Further reading

The topic of empathy is included in many psychology books. Two that give it special focus are Maia Szalavitz and Bruce D. Perry's *Born for Love: Why Empathy Is Essential – and Endangered* and Frans de Waal's *The Age of Empathy: Nature's Lessons for a Kinder Society*. For a wider consideration of the issues, Paul Bloom's *Against Empathy: The Case for Rational Compassion* raises questions about the misapplication of empathy.

Attunement, also covered in many general works, receives special attention in the context of neurological function and mindfulness in Daniel J. Siegel's *The Mindful Brain: Reflection and Attunement in the Cultivation of Well-being*.

In *The Neuroscience of Human Relationships: Attachment and the Developing Social Brain*, Louis Cozolino explores what he calls "interpersonal neurobiology", the concept that the brain is a social organ built through experience. This exploration includes examining mirror neurons and the biology of attachment, and also the healing power of relationships.

An accessible introduction to attachment in infants is contained in Sue Gerhardt's excellent book *Why Love Matters: How Affection Shapes a Baby's Brain*. In greater clinical and theoretical depth are Peter Fonagy's authoritative works *Attachment Theory and Psychoanalysis*, which focuses on the relationship between attachment theory and psychoanalysis, and *Affect Regulation, Mentalization, and the Development of the Self* (which he edited).

Chapter 9

Professional relationships and expectations

"The doctor will see you shortly. Try
not to disappoint him"

Credit: CartoonStock.com

Expectations of professional relationships

Expectations about the professional personally

Clients' expectations may include some or all of the following:

*   *Skill and expertise:* Self-evidently, the point of consulting professionals is usually to receive skilled, expert service.

    In many professions, professionals will have some accrediting qualification confirming that they have trained and reached an acceptable level of competence. It does not indicate the level of their skill, but like the driver's licence that allows one to go onto the road alone, it is a helpful, often essential, starting point.

    All professionals need to maintain up-to-date knowledge of their field, develop expertise, enhance existing skills and gain new ones. Some professional bodies demand continuing professional development (CPD); but whether or not this is formalised, it should be a part of every professional's DNA that he or she chooses to do this in any event. Maintaining skills and expertise must be any professional's top priority.

> Wisdom is not a product of schooling but the lifelong attempt to acquire it.
> (Albert Einstein, letter to J. Dispentiere, 24 March 1954)

- *Judgement:* This will be a combination of intuition and analytical skills. It may be a product of age and experience; but some people are lucky enough to have it from early on: wisdom, it is said, is not measured by the length of one's beard.

  As professionals, we can enhance the quality of our judgement by effective listening, thorough preparation, attention to detail, adopting a reflective approach, seeking support where needed, extending our knowledge and experience, understanding people, psychology and patterns of behaviour – and learning from our mistakes.
- *Acting in the client's best interests:* This is a primary professional requirement. Clearly a professional should not continue to act if there is a material conflict between his or her interests and those of the client or if for any other reason he or she is unable to make the client's interests the top priority.
- *Professional demeanour:* This does not refer to some imagined professional pomp and formality, but rather to the circumstances, culture and expectations.

  The degree of formality appropriate is a matter of culture, judgement, mutual respect and personal authenticity. Maintaining formality may help with maintaining boundaries, though many professionals are able to be informal and friendly and yet fully professional.

  Ultimately, excellence of skill and service trumps perceptions of demeanour: if one is clearly skilled and competent, any differences from an expected norm may be more readily accepted. However, a poor initial client impression can become self-fulfilling and it may be harder to gain the client's confidence (see "the Golem effect" below).
- *Empathy and attunement to the client – listening effectively:* It is fundamental for professionals to have a proper understanding of the client's needs, concerns and aspirations by active listening and appropriate response.
- *Integrity:* Clients expect the professionals they consult to be honest with them and not to mislead them or take advantage of the relationship. This includes telling them if they have doubts about any aspect of the work, however difficult this may be to do.
- *Clear communications:* There should be clear communications, whether oral or written, in language that is understandable without being patronising – as addressed in Chapter 10.

- *Professional energy:* This may be viewed as the ability of a professional to "make things happen" effectively. A medical professional is expected not just to diagnose, but to be able to arrange for treatment and follow-up; a legal professional should be able to advise on and implement best strategy. The professional should be a "self-starter" and not only know what needs to be done, but should be able to go ahead and do it.
- *Proper and fair charging:* The public generally expect that private professionals will charge a fair and proper fee. Costs should be clearly agreed in advance or where there are imponderable future elements, clients should be given information enabling them to make a realistic estimate, with regular updates.
- *Confidentiality:* The client is entitled to expect the professional to maintain strict confidentiality about the client's affairs.
- *Other personal expectations:* Other expectations may be based on the professional's reputation or marketing, public perceptions, or the client's own beliefs.

Expectations about the professional environment

A professional environment may be physical and/or psychological. The physical environment relates to the premises from which the professional works and the resources that support his work – including secretarial, technological and administrative back-up. With increasingly sophisticated technology, expectations of immediacy of response have also increased.

Professional social networking has also increased and for many people is now integral to their practices. Similarly, information resources and relevant links may be available online; and for most professionals, a web presence is essential.

There are of course no objective criteria for professional premises: everything depends on context. A law firm servicing large corporations and wealthy individuals is likely to have different needs, and the clients different expectations, from a neighbourhood law firm undertaking publicly funded work and dealing with local issues.

> A client, used to his solicitor working in a small, neighbourhood firm, when first consulting him at plush City offices to which he had moved was heard to say: "What smart new offices these are. I suppose I'll be paying for these in my fees!"

Is the client put at ease when meeting with the professional? Are the reception, waiting arrangements and meeting room client-friendly? Has the professional ensured that s/he will not be interrupted by incoming calls? Is there hospitality for the client – tea or coffee or even just a glass of water? These can be implemented on a shoestring budget: they just require thought and sensitivity.

The psychological environment refers to the client's feelings about the professional's set-up. Is the environment secure and calming and is there adequate time to deal with the issues? Clients' conscious or unconscious awareness of the psychological environment will at some level inform them whether or not their experience was positive and productive.

Expectations about the work to be done

Everyone will want the best possible professional outcome. Sometimes this will be specific and predictable, for example preparing a tax return, drafting a will or building a conservatory, but sometimes not. When consulting a doctor, instructing a lawyer on a dispute or calling in social services, one doesn't necessarily know the outcome.

This is where the professional's judgement, experience, empathy and communication skills will be particularly important. People like certainty, albeit that this is rarely possible, and are not trained to manage uncertainty. Consequently, the professional may find himself having to manage the client's expectations in the context of an uncertain outcome.

Managing clients' expectations

Difficulties will arise where there is a mismatch between the client's expectations and the realities of what can be achieved. The best available outcome may fall short of that anticipated by the client, which can lead to disappointment and recrimination. Part of the professional's task is to manage the client's expectations by trying to ensure that these are reasonable and realistic.

- A professional should try to understand the client's requirements, not necessarily just on the basis of what is presented, but also any underlying expectations. Misunderstandings can easily arise because the professional and the client may each be making different assumptions, so it is worth spending a bit of time checking one's understandings.
- Where expectations are unrealistic or unreasonable, the professional needs to say so – with sensitivity but unambiguously. This carries the risk that the client may feel that you are not committed to him or her. Nevertheless, it remains your duty to be realistic: perhaps there are better ways of achieving the client's goals; perhaps they are unattainable but others can be explored; or perhaps the client simply needs to be helped to accept the true position.
- Not uncommonly one's professional view may be that a client's position is not so much wrong as uncertain, that while there is a prospect of achieving the goals, the risks are higher than the client perceives. Here again, there is a duty to make those risks clear, perhaps to quantify them insofar as that can be done. Lowering expectations to discount risk may be a legitimate thing to do;

but doing so purely by way of insurance against not achieving a client's legitimate and achievable goals would be questionable.

The power of expectations

There is a credible view that our thoughts influence what happens to us, not just at a conscious level, but also unconsciously. Certainly, that is the basis of the placebo and nocebo effects and the Rosenthal (or Pygmalion) effect, described in Chapter 5: the phenomenon that the greater the expectation placed on people, the better they are likely to perform. This principle appears to be applicable to people in many different environments. For example, researchers have found that employee performance in the workplace is influenced by managers' expectations. The corollary (sometimes called "the Golem effect") is that people with poor expectations are more likely to perform badly. Unconscious belief structures govern our thinking and, to a significant extent, our lives.

> We are what we think ... Our thoughts create the world.
> (Prince Gautama Siddharta – the Buddha –
> the founder of Buddhism)

In his fascinating book *Predictably Irrational*, Professor Dan Ariely writes about the effect of expectations and "why the mind gets what it expects". His experimental research has led him to the proposition that when we believe that something will be good, it will generally be good, as well as the corollary that when we think it will be bad, it will be bad.

By way of example, one study involved serving coffee in two different environments: one had beautiful condiment containers adjacent, the other had styrofoam containers. Although the coffee was identical, those blind-testing the coffee rated it significantly higher when drinking in the beautiful container environment than when drinking it in the "cheaper" environment, and would have been willing to pay more for it. As Ariely observes: "When the coffee ambience looked upscale ... the coffee tasted upscale as well."

Other experiments have demonstrated that if we believe a painkiller is strong, effective and expensive, it will work better than if we think that it is a cheap option. Experiments have also shown that expectations affect our views and behaviour about people based on the stereotypes that we have – our expectations about them. Our preconceptions and expectations create an unconscious bias and effect that influence our actions.

It is worth being aware of these unconscious forces when reflecting on our clients' expectations, and also those unconscious expectations, beliefs and biases that we may have as professionals, believing that we are truly objective and rational.

Client-centredness (person-centredness)

The concept of client-centredness (person-centredness) was conceived by Carl Rogers, one of the founders of the humanistic approach to psychology. This concept, although originating within a psychological context, has relevance in many other fields – as Rogers himself envisaged. They include the following (adapted to make them more generally relevant):

Congruence: Rogers defined congruence as "a matching of experience, awareness, and communication" and explained that this meant that a person's deepest feelings matched what he was saying. Incongruence, on the other hand, arises where there is a mismatch between what a person is saying and what he is feeling. An example of incongruence is someone who is visibly angry in a discussion, as is clear from his tone of voice and volume, his flushed face, his clenched fist and his other body language – yet when it is suggested that he is angry he denies this: "I'm not angry, I'm just explaining this to you."

Congruence includes a correspondence between the professional's personal and professional views and in his or her relationship with the client, being trustworthy and consistent, sharing common goals, and genuinely supporting the client in moving towards those goals.

Genuineness: The concepts of genuineness and congruence are closely related. Genuineness refers to the professional not importing some image or persona ("this is how a judge/lawyer/therapist/doctor/teacher/nurse/banker should be") but being his or her authentic self, deeply involved and sharing his or her own experiences openly with the client where appropriate.

Client empowerment: In a therapeutic context, this involves facilitating the client's growth, development, self-awareness and inner strength. More generally, it ties in with the concept of empowerment as a reaction against the dominance exerted by professionals and the relatively subservient role played by clients and patients. From the professional's perspective, it involves respecting and having due regard to the client's or patient's wishes and priorities, even if having to question or challenge these, and viewing the relationship as being in the nature of a team rather than maintaining professional dominance.

In his 1961 book *On Becoming a Person*, Carl Rogers made the fundamental observation that it is the client who deeply knows and understands what his issues and problems are and which direction to go to address them.

Accepting the client as s/he is: In a therapeutic context, Rogers calls this "unconditional positive regard" – acceptance of the client without judgement. This seems to be a useful general principle for virtually all professions.

Empathetic understanding: The concept of empathy surfaces again, pulling the various strands together.

These Rogerian principles can provide a useful foundation for establishing good working relationships with clients.

Transference and countertransference

The concepts, coming from psychoanalytical theory, may potentially arise in other kinds of professional relationships, so it is helpful to have an understanding of them.

Transference

In psychoanalysis, people may unconsciously transfer the feelings, perceptions and desires that they had towards early significant figures in their lives onto the analyst. This transference forms a cornerstone of psychoanalytical practice. So, for example, the person in analysis, the analysand, might unconsciously respond to the analyst as if he were her father, and the analyst might use this awareness as part of the therapeutic process.

Transference may well arise in other professional relationships, for example where a wife in a divorce complained to her (male) lawyer, who was about to go on holiday and leave the case in the hands of a colleague, "That's right. Leave me just like my husband did!"

Problems can arise with transference for example when the client views the professional in an unrealistic and inappropriate light, as the strong and wise mother figure or the protective father figure, looking to him or her to "make it better" and solve whatever problems the professional has been engaged to deal with. These unrealistic expectations are likely to lead to disappointment and reaction.

Countertransference

Countertransference is the corollary of transference, arising on the part of the analyst who experiences transference feelings towards the analysand. This can be helpful in a clinical context, where the therapist is aware of it and can use it to inform himself as to the reactions that this client is causing. However, it can be harmful where the therapist is unaware of what is happening or allows it to happen to meet his own psychological needs.

Translating this to other professions, countertransference may account for a professional becoming angry with the way that a client functions as it reminds the professional of some other person in his past. Or it may explain why a professional adopts an excessively protective role towards the client or has warm (or hostile) feelings in some cases.

Professionals should take care not to allow transference and countertransference to develop inappropriately. This may require the establishment of careful professional boundaries, which in turn necessitates understanding these concepts and maintaining a heightened vigilance of the professional's own reactions to the client, whether positive or negative.

Authority, power, trust and dependence

These concepts stand independently of one another, but may also be interconnected.

Authority

Professional authority may have at least two different aspects:

- There is the hierarchical authority that some professionals have in the organisation in which they operate, for example a consultant or matron in a hospital, a senior partner in a law firm, or indeed the autonomy of an independent practitioner in any field. This kind of authority generally carries with it power – to give directions and to make decisions.
- There is the authority that professionals generally have as experts in their fields, the possessors of specialist knowledge and skill and superior competence. This recognition and respect given to the professional by the client may create a form of power.

> Knowledge is power.
>
> (Francis Bacon, *Meditationes Sacrae*, 1597)

Clients will usually want their professionals to have some personal and professional authority, which in turn gives the client a sense of confidence. That authority needs to be solidly grounded: it does not mean assuming a "professional" air or pretending to know what one doesn't. It can be maintained just as much by acknowledging what one does not know and what will need further consideration and enquiry as by having immediate answers.

Power

In a professional relationship, the concept of power can manifest itself directly (*positional power*) or indirectly (*personal power*). Who makes the necessary decisions and what is the relationship between the professional and client or patient in this process?

Direct power, which links to *positional power*, arises as a result of the authority that comes with an official role, commonly as part of some institutional system. For example, managers generally have (limited) administrative power in relation to their employees. Institutional systems give power to people to enable them to carry out their functions – such power is positional rather than personal.

Indirect or *personal* power arises through the professional's personal authority, linked to experience, expertise, charisma, trustworthiness and communication skills, creating an influence which the client or patient cannot match and needs to accept.

Of course, there can be a hybrid of these different kinds of power: someone with positional power may well have the expertise, charisma and other qualities to be able to influence the client or patient in the decision-making process rather than having to exert power directly.

And how does money influence the power relationship? Consider the billionaire who wished to consult a solicitor about a non-urgent personal issue and who demanded an immediate meeting. The expectation was that the solicitor would rearrange his schedule to see this wealthy new client. Clearly, this power relationship would be different from one where the client did not have such financial resources.

The professional power relationship can be complex and subtle, and may be affected by a combination and interplay of factors, including:

- the official status of the professional and the power arising by virtue of his or her position;
- but limited by any constraints on the exercise of power that may be built into the system and the power of the client or patient to appeal to higher authority;
- the authority, standing, experience and expertise of the professional;
- at a personal level, the professional's charisma, trustworthiness and communication skills;
- the vulnerability of the client or patient in the circumstances of the relationship;
- the nature, complexity and uncertainties of the professional task and the degree of dependence that the client or patient has on the professional to carry it out;
- the level of professional mystique that the client or patient may have to penetrate;
- the financial and other resources of the client or patient and the ability to change professional representation and/or to seek supplementary professional support;
- the personal circumstances of the client or patient, including factors such as ability to articulate their views clearly, personal sense of authority and self, educational and social standing and cultural factors relating to acceptance of authority;
- external factors such as the level of third-party support that clients or patients may have or be able to get, whether personal or organisational, and the potential accountability to which the professional may be subject.

Power also needs to be seen in the context of the emergence of a client and patient empowerment culture. Professional power dynamics may be in the process of change.

Trust

The client or patient trusts the professional to deal with matters and problems that he or she cannot address personally. This is generally inherent in the professional relationship.

There is also a deeper kind of trust that the client or patient needs to be able to place in the professional, a sense that the professional is not only skilled and expert in his or her field, but understands the critical aspects, needs and experience of the client or patient. This is a sense that the professional "knows who I am and understands me and what I am looking for".

Establishing this deeper level of trust distinguishes those professionals who operate formally and impersonally, albeit technically proficiently, from those who relate more personally to their clients or patients. For a professional to have that relationship of trust and rapport and to communicate it to the client or patient requires a number of interrelated elements including empathy and reflective function as well as communication and interpersonal skills.

There is also a concept of *epistemic trust*, which is trust in the authenticity of knowledge and information that is passed down from one person to another. This kind of trust allows those receiving information and knowledge to set aside any scepticism and reservations, and to accept the information and knowledge as reliable. In the professional context, epistemic trust may not be automatic but may need to be earned.

The ethical principles applicable to the counselling relationship, as contained in the Ethical Framework of the British Association for Counselling and Psychotherapy (BACP), have a universal relevance to all fields of professional activity. The core ethical principles are as follows:

> Being trustworthy: honouring the trust placed in the practitioner.
> Autonomy: respect for the client's right to be self-governing.
> Beneficence: a commitment to promoting the client's wellbeing.
> Non-maleficence: a commitment to avoiding harm to the client.
> Justice: the fair and impartial treatment of all clients and the provision of adequate services.
> Self-respect: fostering the practitioner's self-knowledge, integrity and care for self.
>
> (BACP (2016) The Ethical Framework for the Counselling
> Professions. Lutterworth: BACP)

Dependence

It may be largely inevitable that clients who consult professionals will develop some degree of reliance on that relationship. Much depends on individual factors including the personality and vulnerability of the client; but even mature professionals consulting other professionals may to some extent be in this position.

At one level, professional dependence has obvious and understandable roots in the nature of the professional relationship. People who feel uncertain and vulnerable are going to look to their own "expert" for support and guidance.

However, many professions shroud themselves in mystique and jargon, lending themselves to professional dependence, with a professional culture and language that the professionals may take for granted, but which can be a mystery to laypeople.

The following pragmatic steps, insofar as they may be appropriate to the particular circumstances and level of dependence, may help in dealing with dependent clients:

- considering with the client what informal support systems he or she has, for example from family and friends, and whether these can be drawn upon;
- considering with the client whether counselling or therapy might be helpful (sometimes better understood as "obtaining professional support in difficult times");
- discussing cost implications of extensive support from the professional with the client and agreeing how the client's financial resources can be most efficiently used.

Culture and gender

Culture

Cultural influences affect people's world view, how they see things, what their values are, how they make decisions and may influence the way in which the professional views the client or patient, and vice versa. With many countries increasingly having a culturally diverse population, the probabilities of the professional and the client or patient having different cultural backgrounds and belief systems is similarly increasing.

Culture is not necessarily synonymous with nationality, ethnicity, race or religion, though it may arise from and relate to any of these. People and society group themselves in many different ways, whether by commonality of religion, nationality, sexual orientation, ethnicity or background, or whether by sharing a professional, business, social, workplace or geographical experience or history. So culture can take many different shapes and forms.

Culture can be complex, for example where one's religious cultural background conflicts with one's political and social beliefs. It can be easy to fall into the mistake of stereotyping people based on their ethnicity, religion or culture, when the reality may be far more complicated.

The professional cannot be expected to be aware of all the cultural influences that may arise in client or patient relationships but the following may help in managing these:

- awareness of and sensitivity to cultural diversity in its widest sense;
- willingness to learn more about the other's culture, which may include asking the client or patient to explain these in greater detail as necessary;
- respect for values that may differ significantly from the professional's own and discussing these with sensitivity and respect;
- avoiding making any assumptions, generalisations or stereotyping but rather treating each client or patient as an individual with his or her own views and needs rather than a member of a group;
- where appropriate, undertaking some prior research into the relevant cultural norms may be useful – but always taking care to avoid making assumptions.

Ultimately one is working with an individual, with individual beliefs, views, traits and needs, transcending any differences of culture, race, religion or ethnicity. One needs to have an awareness of how cultural norms may differ, of cultural diversity and an insight into one's own attitudes in this regard. But fundamentally if one works with empathy, authenticity and sensitivity, cultural differences will largely melt away into insignificance.

> Tolerance, inter-cultural dialogue and respect for diversity are more essential than ever in a world where peoples are becoming more and more closely interconnected.
> (Kofi Annan, former Secretary-General of the United Nations)

Gender

In addressing gender issues for professionals, there is the risk on the one hand of generalising into stereotypes and on the other hand of ignoring some patterns that do exist.

Patterns: One of the difficulties in identifying patterns is that they generally only show a trend and there will always be exceptions, sometimes significant, which challenge the existence or validity of the pattern.

So, for example, one may observe that men tend not to ask for directions when driving, whereas women will readily do so. However, there are also generally men who will observe that they readily ask for directions and women who do not do so.

This observation is an example of the kind of pattern that gets established as a result of conditioning and gender expectations when growing up. This may arise from families, schools, peers and society generally. Yet this is not always the case so it is perfectly possible for some, perhaps many, people not to experience this.

Communications and "language": John Gray wrote *Men Are from Mars, Women Are from Venus* with a light-hearted allegorical proposition that men originally came from Mars and women from Venus, and that while they have both learned a common language, they basically speak different languages and hence misunderstand one another.

The broad thesis of Gray's book, and indeed a widely held view, is that men and women have different ways of communicating because of their different values, approaches and conditioning. So, for example, men may be perceived as tending to be rational, women as emotional, men valuing competence with women valuing relationships, and women easily multi-tasking whereas men are better at working – and reasoning – sequentially.

On the other hand, in *The Myth of Mars and Venus: Do Men and Women Really Speak Different Languages?* Professor Deborah Cameron debunks what are described as the myths about language and the sexes. She believes that the position is more complicated and that perpetuating the myths can have detrimental effects, for example in the workplace, and that differences of language use and style of communications may arise just as much, if not more, between members of the same sex as they do between the sexes.

Brain and genetics: Research and brain scan imaging reflect that differences in structure, size, composition and wiring exist between male and female brains; but there is no consensus that these differences are significant, with contradictory results and views; and if they do differ, the effect of this on behaviour is neither clear nor agreed.

This whole topic tends understandably to be sensitive and controversial. What should be less controversial is, first, that there are many stereotypes and clichés about how women and men function, and, second, that there are gender disparities in earnings, career progression and representation in some of the most senior positions in business, politics and other fields.

Negotiation: Research undertaken by Professor Linda Babcock, as outlined in her book co-written with Sara Laschever *Ask for It: How Women Can Use the Power of Negotiation to Get What They Really Want*, indicates that women do not actually ask for what they want and need, whereas men have no reservations about doing so. Professor Babcock's research showed that men initiate negotiations to advance their interests about four times as frequently as women do, with adverse consequences for women.

Some basics: In this complex and sometimes confusing and contradictory environment, it may be worth reminding ourselves of the following:

- The primary and overriding consideration in all professional relationships is that we are dealing with an individual and not a stereotype. As with cultural differences, we should avoid making any assumptions, generalisations or stereotyping and treat each client or patient as an individual with his or her own views and needs.

- Irrespective of gender, if it seems necessary we can support individuals, for example by facilitating discussion to ensure that questions are not left unasked and issues not left unaddressed.
- Professionals need to understand people's different ways of functioning, which may differ significantly from the professional's mode. Responding sensitively does not mean mimicking an emotional response to an emotional client. Rather it means being respectful of the client's way of being and communicating, and responding in an appropriately empathetic way.

With gender as with culture, the key lies in practising one's profession with empathy, authenticity and sensitivity. All the rest is gloss.

Further reading

While Dan Ariely's *Predictably Irrational* has only one chapter, "The Effect of Expectations: Why the Mind Gets What It Expects", dealing with expectations, much of the book is based on the effect of unconscious thinking and attitudes and is a very good read.

In relation to the support and management of business customers, *Managing Expectations: Working with People Who Want More, Better, Faster, Sooner, Now!* by Naomi Karten is adaptable to professional circumstances.

Central to client-centredness is Carl Rogers' classic *A Therapist's View of Psychotherapy: On Becoming a Person*, one of the foundations of humanistic psychology.

Books on gender issues include John Gray's *Men Are from Mars, Women Are from Venus*; Deborah Cameron's *The Myth of Mars and Venus: Do Men and Women Really Speak Different Languages?*; Lewis Wolpert's *Why Can't a Woman Be More Like a Man?*; and Linda Babcock and Sara Laschever's *Ask for It: How Women Can Use the Power of Negotiation to Get What They Really Want*.

Deborah Tannen's books *You Just Don't Understand: Women and Men in Conversation* and *Talking from 9 to 5: Women and Men at Work* both effectively cover the issue of communications with gender understanding.

Chapter 10

Enhancing professional relationships

Communication and other interpersonal skills

"To be understood by another person, one must not authorize validity to the very prospect of invalidation which has the potential to assume its own assumption of deficiency within the very milieu of the message. *That is the key to clear and effective communication!*"

Credit: Glasbergen.com

Essential communication skills

Professional skill and expertise, judgement, integrity and empathy may be critical but unless one can communicate effectively, much of the benefit of these attributes can be lost. Communication skills grounded in empathy will support all kinds of professional practice.

Active listening

In all communications, and especially for a client or patient in a professional relationship, it is very important to be heard, and to feel and know that you are being heard and properly understood. This is the cornerstone of effective communication.

Active listening involves allowing someone to speak without interruption, giving thoughtful attention to what is being said, picking up the nuances and any underlying feelings or concerns, and acknowledging and responding appropriately.

This doesn't mean that one cannot seek clarification while listening or make an appropriate comment or observation, as long as it is sensitive to the speaker. Some professionals just go through the motions of listening, while thinking about their response. It may take some practice to listen actively, to suspend judgement and to defer responding until fully understanding not only what has been said but the underlying feeling; but as it becomes more familiar to do so, the skill becomes more effective.

Of course, active listening can be time-consuming and it may not always be practicable to do this as fully as one might wish. A doctor with a short fixed-time slot may not be able to afford the time or a lawyer conscious of his hourly rate may need to be time-conscious. Helping the speaker to maintain a focus, probing with questions and cutting short discussion when appropriate are not necessarily inconsistent with active listening. Where one is fully engaged, most clients or patients will understand if the professional needs to keep control of the time. What most do not appreciate is being listened to perfunctorily.

> The American poet and novelist Alice Duer Miller referred to listening as taking a "vigorous, human interest" in what is being said. And in a message for the 2016 World Day of Social Communications, Pope Francis said that listening "is much more than simply hearing … [it] is about communication, and calls for closeness" (© Libreria Editrice Vaticana).

Observing non-verbal communications

Non-verbal communications comprise a range of unspoken ways of sending messages, whether consciously or more usually unconsciously, including:

- body language such as facial expression, posture, gestures and actions;
- eye contact and direction of gaze;
- voice tone, volume inflection, silences and hesitation;
- issues around the maintenance of personal space.

Most of us are likely to have a natural ability to observe someone and pick up things that have not been said but are merely hinted at. For example, a client looking at a watch may be as pointed as actually saying: "I think that we're using time ineffectively here." But our instincts may not always be sufficient to support our observations. In particular:

- Differences of culture may affect our understandings of non-verbal cues and clues. For example, in Western culture one shows straightforwardness and honesty by looking a person in the eye when talking. However, in many

Asian and Middle Eastern cultures eye contact may be thought to be disrespectful. There may be subtle cultural protocols that require special understandings, even within cultural and ethnic groups in the West.

- Mirror neurons have a role in helping us to attune to the emotional states of others. Shortcomings in the brain's mirror neuron circuitry are likely to have the effect of limiting our capacity to understand non-verbal signals and cues. So for example being on the autism spectrum may involve some malfunctioning of the mirror neuron system.

- Our innate ability to understand others may be enhanced by learning more about non-verbal communications and by mindful face-to-face interaction with others – and may be diminished by the increase in the use of social media, texts, e-mails, mobile-phone calls and other media that do not involve face-to-face communications.

Professionals can treat non-verbal communications as part of their dialogue, responding in some appropriate way as if it were a spoken comment (e.g. "I notice that you looked puzzled when I mentioned that the course you're proposing to follow had real risks attached to it, and I'm wondering whether I've explained those risks to you sufficiently clearly") or perhaps by storing it in their memory as data received that might later be relevant.

We should also be aware that the common professional tendency to take notes, ask questions and express our views may sometimes make us insensitive to the nuances of our client's or patient's communications and unspoken responses.

Fie, fie upon her!
There's language in her eye, her cheek, her lip,
Nay, her foot speaks; her wanton spirits look out
At every joint and motive of her body.
                    (William Shakespeare, *Troilus and Cressida*)

Acknowledging

People generally need an acknowledgement that they have been heard and understood. This does not necessarily mean agreeing with them, nor does it mean patronising them. It may simply be some form of reaction that confirms that the professional has heard and understood their words, views or feelings, whether verbal or just by way of a nod.

Care needs to be taken that acknowledgement is not misconstrued as agreement, that active listening is not misunderstood to signify agreement with what is being said.

Helping people to hear

Sometimes during a professional exchange people may physically hear what is being said, but not take it in properly. Perhaps they are preoccupied with their own thoughts and concerns or with what they want to say or ask. Perhaps they are experiencing information overload. Or in many such cases, perhaps their stress or anxiety levels are so high that they simply cannot process what they are hearing.

We know that when people experience stress, anger or fear, the left side of the brain, with its cognitive functioning and memory, gives way to right-brain activity, which in turn results in stress hormones such as adrenaline and cortisol being generated. The result is a "fight or flight" or dissociation response.

Seeking advice from a lawyer, consulting a doctor about an illness or struggling to understand some financial or technological arrangement may well provoke a stress reaction. Indeed, current living bombards us with so many concerns that we may have become sensitised to producing a fear reaction readily in our bodies.

So we should not be surprised to find some clients failing to function from their optimal cognitive base. It may be necessary to reiterate advice and perhaps check that it has been properly taken in. There are many situations where things are said that do not register and may need reinforcing, in discussion or where appropriate, by written confirmation.

Summarising

Summarising can help both to provide the client or patient with a crisp précis of what has been discussed and to ensure that the professional has understood the position properly. It may also be a tool in "helping people to hear".

Summarising is not, however, mere parroting what has been said, but involves careful, accurate and succinct paraphrasing.

It is obviously not necessary or appropriate to summarise everything discussed, particularly as the discussion goes along. That would be excessively laborious and annoying. However, an occasional summation, especially at the conclusion of a meeting, can be very helpful, and more especially if tasks are being allocated.

Questioning

Of course, the primary purpose of asking a question is to get an answer – to establish information or views and to clarify facts. However, questions can be used for other purposes; for example to help promote reflection, to confront perceptions, to widen a field of discussion or perhaps to divert discussion from one topic to another. A question may also be strategic, where you know the answer but wish the client to arrive at the answer himself.

There is also a view that instead of expressing an opinion on any situation, one can ask questions that allow people to consider issues needing to be examined, and perhaps allow them to reach their own conclusions.

Questions may take different forms and may be:

open or general, allowing for any kind of answer, for example "What should we do now?";
closed, usually calling for a yes or no response, for example "Have you taken your medication today?";
focused, which call for a precise reply, for example "What time did that happen?";
directed to a specific person;
undirected, asked generally to everyone present;
leading, which suggest the answer such as "You knew that was wrong, didn't you?";
hypothetical, which contemplate possibilities, for example, "How might it be to give that up for two weeks and see how you feel then?";
reflective, which encourage reflection, such as "Do you believe that your actions may have helped to calm the situation?";
rhetorical, in the nature of musing with no answer expected, for example, "How do people get into such crazy situations?";
minimal prompts, to seek supplementary information without specifically asking, for example repeating as a question a word or phrase used by them.

Questions can have their own inherent power and value, especially when thoughtfully raised. They can indirectly indicate a professional's line of thinking and can influence the answers received, which can place greater responsibility on the professional to ask questions with care. Tone of voice and phrasing can have more effect than one might imagine. This humble device, the question, is rather more complex that might initially be realised.

Reframing

Reframing refers to a way of changing the frame of reference against which anything is viewed, so that it is given a different and usually more benevolent perspective. So, for example, where someone is referred to as "mean", this may be reframed as "careful", or being told that "she nags me about my diet" may be reframed as "so she is expressing a concern for your well-being".

Reframing can relate to individual words or expressions, or more generally to concepts and ways of seeing events and experiences.

Reframing should not be used so as to change meaning but rather to enable something to be seen through a different lens. If the reframe does not sound and feel right to the person whose perspective is sought to be changed it will not be effective.

Avoiding professional jargon and mystification

Sometimes professionals may be so used to their own language, system and culture that they might wrongly assume that their clients are on the same wavelength.

Where terms, abbreviations or acronyms are familiar to the professional, there may be an assumption that clients are similarly familiar with them.

There is a need to communicate in simple, understandable language, even when discussing complex subjects. Professionals can help their clients by providing simple explanations in non-technical terms, appropriate to the circumstances and without being patronising, and by writing letters in straightforward and simple terms rather than using jargon.

Organisations promoting simplified professional language include "Clarity" (an international association promoting plain legal language), the Plain English Campaign, Plain Language Association International and the Plain Language Commission.

References in these Regulations to a regulation are references to a regulation in these Regulations and references to a Schedule are references to a Schedule to these Regulations.

(Statutory Instrument 1991 No. 2680, The Public Works Contracts Regulations 1991, Part 1, 2.4, page 4)

Some other interpersonal skills

Establishing rapport

As with so many other aspects of the professional relationship, empathy is a critical component of effective rapport. Being able to "tune in" to the other person's thoughts, feelings and aspirations is one of the keys to establishing positive rapport. That is generally enhanced by a commonality of beliefs, aspirations or background and of ways of being and relating – "being on the same wavelength".

Authenticity is an essential ingredient of rapport; so any action taken to develop rapport must feel comfortable and authentic to you. Subject to this qualification, the following are some of the things one can bear in mind when establishing rapport:

- Without being inappropriately over-familiar or unprofessional, the tone of the conversation can be friendly and informal, as if advising a friend over a cup of coffee.
- Use the other person's name in conversation, but not excessively. In some cultures, using first names is a given; in others it might be inappropriate without permission. However, rapport can be established even in more formal situations.
- If there is any commonality, for example of background or common interests, this may be taken for granted or you may want to touch on it briefly to establish the connection.

- Active listening and acknowledgement are important, as is a genuine interest in what you are being told.
- Remember the key features of what you are being told and be able to discuss these, using names and details that show that you have understood and remembered these.
- Body language is important; but it is more important that it should be relaxed yet still maintain professionalism, rather than that it should be studied.
- Be sensitive not only to what is being said, but the mood. Be prepared to respond to the mood and tone as well as the words.

Rapport sits alongside trust and cooperation in the professional relationship.

Maintaining professional presence and professional energy

Professional presence represents personal authenticity, empathy, expertise, judgement and skill as reflected in the way that we manifest these in our demeanour and our relationship with our clients or patients and how they see us.

Some professionals may assume a "professional" persona at work, becoming what they believe is expected of them in that role. But "putting on a show" of having professional presence would be inauthentic and is unlikely to be experienced as genuine. Being comfortable with who we are, having a genuine interest in our client or patient, maintaining boundaried empathy, demonstrating the skills outlined in this chapter – these can all combine with expertise, integrity and judgement to present a professional presence that can give the client or patient confidence and establish the foundation for a good professional relationship.

This is not to suggest that we cannot consciously and mindfully improve the quality of our professional presence. That may be achieved, for example, by developing and improving our interpersonal skills, being aware of our own body language and perhaps undertaking a programme of self-development. If we are confident in ourselves and what we say and do – even while acknowledging uncertainty where this is appropriate – this is likely to be reflected in the confidence that our clients or patients have in us.

This may be expressed as the quality of energy that we bring to a situation – not energy in the sense of being vigorously active or doing lots of things, but rather a qualitative concept reflecting the entire way that we function as professionals and the approach we have to our work and relationships. It is a holistic combination of commitment to applying ourselves diligently, skilfully and proactively to what we are doing while exhibiting a high quality of professional presence. Intangible, it can be felt by a client when it is present.

Managing clients' expression of emotions

People will from time to time be upset, angry, frustrated or apprehensive. In such situations, their capacity for reasonable, logical discussion and decision-making is likely to be adversely affected. Professionals may be guided by their own instinctive responses as to how to react. In addition, the following guidelines may help:

- Professionals working in fields where people may feel vulnerable or apprehensive, and where strong emotions are likely to arise, have a special need for self-awareness and it would be helpful for them to undertake some training in working with emotions.
- Except in a counselling or therapeutic context, it is not usually productive to try to conduct a substantive discussion with someone in the grip of strong emotions. Where practicable, this may need to be temporarily deferred.
- In some cases it may be necessary to discuss, with sensitivity, the cause or underlying reason for the emotion. In others this may not be appropriate. In either event it may be sufficient to acknowledge the emotion and allow some space for the person to collect themselves and continue with the task in hand. Pausing for a cup of tea can be helpful. If intense emotions do not subside, a postponement of any discussion may be appropriate.
- It should be borne in mind that talking about traumatic events can rekindle the feelings; and there is also a necessary caution here about opening up feelings if one doesn't have the skill or knowledge to be able to help close them down again. The operative guideline would appear to be: proceed tentatively and sensitively and err on the side of caution.
- If wishing to help someone back from strong emotions, it can be helpful to engage them sensitively with some simple, practical, factual matters that require them to use their logical processes to answer. This helps to restore cognitive abilities.

Understanding the value and use of symbolism and metaphor

Symbolism

For each person, words and physical things may have a deeper and more profound meaning going beyond their superficial content. Some may be widely shared, for example a national flag that symbolises belonging and identity or a wedding ring that symbolises commitment. Others may be more personal, for example a book that may symbolise one's belief in the values expressed in it.

Symbols are used in a multitude of ways in everyday life. Language itself is a way of symbolising meaning; using a computer keyboard necessitates understanding symbols.

> A word or image is symbolic when it indicates something more than its obvious meaning. In *Man and His Symbols* Carl Jung explained that we used symbolic terms to represent concepts that we cannot easily define or comprehend.

Symbolism can be significant in managing different situations, including endings. We may take one example in the legal context. A complex divorce settlement was agreed but broke down on the issue of who was to receive a particular ornament that had been given to the husband as a gift. The wife's position was that if the person who gave it to him had known how he would behave, it would never have been given to him. This created deadlock in the whole deal. The ornament had become a symbol of who was right and who was wrong in the marriage. It also symbolically represented the ending of the relationship and "the last straw", each feeling that they had conceded enough. In the event, a symbolic solution was necessary, involving making a joint gift of the ornament to one of the children.

Symbolism may help to explain the significance placed on acknowledgements and apologies and the importance of forms of restitution in legal disputes.

Professionals need to take symbolism seriously and where necessary to seek creative and perhaps symbolic solutions that recognise and respect this symbolic power.

Metaphor

A metaphor is a figure of speech based indirectly on symbolism. It compares two dissimilar things and reflects their commonality. Metaphors can help clients and patients understand complex processes by giving them an analogous and comprehensible frame of reference.

For example, war is a common theme that arises in different professional situations. Patients may be told to "fight the battle against cancer", that we need to "attack the cancer cells" or that a disease has "invaded" their body. Litigants in a legal context may be told of the "arguments in our armoury" or "this will blow up in their faces". More generally, we hear about workers "on the front line", people "trouble-shooting" and that "we're right on target".

Using martial metaphors can create a confrontational way of thinking for people. Perhaps this may be appropriate in some situations, but it may be counterproductive where more temperate counsel is needed, where people may need to be calm rather than aggressive. So, for example, a "toolkit" can provide a better metaphor than an "armoury" where appropriate. It is important to be aware of the culture of thought that metaphors can create.

Another common metaphor is that of a journey. We may be at the crossroads. The road may be rocky but one can cross over it to reach a smooth path ahead. There may be unexpected detours. We will cross that bridge when we come to it.

Metaphor can capture the client's own imagery or create fresh ways of seeing things. In a case where a claimant in a dispute had established most of the necessary elements of the legal claim but missed one essential one, and hence his claim would not attract maximum damages, a lawyer was able to suggest to him that the lottery required the winner to get six numbers. Five correct numbers would result in some payment but not "the big one". To succeed in recovering significant damages he would need to be able to produce the sixth number – if he could. This brought the principle home to him directly and effectively.

> The greatest thing by far is to be a master of metaphor; it is the one thing that cannot be learnt from others; and it is also a sign of genius, since a good metaphor implies an intuitive perception of the similarity in the dissimilar.
>
> (Aristotle)

Some communication practicalities

Terms of engagement

Formalities for engagement may vary between signing a written agreement with detailed specifications, terms and conditions to just orally agreeing the outline of what is required and some basis for remuneration. The clearer the terms at the outset, the less potential there is for later disagreement.

Certainly some kinds of work demand a clear specification, such as setting up an IT system or designing a house. Also, there may be professional obligations to record terms; for example, commercial and family mediators generally have organisational and code of practice requirements to have a written agreement to mediate.

Where a professional relationship is being established, various elements may need to be covered including the work required to be done, the basis and arrangements for remuneration, confidentiality if applicable, complaints procedures and reference to any relevant code of practice, limitations on professional liability and termination of appointment.

One way to record terms effectively and informally is by way of a Letter of Agreement, from the professional to the client or patient, recording the terms clearly and perhaps with relative informality, requiring counter-signature of a copy to record agreement with its terms.

Some practicalities concerning communications

Where the professional work is to be done over time, interim reports may be necessary to keep the client informed of developments. Similarly, it is important to keep the client regularly informed of the incurrence and escalation of costs. Ordinarily, arrangements will have been made about how and when these are to be paid, where applicable.

Where interim communications are likely to be needed, arrangements for these should be clear and specific – whether to be in writing and/or on the telephone, whether e-mail or any other electronic format is acceptable and if so at what address and whether privacy and confidentiality can be assured.

Where issues are being reported by letter or e-mail that are likely to lead to the clients wishing to establish urgent contact with you, it can be very frustrating for them if you are unavailable for any length of time afterwards – and indeed some clients are unhappy about receiving such communications late on Friday or on Saturday morning if it means that they cannot contact you for some days. Where practicable, timing can be important.

Living as we do in an age of instant communication, prompt responses to e-mails, texts, phone messages and other communications may be expected. If you can't respond substantively reasonably quickly to incoming mail or messages, an acknowledgement that it is being considered and that a response will be forthcoming may be helpful.

If you are going to be unavailable during a period when a client or patient is likely to need to contact you, it is good practice to set up alternative arrangements to deal with any urgent aspects. This is thoughtful and caring practice.

Further reading

Gerard Egan's book *The Skilled Helper: A Problem-Management and Opportunity-Development Approach to Helping* has had many editions over many years, a tribute to the timelessness of its underlying theme. It has a substantial section dealing with communication and relationship-building skills.

The topic of communication skills for lawyers (covering much wider territory including emotions, psychology, intuition, meaning and values) is effectively addressed in Professor Marjorie Corman Aaron's *Client Science: Advice for Lawyers on Counseling Clients through Bad News and Other Legal Realities*.

Allan Pease has written a number of helpful books on non-verbal communication, notably *Body Language: How to Read Others' Thoughts by Their Gestures* and, with his wife Barbara, *The Definitive Book of Body Language: How to Read Others' Attitudes by Their Gestures*.

James Lawley and Penny Tomkins' *Metaphors in Mind: Transformation through Symbolic Modelling* has been well reviewed in both a therapeutic and more general context.

Some of the skills outlined in this chapter have drawn on the section on mediation skills contained in *ADR Principles and Practice* by Henry Brown and Arthur Marriott.

Chapter 11

Balancing professional and systemic tensions

The essential tension of opposites

Conflict and change

It may be said that all aspects of life comprise balancing the essential tension of opposites, and that professional life is another manifestation of this.

This concept is widely known in philosophical terms. For example, the Chinese concept of *yin* and *yang* (the symbol shown above) represents the juxtaposition of opposites: day and night, tranquillity and aggression, feminine and masculine, soft and hard, wet and dry. When opposites are in equilibrium, harmony, well-being and good health result; when they are not, there is conflict.

Conflict is often perceived as negative and destructive, and indeed uncontained conflict may manifest itself in challenging ways and sometimes in violence or war. Conflict is, however, an integral part of human behaviour, and there could be no movement or change without it. All decision-making contains an element of conflict; exchanges of ideas involve conflict; the democratic process is built on the basis of the normalcy of a conflict of ideas and interests.

In *A Sudden Outbreak of Common Sense: Managing Conflict Through Mediation*, Andrew Acland suggests that "the purpose of conflict is related to change … all conflict is about the attempt to achieve or resist change".

In *Staying with Conflict: A Strategic Approach To Ongoing Disputes* Bernard Mayer writes that "Conflict is essential to everyone's growth and survival. It is the vehicle all of us use to face our most significant challenges. Conflict is our stimulus to attack problems and gives us the energy to overcome our powerful inclinations towards passivity."

So conflict and the tension of opposites serve a positive purpose in helping us to make decisions, move forward and effect change; and when equilibrium is established, it can bring about harmony and well-being. But there are many different elements to balance, both in personal and professional life, and this can be difficult: the prospect of achieving equilibrium in all respects and at all times is remote and few if any of us is likely to achieve this.

Perhaps the best we can aim for is to be conscious of the choices we have and try to make them in the best way possible at the time. In any event, circumstances change and decisions have to be made and re-made under different conditions from time to time.

Quite often our circumstances and needs feel so pressing and our options so limited that we may not identify our choices clearly. This chapter is about highlighting some of the tensions, conflicts and competing demands that may face professionals, and about bringing them into consciousness so that their implications and their alternatives can be explored.

Systems and change

Although we are individuals, we are also a part of various different systems. We probably function within a family system, and in our work we operate as part of a professional, institutional or commercial system. We live within national government and local authority systems, healthcare and legal systems and we will have passed through an education system – or as teachers, academics or administrators we will be a continuing part of it. In our relationships we are part of a social system. We are surrounded by systems.

Many of us will understand the power of systems if we have tried to change them. Systems and organisations tend to have an inbuilt resistance to change. *Homeostasis* is a property of living beings that seeks to maintain them in a stable and constant condition. This serves a positive function in allowing them to function effectively despite environmental changes.

One can think in terms of homeostasis in relation to the general tendency of systems and even individuals to try to preserve the status quo against what might otherwise be frequent pressures for change from various sources. Indeed, in the twenty-first century, it does seem that changes in all fields are happening more quickly than ever before and that life is ever more challenging. Small wonder that we may like to hang on to established ways of working and being, and try to maintain some certainties (however illusory these may be).

This chapter will consider some specific tensions that exist for professionals, including those that arise when attempts are made to change or challenge systems.

Profession v. business

One significant change to professions over the years is perhaps the feeling that many traditional professionals seem to have lost their sense of pure dedicated professional direction and have adopted some of the practices of trading businesses.

Traditional professions, for example, would not at one time advertise but now in the UK and many other countries law firms and accountants are advertising in the media and many have marketing directors; websites "sell" professional services; incorporation and limited liability are now possible for various professionals in the UK and other countries; business development and revenue generation have become critical and competitiveness and "rainmakers" are highly prized; web and social networking have become an increasing feature of establishing a professional reputation.

Professionals in the private sector have always had to conduct their work as a business in order to make a living. So there will be no surprise that professions need to work according to business principles. What concerns some professionals, however, is the fact that many practices in the private sector have become increasingly driven by market forces rather than by "pure" professional constraints. And in the public sector, professionals are often not exempt from pressure to work within tight budgetary constraints and to maximise their output.

A professional practice can combine a high ethical standard with a successful business; these are not mutually exclusive. And it is not a corollary that to have a committed professional practice one needs to run an unsuccessful or commercially indifferent business.

The following are some of the main considerations in relation to the tension between maintaining a professional way of working and running a business:

- Many people enter professions with a sense of purpose and dedication, with a strong motivation to perform a useful service. Of course, they would expect to make a reasonable living, but running a highly profitable business may not necessarily be their primary objective. For medicine, nursing and related professions, this may be to help with some form of healing. For law, it may be a sense of justice and fairness.

  People with such ideals can be disillusioned to find that a vigorous profit motive prevails. This can be compounded by having to cope with the inevitable pressures and stresses of professional life. On the other hand, long-term financial struggle is likely to be unsustainable for most people however fulfilling the actual work may be.

- Most professionals will regard the nature of their relationship with clients to be very important. For many, values such as integrity, loyalty and commitment to the client, competence, respect, care and caring will be critical, and if these are compromised by the need to maximise profit, that may be unacceptable.

- The desirable balance it would appear lies between maintaining values on the one hand, and making profits or at least balancing the budget on the other.

Professions are distinguished from businesses in that the professional relationship is one in which the professional (dentist) holds considerable power, as a result of knowledge, over the individual (patient), placing the patient in a vulnerable position. Thus, the need exists for the dentist to place the patient's interest at a level equivalent to or above that of his or her own. The professional dentist's primary motivation and responsibility is, or should be, "caring" for patients ... Professionals focus on serving, with financial rewards derivative from serving well. Businesses focus on profit, with serving being the means to that financial end.

(David A. Nash, D.M.D., M.S., Ed.D. and William R. Willard Professor of Dental Education, in a 2004 letter to the *Journal of the American Dental Association*)

In a 2015 article in the *Journal of the American College of Dentists*, Professor Nash observed that while there were relevant business dimensions to operating as a learned profession, "the marketplace model of selling cures undermines the traditional learned professional model – a model rooted in a tradition of caring".

Public professional persona v. private persona

Read about "professional persona" on the web and you will find articles that tell you about the need to "build a professional persona" and that "the way people will perceive you in the workplace is as much a product of your appearance, presentation, attitude, and communication skills as it is of your performance". A good professional persona will provide a basis for people "to believe in you and to have confidence in your abilities".

This is not a revelation. We all know that the way we come over to people will affect how we are perceived as professionals. Our demeanour, bearing, tone of voice, level of confidence, language and the way we dress and present ourselves will affect perceptions of us.

The Rosenthal effect outlined in Chapter 5 is a significant factor in the way that people respond to professional input: a doctor, for example, has the authority of his qualifications and experience and will use authoritative and reassuring language to generate confidence. A teacher whose natural style is friendly and relaxed may quickly need to develop a firm and tough persona to be able to deal with challenging pupils.

To what extent, then, do we, consciously or unconsciously, adopt a professional persona and how far removed might this be from our natural personalities? Do these distinctions become integrated into our lives? How does this affect us? The following are some considerations.

An appropriate level of professional demeanour

We have seen that clients, patients and colleagues generally expect an appropriate professional demeanour, but what this means will vary. Some people may expect a high level of formality, others may prefer the professionals they engage to be informal and personable – as long as they know that the professional has all the necessary qualifications and skills.

What is appropriate?

Organisational and individual culture will both affect attitude and professional persona. A City law firm, for example, may expect its lawyers to dress formally (except perhaps for accepted "dress-down" days) and maintain a formal demeanour. Those in a local community practice, however, may be more informal, and casual dress may be the norm.

Informality should never be confused with sloppiness. Indeed, those who maintain an informality of dress and demeanour may arguably need to be even more professional in what they do: without the "props" of formality, their skill, abilities and commitment will need to shine through the informality of their approach.

The professional's judgement and natural inclination should supplement cultural norms in establishing the "appropriate" level of demeanour, tone, level of formality and authority.

Inter-relationship of personal and professional personae

Can we separate our professional and private *personae*? How far do each of these reinforce one another?

It would hardly be surprising to find a link between the work one does and the personality one has. After all, our personality is likely to be a strong motivator in our choice of career; but other factors (such as financial considerations, family and social pressures and assumptions) may supervene, and it is these that may result in a disjunction between work and personality.

The more one works in a particular way, the more that is likely to rub off on one's personal life. Understandably one's personal being can be subverted to a professional image of how one understands one's role to be; and this can be reinforced by the expectations – real or assumed – of colleagues, clients, friends, family and everyone with whom one has to deal.

In mediation training, some lawyers adopt a judicial bearing when role-playing the mediator. At the end of a role-play, people commonly relax visibly and sigh with relief. Feedback indicates that a better way to mediate might be in the relaxed mode that they showed after the end of the exercise, rather than the studied, judicial style shown in the role-play. One Queen's Counsel observed: "That's just what my wife tells me! She says I sometimes behave as though I'm cross-examining a witness or sitting as a judge when I talk to friends."

Sometimes we may just need to remind ourselves that we will be more congruent if we can adopt our natural persona in our professional lives. We can "catch ourselves" when functioning in a studied professional mode, and shift to a more personal mode as a conscious act. This doesn't mean abandoning a professional demeanour but rather reflecting that demeanour in a way that feels authentic and resonant with our personalities.

Tradition v. change: challenging the system

Systems thinking

Systems are inherent in all aspects of life and exist in many forms.
A systemic perspective

> implies that there is a whole multiverse of different perspectives from which to view a person's individual problems: individual, couple, family, extended family, social setting, cultural and religious context, economic and political larger system. This multi-level and multi-contextual view of a person's or family's predicament is what can be summarised as a "systemic perspective".

This quotation from Alan Cooklin, Neil Dawson and Brenda McHugh's *Family Therapy Basics* is written in a family context but applies to all walks of life and all contexts.

The systemic approach, which seeks to understand how the system works so that changes for the better can be made by taking these workings into account, has been applied in a number of areas over decades. These include the environment, families and society, management, health, information science, engineering and computing.

The systemic view is that people who are part of a system are not simply autonomous entities who happen to be together, but, as suggested by William Bridges in *Transitions: Making Sense of Life's Changes*, are parts of a larger whole, affected by whatever may happen to that whole.

Peter M. Senge, author of *The Fifth Discipline: The Art & Practice of the Learning Organization*, considers that the complexity of current life demands that we are able to see and understand the structures that underlie complex situations. He sees systems thinking as a conceptual framework that can clarify patterns and help understand how to change them. Learning organisations – those that encourage personal mastery and vision – will expect "creative tension" between existing conditions and the vision of what might be wanted.

Challenging and changing systems

The conflict between maintaining the system and seeking change and development is a manifestation of a wider conflict in life: how individuals, organisations and systems identify the need for change and manage – or fail to manage – the process of changing.

Homeostasis is just a convenient way of representing the tendency to protect the status quo, and the position is inevitably rather more complicated. Some of the factors that explain this tendency include the following:

- Systems, organisations and individuals need stability and consistency, and it is right that they should protect themselves against the risk of frequent and potentially destabilising change and that they should only consider change when it is clearly the right thing to do.
- Tradition and ritual can serve a positive function in carrying down inform-ation, practice, wisdom and guidance from the past and in providing symbolic meaning. Where these are of value, few will wish to abandon them simply for the sake of innovation. People may be properly jealous of their traditions and rituals.
- Change is challenging and potentially uncertain and frightening and the volume of demand for change can feel overwhelming. Many of us are creatures of habit, and we develop patterns of behaviour that suit us: we do not necessarily welcome disruption to our ways of being and functioning, especially if they seem to serve us well.
- Change often involves a resource cost, which may be of time and energy and not uncommonly also a material or financial cost.
- While some may consider change desirable, there will be others with vested interests in maintaining the existing position. Vested interests may take various forms: attitudinal (preferring an existing way of functioning), financial, hierarchical, ideological or personal.
- Change can be for the better, as is commonly intended, but the "law of unintended consequences" suggests that there may also be other effects, sometimes significant and not always desirable or positive. There may be underlying reasons to be wary of change.

> When an alternative dispute resolution programme, including media-tion, was first mooted for the UK, a London City lawyer observed: "Our legal system has managed to develop very well over many hundreds of years. We really don't need to rush into this."

The medical profession is understandably wary about adopting new practices and approaches. This applies both to the system of healthcare delivery and to issues like accepting complementary practice alongside conventional medicine. Many people subscribe to osteopathy, acupuncture, chiropractic, homeopathy and other complementary practices, but there is a variation among medical practition-ers as to their efficacy and acceptance. Systemic change may require practitioners to give more time to patients (though there are real time and budgetary constraints) and to explore the possibility that healing may occur through unorthodox and sometimes unexpected procedures.

All professions face similar issues. The following are some considerations as to striking the balance between maintaining an established approach and adopting innovation and change.

The value of tradition

Tradition has an important role in preserving and venerating good things that have been carried down from the past. It protects against arbitrary and whimsical changes to the established order. It has the capacity to enhance respect for the way things were.

The Hippocratic Oath that doctors take to practise medicine ethically dates back to the fifth-century BC. Traditional methods of painting and sculpture have continued from the past to the present, as have traditional forms of Eastern medicine and healing. Traditional rural skills such as making dry stone walls, hedge-laying and cobble-stoning have changed little over the years and this is much appreciated: there is no audible call for these to be modernised.

The downside of tradition

Tradition can also preserve practices that are undesirable, unsatisfactory and outmoded. Slavery may have been an established tradition in many parts of the world, and its abolition was vigorously opposed by many; but the mere fact that it was traditional did not justify it.

Many "traditional" gender assumptions that were widely accepted are now becoming largely superseded, though progress is patchy. Traditionally, men were viewed as breadwinners and women as caregivers, but this is no longer necessarily the case. Men are increasingly found in roles that were not necessarily "traditional" such as primary school teaching, nursing and social work, and women are increasingly active in a wide range of professional roles including science, engineering and technology.

Traditions that no longer serve any purpose need to be re-evaluated – not automatically discarded, but also not automatically retained simply because "things have always been done that way".

Recognising and managing concerns about change

Change needs to be managed thoughtfully and sensitively. This necessitates being keenly aware of and responsive to people's concerns and dealing with them in an understanding way; communicating honestly, openly and effectively with them and involving them in decision-making as far as practicable; helping people to deal with their uncertainties; taking people through the process patiently; and being adaptable so as to be genuinely responsive to any concerns expressed.

Credit: Grantland

Other competing professional tensions

Other professional tensions may arise, including the following.

Work pressure v. need for self-care and leisure

When work pressures are substantial, professionals may neglect their own well-being, work long hours, forget family responsibilities, and take less time for leisure and self-care. This is understandable, not least because conscientious professionals will want to give the client or patient proper attention, even if this sometimes places a burden on them.

Of course this is a common and inherent part of professional life and there are times when the needs of the situation demand this kind of prioritisation. But if it becomes a pattern rather than an occasional need, then one does need to step back and examine whether one has the balance right. Apart from the stress and potential health issues that this entails, one of the later regrets of chronically busy people is that they find that they have missed important times in the lives of their families, that children have missed having them as an integral part of their growing up and that relationships have been placed under strain.

Self-care is an important component of professional life.

Budgetary constraints v. quality of care

Constraints that budgetary restrictions may place on the level and quality of professional care may arise in some parts of the public sector such as social care and welfare, healthcare and perhaps education. Various of these resources might see their budgets reduced in difficult economic times. The effects of these constraints may also be felt in the private sector when the economic environment is a challenging one.

Professionals affected by this may find that they have to do more work for the same remuneration, have less support and greater expectations placed on them.

Leadership v. democratic decision-making

When working in teams, whether formal or informal, there can be a tension between the responsibility of the team leader or the senior member for whatever task is in hand and the needs of the team for participation in decision-making.

Ultimately it is a function of leadership to ensure that everyone on a team feels that their contributions are properly regarded and their views properly taken into account, even if they do not prevail. And it is a further function of leadership to know when exceptionally to override the views of others in the interests of a greater good.

Professional v. personal values

As professionals we may well find that ways we are required to work or the behaviour or attitudes of our colleagues or clients do not always accord with our personal values. These may create moral or ethical dilemmas for us. How far do we allow our value judgements to impact on our professional duties? If clients wish to behave in a way that we find morally unacceptable but legally permissible, do we decline to continue working for them? This is a personal decision that each of us must make in accordance with our beliefs and individual circumstances.

Further reading

One of the originators of *general systems theory*, Ludwig Von Bertalanffy wrote his book of that name in 1968. An updated version *General System Theory: Foundations, Development, Applications* was published in 2015.

Thinking in Systems: A Primer written by Donella Meadows with a more recent edition edited by Diana Wright has been extensively and positively reviewed, providing an overview of thinking in systems and systems-based problem solving.

Peter Senge's *The Fifth Discipline: The Art & Practice of the Learning Organization* sold more than two and a half million copies in its first edition. A revised edition was produced in 2006.

William Bridges, author of *Transitions: Making Sense of Life's Changes*, has also written about organisational change, with particular reference to the psychology and personal side of change, in *Managing Transitions: Making the Most of Change*.

Also helpful in understanding and effecting change in both a work and personal context is David Straker's *Changing Minds – in Detail: How to Change What People Think, Feel, Believe and Do*.

Chapter 12

High conflict personalities

Credit: Len W

Understanding high conflict personalities

What is a high conflict personality and how does it manifest?

As professionals we will periodically encounter difficult people, but one stands out from the others, leaving us feeling frustrated and impotent – unable to reach him (or her – there is no gender bias) or to find any way forward from a stuck position in any form of conflict, disagreement or dispute because of the total intransigence of his views and beliefs. This is the "high conflict personality".

The high conflict personality's main attribute is the complete certainty about the correctness of his views and beliefs – the unshakeable attachment to a "world view" about anything – while to others it may seem that this view, while presented strongly and with apparent logic, is based on some false or questionable premise and produces a potentially distorted result. Facts seem to be viewed through a somewhat misshapen lens.

He sees things in stark black and white, with no shades of grey, and expects that others – including anyone advising him or who might have to adjudicate any dispute or disagreement – will support his views and vindicate his position.

Consequently he sees no reason to acknowledge the possibility that any other views may have any validity, or to compromise.

The term "high conflict personality" may conjure up the image of someone who is hostile, aggressive and argumentative, whereas the person with these traits and personality may present himself calmly and apparently rationally, but simply with no capacity for insight into other views. Communications may be civil and extensive but get nowhere. He will not uncommonly cite others in vindication of his views and position, sometimes quite inappropriately. He may also blame others for any problems, without recognising any possible element of personal responsibility.

Of course people may hold strong views without having high conflict personalities. What marks this out is the absolute certainty of the conviction, the sense that other views are simply not acknowledged, the logical but flawed nature of propositions and the stress and frustration this induces in those working with this situation.

The emotional energy needed in dealing with such personalities feels far greater than when working with most other clients or patients, which is another indicator of this personality.

It can be important to understand how people with high conflict personalities function and how this impacts on professionals; but there can be difficulty in identifying such people, partly because we do not aim to do this by way of any "diagnosis" – which would be inappropriate – and partly because they may come from any kind of background or occupation, can be charming, successful and personable, and can present themselves in a reasonable light. The "high conflict" identification may only manifest itself after working with the person for a time and the particular conflictual aspect has arisen.

Perhaps half of all legal cases that go to trial today involve one or more parties with a high conflict personality. In these cases, the conflict is driven more by internal distress than by external events … personalities drive conflict.

(Bill Eddy, *High Conflict People In Legal Disputes*)

Why professionals might need to know about high conflict personalities

A professional may encounter a high conflict personality in a number of possible ways – perhaps as a client or patient, or as an employer, employee, co-worker or colleague, or perhaps someone with whom one might need to negotiate in some other capacity; or perhaps one might find oneself in dispute with such a person.

What makes it particularly important to understand this personality type is that ordinary strategies and rational reasoning will not usually be effective and might indeed be counter-productive; some specific understandings and strategies may be necessary, which might feel counterintuitive without an awareness of the rationale for them.

We should start with trying to understand the underlying basis of high conflict personalities.

Why do some people have high conflict personalities?

Our concept of high conflict personalities arises primarily from two sources. One is the work on the link between enmeshed couples, conflict and disorganised attachment developed by the authors of this book together with Professor Peter Fonagy, and the other is the work on the link between high conflict and certain personality disorders and traits developed by US mediator Bill Eddy and the High Conflict Institute that he co-founded.

Having regard to both these sources, it seems likely that three personality backgrounds, which overlap one another, are linked to and lie at the root of high conflict:

- attachment disorganisation;
- personality disorder;
- maladaptive personality traits.

Attachment disorganisation

Chapter 8 outlines attachment theory and explains the reflective function, or mentalisation (based on mirror neurons), which enables people to understand their own and others' mental states and feelings.

Most people have a reasonably functional attachment system. However, for a small minority of people, perhaps 5–10 per cent or fewer, the level of insecurity is so great that the system becomes dysfunctional and "disorganised".

Professor Fonagy suggests the analogy of a central heating system, the efficient running of which compares to secure attachment, serving the purpose well and effectively. However, the heating system may work, but not at its best, for example with a malfunctioning timer or thermostat: it provides heating but not entirely satisfactorily. This is akin to insecure attachment. However sometimes there is a fundamental flaw in the system, so serious that it not only fails to work at all, but threatens to overflow and flood the house, with seriously damaging consequences. This is analogous to disorganised attachment.

For a person with disorganised attachment, trust may simultaneously and para-doxically exist in an extreme form alongside its extreme opposite, paranoia. Such a person is likely to make unconscious attempts to turn the professional adviser into a kind of substitute attachment figure – pushing professional boundaries and with unrealistic expectations including a demand for highly partisan personal support. Indications of trust and expectation ("I have the best lawyer in the City") may shift to mistrust bordering on paranoia ("My lawyer has let me down badly and I won't pay his fees").

There appears to be a direct link between disorganised attachment and high conflict.

> Strategies that work so well with usual clients create the most difficulty with that kind of person [from the disorganised attachment group] ... You have to be aware that if you use the same strategies as you use normally when you work with an individual that comes from this group you are likely to create more problems than you solve.
>
> (Professor Peter Fonagy, speaking on the DVD
> *Managing Difficult Divorce Relationships*)

Personality disorder

We observed in Chapter 7 that personality may be described as the distinctive manifestation of an accumulation of individualistic qualities, traits, beliefs, attitudes and characteristics that each one of us has, and which together help to define who we are and how we relate to others and to our environment.

Where someone's personality makes it difficult for them to live with themselves and/or others and they cannot change or control those ways of thinking, feeling and behaving, with consequential difficulty in making or keeping relationships or getting on with others, the Royal College of Psychiatrists considers that the person may have a personality disorder. The categories of disorder that seem to be most closely linked with high conflict are anti-social, borderline or narcissistic.

Although the categorisation of personality disorder is the model adopted by the American Psychiatric Association (in its *Diagnostic and Statistical Manual*, 5th edition, DSM-5) and widely used internationally, including in the UK, there are strongly held views that a system that categorises personality disorders without regard to other considerations is not satisfactory.

So, for example, Professor Thomas Widiger favours a dimensional model which would view personality disorders as "maladaptive variants of general personality traits". This dimensional model could have regard to the "Big Five" personality characteristics outlined in Chapter 7. In effect, everyone has these traits across a spectrum and there could be criteria for each that could guide clinicians in assessing whether anyone has moved over a threshold into the territory of personality disorder.

Two points must be emphasised. First, it would be entirely wrong and inappropriate (unless a mental health professional is undertaking a diagnosis) to attempt to diagnose or "label" anybody as having a personality disorder; and second, not all people with personality disorders will be involved in high conflict disputes. Rather it is likely to be from this category of people (among others) that high conflict may emerge. Within these categories, there are those who cannot see that any fault for anything lies within themselves, who blame others for things that go wrong. Bill Eddy describes these as "persuasive blamers" whose denial of personal responsibility and cognitive distortions links them closely to high conflict disputes.

Maladaptive personality traits and systemic influence

Instead of seeing high conflict in terms of personality disorder, it may be more helpful to regard people as having a collection of personality traits, some of which may be somewhat maladaptive – as broadly envisaged by Widiger.

This viewpoint would regard everyone as having a combination of traits on different spectra, with functionality at one end and maladaptive and dysfunctional traits at the other end. On this understanding, a high conflict personality may arise where someone's traits are maladaptive in the anti-social, borderline or narcissistic direction.

There is also a systemic perspective on the possible state of mind of a client or colleague. This would suggest that a person's behaviour is not controlled only by personality, but also by the social system in which they function and the inter-personal influences to which they are subject. Patterns of behaviour and interaction within a system – family, corporate or any other – and social and family history may have a significant effect on individual behaviour.

Links between attachment, personality traits and disorders, and high conflict

Around the turn of the century, the authors of this work observed the overlap of characteristics and patterns between people with attachment insecurity and those with relationship issues involving many of the attributes of high conflict, which was developed with Peter Fonagy into a link with disorganised attachment in their 2006 book *Managing Difficult Divorce Relationships: A Multimedia Training Programme for Family Lawyers*.

In the US, Bill Eddy observed an overlap of characteristics and patterns between people with personality disorders and traits, and those manifesting high conflict, which he developed in his books including *High Conflict People in Legal Disputes* and which was further developed by the US High Conflict Institute, which he co-founded.

This raised the question as to whether there might be a link between disorganised attachment and personality disorders, which might bring both observations in synch with one another; and indeed a number of psychologists, psychiatrists and other mental health professionals have observed the probability of links between insecure and disorganised attachment on the one hand and personality disorders and traits on the other.

Consequently, while there are also other factors, it seems that brain development during the first two or three years of life, and the nature of attunement and attachment security (or insecurity) experienced during this phase, may provide at least some of the origins of personality disorders and maladaptive traits – and of high conflict.

Cautions and reservations

This is a relatively new field in which it would be inappropriate to be dogmatic. Furthermore, there are different views and some controversy about the nature of diagnosis of personality disorders and the reliability of any single model. Practical experience of working with high conflict and current thinking about attachment and personality disorders seem to support the views expressed in this chapter, but they must necessarily remain tentative.

There are a number of further cautions and reservations:

- As previously emphasised, it would be wrong for professionals outside of specialist mental health fields to diagnose or "label" people. Even mental health professionals can have difficulty doing so. It follows that it would be wholly inappropriate to probe into personal histories or attachment or personality issues.
- It is also inappropriate to share any insights or speculation about high conflict or its possible causes with those involved, which would in all probability – and quite understandably – not be well received. Any such thoughts or insights should be maintained as private working hypotheses.
- The mere fact that someone holds strong and unshakeable views is not necessarily an indicator of high conflict. There may be other reasons for this, for example different perceptions of fairness or of legal entitlement, or commercial or strategic considerations. And the fact that someone may be "difficult" does not mark him out as "high conflict". Various ways of being difficult are examined in the next chapter.
- More generally, professionals need to be careful about making assumptions about people, particularly when dealing with high conflict personalities. People who present themselves as reasonable and charming may well have complex personalities with high conflict traits, while others who appear to be difficult and "stuck" may well have justification for their positions, however unreasonable those may seem to be.

George Bernard Shaw observed "the reasonable man adapts himself to the world, the unreasonable one persists in trying to adapt the world to himself. Therefore all progress depends on the unreasonable man." This does not, of course, preclude the possibility that the unreasonable man responsible for progress might have a high conflict personality.

Strategies for professionals working with high conflict personalities

Maintaining empathy and emotional sensitivity and being conscious of communication skills remain critical components in working with anyone including high conflict personalities. However, some other strategies are particularly relevant to high conflict.

Boundaried empathy

High conflict personalities with their background of disorganised attachment and maladaptive traits tend to ignore professional boundaries and limits, sometimes using charm, manipulation or bullying to achieve this. This pressure to go beyond one's proper role – not necessarily illegally, but rather inappropriately and uncomfortably – can happen quite subtly, so professionals need to be fully aware of this tendency and watchful in case it should arise.

Disorganised attachment carries with it the likelihood that the client may seek a strong attachment bond with the professional and expect the professional to "care for" him or her, going well beyond what is realistic or proper. For this reason, high conflict personalities may need to have clear lines drawn for them from the outset. Professor Fonagy suggests telling them early on: "I can do A, B and C, but I can't do E, F and G." If at any later time they try to push one beyond one's limit, they can be reminded of these lines.

There is, however, no inconsistency between having clear structures and boundaries, and maintaining empathy with the client. On the contrary, an empathetic relationship remains as critical when working with high conflict personalities as with any other client. This is where the concept of "boundaried empathy" has particular significance.

Empathetic objectivity – or reason and compassion

Professor Fonagy points out that whereas many professionals would wish to be viewed as likeable and be liked by their clients, this is not a good idea when working with high conflict personalities, as those with attachment disorganisation may well see anyone doing this as a new attachment figure, with the risks of shifts between trust and paranoia.

It is better to maintain a rather more professional stance, with empathy and informality as appropriate, but avoiding an unduly close personal relationship. The aim would be for "empathetic objectivity".

Having regard to the views of Professor Paul Bloom as outlined in Chapter 8, we might perhaps reflect this as having cognitive empathy and applying reason and compassion in order to arrive at a course of action that is likely to lead to the best available outcome.

Structure and records

Professionals should take steps when working with high conflict personalities to minimise the risk of misunderstanding. There are a number of ways of doing this, for example:

- being clear about one's role and the scope and nature of the work one is undertaking;
- being clear and specific about costs and keeping the client up to date with these;
- being clear about arrangements for communications;
- making and retaining working notes and records, and where appropriate providing written notes or summaries to the client.

This structure and formality provides a sound basis for the professional relationship.

Small steps

Progress in huge leaps may be unlikely, so one should allow for small incremental steps. This may translate into tolerance for change to aspects one may have thought to be already addressed. Reviewing and seeking to revise aspects already agreed is not uncommon in high conflict situations.

It follows that a professional may need to be patient and to help the client to exercise patience. It may be necessary to allow more time for whatever service one is providing.

Proactivity

The professional may need to be proactive in proposing ways of dealing with any conflictual situation that may arise. This should, however, not be confused with heavy-handedness, which is to be avoided, and should not be allowed to interfere with maintaining a sensitive working relationship with the client.

Dealing with a client's "world view"

A professional working with a high conflict client may need to manage the client's world view, which may well be based on cognitive distortions. This can be one of the most difficult aspects of the professional relationship.

This can be done in a way that is both respectful and appropriate, that neither accepts nor criticises those views. A high conflict personality will expect support for his views from his professional adviser and will not take kindly to criticism or rejection. So it may be difficult to respond effectively to a distorted world view. The professional will need to listen respectfully and empathetically, without criticism, but without losing objectivity.

Professor Fonagy suggests that it may be necessary to treat the client's world view as correct and reasonable and explore what the consequences would be if that were the case, but without suspending critical judgement. There is a paradoxical aspect to this, but this may be inherent in dealing with high conflict personalities.

Helping with understandings and responses

High conflict people generally have difficulty in appreciating the views and thinking of others. Reflective function (and mirror neurons) may not be wholly efficient and some support may be needed to help interpret and convey thoughts, ideas and feelings, insofar as appropriate.

The professional can try to help the client with gaining a better understanding of the thoughts and feelings of others and in expressing himself more effectively.

Helping decision-making inhibited by strong emotions

A person caught up with strong emotions is likely to have difficulty in functioning in a logical and rational way: the person may be in "fight, flight or dissociation" mode, cognitive functions may be temporarily impaired and it may be difficult to move forward with decision-making.

It may be necessary to help the person back into left-brain mode, in which he can deal with the practicalities of the situation. The strategy for this applies equally to high conflict people as it does with all others. This may entail taking a break, short or long, and perhaps engaging the person in simple cognitive tasks, such as form-filling or providing basic data. While allowing expression of feelings may be cathartic, we have observed that dwelling on anger may in fact have the opposite effect of reinforcing it and holding back effective negotiations – hence helping a person back to task at some early opportunity can be helpful.

> Daniel Goleman, author of *Emotional Intelligence*, has observed that if a so-called "cooling-down period" simply continues with the same line of discussion or thought that gave rise to the anger, then it will not be useful as each such thought just rekindles that anger.

Seeking third-party support where appropriate

Working with a high conflict personality can be exhausting, stressful and hugely demanding on one's time, energy and resources, going well beyond the requirements of working with clients or patients ordinarily. It is in the nature of this relationship that the professional can feel manipulated or bullied by the client, pressed to work in a way that doesn't feel right or appropriate and sometimes trapped by the professional commitment.

Professionals might feel very lonely facing such situations and could find it helpful, and sometimes necessary, to talk confidentially to someone independent of their immediate circumstances. Chapter 18 outlines various kinds of resources that might be available to support professionals, such as liaising with a supervisor, consultant, coach or mentor.

However, these resources are not necessarily available, readily or at all, in which event speaking to a senior colleague or to someone with relevant experience may well be the way forward. It is by no means a failing to do so; on the contrary, seeking such support may be entirely appropriate for both the professional and the client or patient.

High conflict endings

The insights about high conflict and the strategies suggested in this chapter should provide some help to professionals in dealing with these personalities.

It is, however, in the nature of this personality that professional support is not always accepted and that disagreements do not get easily resolved, with the consequence that the client may wish to move to another forum or to another professional, sometimes with criticism and reproach. One should not regard it as a failure if this proves to be the case.

In this event, the ending should be dealt with in a courteous and professional way, avoiding becoming defensive or embroiled in any disagreement about blame. Fall-out from working with high conflict people may be regarded as an occupational hazard.

Further reading

The authors acknowledge the section on high conflict personalities in *ADR Principles and Practice* (3rd edition) by Henry Brown and Arthur Marriott.

The leading works in the field of high conflict are those written by Bill Eddy, including *High Conflict People in Legal Disputes*, which addresses the dynamics of four types of personality disorders relevant to high conflict; *BIFF: Quick Responses to High conflict People, Their Personal Attacks, Hostile E-Mail and Social Media Meltdowns*; and *So What's Your Proposal? Shifting High conflict People from Blaming to Problem-Solving in 30 Seconds*.

For information about personality disorders, see the American Psychiatric Association's *Diagnostic and Statistical Manual of Mental Disorders DSM-5* or perhaps more easily readable is Joel Paris' *The Intelligent Clinician's Guide to the DSM-5*. For an alternative perspective, with reference to the dimensional model, see *Personality Disorders and the Five-Factor Model of Personality* (3rd edition) edited by Thomas Widiger and Paul Costa, Jr.

To read about the links between insecure and disorganised attachment on the one hand and personality disorders and traits on the other see, for example, Allan Schore's *Affect Dysregulation and Disorders of the Self* and Fonagy, Target, Steele et al. "Morality, Disruptive Behavior, Borderline Personality Disorder, Crime, and Their Relationship to Security of Attachment" in Leslie Atkinson and Kenneth Zucker (eds) *Attachment and Psychopathology*.

Chapter 13

Difficult people

"I'm going to train you to 'Confront Difficult People' ...
okay, raise your hands if you're a difficult person."

Credit: CartoonStock.com

Raise your hand if you're a difficult person

Everyone is crazy except thee and me – and sometimes I'm not too sure about thee

Mostly we will work with people who will have individual personality traits and eccentricities, but with whom one can have an "ordinary" working relationship. This chapter, however, addresses a category of people whom we might describe as "difficult".

This raises the question: how do we know whether it's the other person who is difficult, or whether perhaps any perceived difficulty is actually arising from our own attitudes, beliefs, traits, behaviour or perceptions? Raising self-awareness may be necessary. In the event that any of the issues raised in this chapter seem to strike a personal chord about oneself, hopefully this will be positively viewed, allowing for constructive self-reappraisal.

Even if one identifies difficult personality traits in oneself, it remains possible that one will nevertheless also have to deal with people who manifest their own difficult personalities – along the lines of "just because you're paranoid doesn't mean they're not out to get you!"

What do you mean "difficult"?

- *There is a huge array of ways of being difficult.* People can be manipulative, bullying, argumentative, abrasive, abusive or domineering. They can be evasive, negative, unhelpful, disruptive, unresponsive or uncooperative. They can be indecisive or unreliable. They can be stubborn, inflexible, know-it-all, dictatorial or arrogant. They can be hypocritical, mischievous or deceptive. This list could go on and on.
- *There is a "Richter scale" of difficulty.* At the extreme end, people may have personality, mental or emotional disorders or dysfunctions that can make it near impossible to work or communicate effectively with them. At the other end, even reasonable people may from time to time become difficult, for short periods or in a mild way.
- *People can be actively or passively difficult.* Overt difficulty arises for example where someone is challenging, bullying or abusive. Passive difficulty – for example, where someone fails to cooperate effectively and thereby subtly undermines others' actions.
- *People can be consciously or unconsciously difficult.* Factors built into one's personality may be unconscious. One has more control over conscious difficulty, which may include cussedness, being perverse and stubborn, and argumentative (though there may be an overlap where although conscious, it becomes an integral part of a person's personality).
- *Being difficult is a relative concept.* It can only be viewed in relation to something else: another person or other behaviour. It is also a variable concept, in that its nature and intensity can sometimes vary according to how it is received and dealt with.
- *Difficult behaviour is sometimes appropriate.* Terminology can depend on where you are sitting. One person's "terrorist" may be another's "freedom fighter". A "difficult" person may be appropriately challenging dysfunctional systems or behaviour.

Why some people are difficult and some strategies for dealing with them

Cautionary introduction

People are complex and there is seldom only one cause of difficult behaviour or clarity about all the circumstances affecting someone who appears to be difficult. There is a risk that by identifying particular kinds of difficulty, we may inappropriately oversimplify what can be a complex package of circumstances, and that in labelling someone as "difficult", especially falling into some category of difficulty, we may stereotype and perhaps stigmatise them.

On the other hand, understanding the underlying causes of difficult behaviour can help cope with and deal with that behaviour, especially if done with sensitivity.

Subject to these cautions, we can consider the factors that can contribute to people being (or being perceived as) difficult.

High conflict personalities

This has been dealt with in the previous chapter. If there were a hierarchy of difficulty, arguably that kind of personality would go well beyond just being "difficult".

Anger – overt or suppressed

Anger is undoubtedly one of the causes of difficult behaviour, but the anger expressed by a difficult person may just be the tip of the iceberg. Not uncommonly other root causes may underlie the anger, such as disappointment, frustration, fear, anxiety or insecurity.

While overt anger may be expressed in aggressive or hostile behaviour, anger can take other less obvious forms. Cold, steely anger can be extremely powerful. And suppressed anger can sometimes create more problems and difficulties than an openly expressed anger.

In negotiation or mediation "submerged anger can sabotage attempts to reach an agreed resolution, as the anger manifests itself in a disguised form, such as destructive comments or an unwillingness to cooperate with the other party or the process".

(Henry Brown and Arthur Marriott,
ADR Principles and Practice)

The following are some considerations in dealing with anger:

Don't take it personally: Anger is not always caused by the present circumstances, which may well have rekindled some underlying issue; so the first principle is not to take it personally, even though it may be directed at you. This is of course more easily said than done; but in most cases engaging in an angry exchange is only likely to make it worse. If you can disengage emotionally, you can deal with the anger more calmly and dispassionately.

Consider the validity of the anger: You need to try to understand the cause of the anger and consider whether it may be justified. This may need some sensitive probing and active listening. Acknowledging the anger and if appropriate its cause without necessarily agreeing (and without being patronising) can help to calm the situation. If there is a genuine cause for anger, it may be necessary to acknowledge this, to address the problem and if appropriate to apologise; but an inappropriate apology is not going to be right for you or for resolving the situation and should not ordinarily be given just to keep the peace.

Maintain calm – but not by inappropriate concessions: Here again, it may be difficult to be calm in the face of an angry onslaught, but this can help move the angry person into a calmer state. However, you need to maintain your boundaries and to make it clear, in a quiet way, that you are not willing to accept inappropriate behaviour. Nor should you accept unwarranted criticism or make inappropriate concessions with the aim of defusing the anger.

Don't expect rational discussion when anger prevails: As will now be clear, when people are angry the brain goes into fight, flight or dissociate mode and shifts away from its cognitive state. At this time it is not practicable to try to engage in rational discussion, whether about any substantive aspect or indeed about the emotion itself. People need to be helped gently back to cognitive rationality, and meanwhile some cooling off space may be needed.

Non-cooperation and passive aggression

Passive aggression is a personality trait that may take different forms and which in its most extreme form is a personality disorder marked by submerged anger, resistance to authority and a failure to respond responsibly and effectively to requests for appropriate action in a personal, social or workplace context. It is commonly marked by procrastination, sullenness and resentment, "learned helplessness" and "sugar-coated hostility".

An isolated instance may not be easily identifiable as such, for example arriving late for a meeting and delaying discussion; forgetting to bring something needed for some group activity; subtly disrupting plans or confusing issues through ambiguity, misunderstanding and misstatements; or obstructing some project in which he is required to play a part. However, as a pattern emerges over time, it becomes clearer that passive aggression is at play.

A passive-aggressive person may not be conscious of what he is doing and may be genuinely dismayed if confronted by the effects of his behaviour: his world view tends to be that he is innocent and blameless. He may even feel that he is a victim or martyr and seek to justify his behaviour by making excuses and complaints and by shifting blame to others.

The effect of dealing with a passive-aggressive person is that one may feel quite confused about whether one has done something wrong or perhaps inadvertently upset them. The sense is that something is not right, but it is elusive, and because the aggression is hidden, one may not be aware of it and therefore cannot address it.

The following are some considerations in dealing with passive-aggressive people:

Understand the hostility: Once you can identify the behaviour as passive-aggressive it is easier to understand it and make a conscious decision about how to deal with it.

Take practical steps to deter damaging patterns: You may need to formalise requests and arrangements, for example putting them in writing, and making consequences clear. If he does not attend on time, a meeting will start without him. If he does not produce a report, someone else will be briefed to write it. Take control, set out clear expectations and boundaries and do not allow the passive-aggressive person to set the agenda for action – or inaction.

Describe the behaviour without criticism: In some cases it may help to identify to the person how his behaviour is unacceptable – in a straightforward, empathetic way and without being critical: for example "Fred, I would find it really helpful if you could explain to me whether there are any difficulties in your providing the research information that we agreed on. I need it rather urgently and if you can't undertake this I need to understand what the problem is."

Power and control – and Machiavellianism

The Machiavellian personality refers to a behaviour pattern motivated by a wish to exercise power and control over others by means of manipulation through guile, deviousness, deception and opportunism, with sociopathic personalities and a possible personality disorder at the extreme end of the spectrum ("High Machs").

They may be charismatic and may well, consciously or unconsciously, use strategies that may include being charming and personable, but if this does not work, moving to bullying and threat, often implied, and manipulating others, drawing on their goodwill without compunction.

Inevitably, a tendency towards power and control will result in some people achieving positions of authority (though it is obviously not a necessary corollary that all people in authority are Machiavellian). Consequently, difficulties may be exacerbated by the fact that the controlling person has authority over one.

Power relationships may be complex. Difficult behaviour that appears to be controlling may originate in a feeling of powerlessness. It has been said that people who make threats are often in a position of frustrated powerlessness, rather than real power.

The following are some considerations in dealing with Machiavellian personalities:

Tread warily: Identifying this personality can be a challenge, let alone dealing with a person who is charming and glib and uses guile, deception and manipulation as tools for personal advancement. The overriding consideration would be to handle such a person with caution, resist direct confrontation and "watch your back".

Avoid being manipulated: It has been said that "nobody can manipulate you; you can only be manipulated" – the point being that manipulation only works if you allow it to. This demands awareness of a person's manipulative tendency and self-awareness in not succumbing to it.

Assess your relationship with them: If you believe that they are unlikely to change their ways, you may need to consider how sustainable and important your relationship is with them. In some circumstances, it may be advisable to move away from that relationship; in others this may not be feasible.

Consider addressing specific issues: If you are not in a vulnerable position, you might consider indicating to High Machs how certain of their behaviours do not serve their interests – but this would need to be done with care and sensitivity in appropriate circumstances and with due regard to the nature of your relationship with them. It may well be badly received.

Negativity

For some people, "no" is their default response rather than "yes", "perhaps" or "I'll try". This may also manifest in negative criticism of others' ideas without any positive input. This is not necessarily because of a deliberate wish to be difficult, but is often simply part of their personality – without realising how frustrating and challenging this can be for others.

Research has indicated that the human brain actually has a *negativity bias*; that is, a greater sensitivity to negative images, thoughts and feelings than to positive ones, perhaps because of some evolutionary need to be aware of and avoid danger. Bad news, it seems, has a greater impact on our brains than good news. This does not itself explain why some people are so much more negative than others, but it helps put the negativity into context.

Although we may understand the inclination towards negativity, its constant presence is likely to have a negative effect on others, though the negative person may not necessarily realise this. So the following are some considerations for dealing with people who present themselves in this negative way:

Understand the root cause of negativity: There are reasons why some people are so much more negative than others, which tend to be largely grounded in fear; perhaps fear of failure, fear that bad things will happen, fear of not being loved or respected, or fear of humiliation. Negativity can also become a habitual response. Having this awareness can help one to respond more compassionately and supportively to the negativity, where appropriate.

But take care about giving negative feedback: Even if constructively meant, feedback about the negative effects of someone's behaviour or personality may reinforce the negativity rather than encourage positivity.

Detach from the negativity: As it can be quite easy to pick up on another's negativity, you need to be aware of your own reactions and to step back consciously from adopting a negative approach yourself, or a hostile reaction to the negative person. Having a conscious, mindful approach to the relationship and to your own ability to detach from the negativity gives you immunity from it and allows you to function more effectively.

More deadly to morale than a speeding bullet, more powerful than hope, able to defeat big ideas with a single syllable. Disguised as a mild-mannered normal person, the No Person fights a never-ending battle for futility, hopelessness, and despair.

(Dr Rick Brinkman and Dr Rick Kirschner, *Dealing with Difficult People – 24 Lessons to Bring Out the Best in Everyone*)

Ambivalence and indecision

Whereas a passive-aggressive person may procrastinate because of innate hostility, some people do so because they simply can't make a decision and are afraid of the consequences of making it wrongly. This ambivalence manifests in a sense of simultaneously being pulled in two mutually exclusive directions.

Aiming perhaps for the "right" decision when one is not obvious, their dilemmas can be understandable; but when decisions are required and perfection cannot be guaranteed, an inability to take a necessary decision can be very frustrating and often problematical.

When dealing with indecisive clients, the following considerations may be helpful:

Decisions may often have to be imperfect: Quite commonly, whichever option the person may choose may have negative aspects. Indeed, sometimes there are no good options at all and the dilemma is to select "the least bad" one. It may be necessary to identify and articulate this and help relieve the person from feeling he has to make an ideal choice.

The obvious – list pros and cons: This may not immediately produce a solution but may identify which aspects are more important and may open up the issues for consideration and discussion. Sensitive dialogue, without applying pressure, and an analysis of the person's priorities in each list may then help move decision-making forward.

Provide advice and guidance if appropriate: Depending on your role and relationship, it may in some cases be helpful to provide tentative personal guidance; for example: "I can't make this decision for you, but I think that if I were in your shoes I would be inclined to... . ."

But resist taking over the decision: You should guard against making a decision that needs to be made by a client: this would subvert the client and could also expose you to later potential liability if the decision turned out to be materially wrong.

The five-year test: Ask the person to go forward five years and to look back at the decision on the basis that it might prove to have been wrong. Which option could they more easily live with if it was the wrong one?

> I must have a prodigious quantity of mind; it takes me as much as a week, sometimes, to make it up.
>
> (Mark Twain)

Intolerance of other views

Intolerance may arise where someone has an entrenched ideological world view on any topic, which does not brook challenging or questioning. In an extreme form and in combination with other factors, this intolerance may indicate a high conflict personality, but it can exist on its own and simply belong to a difficult person.

But world views are of course not limited to ideological issues. They cover beliefs as to how people, families and society function, what kind of lifestyle and behaviour is or is not acceptable and values and attitudes towards all aspects of life, right down to the minutiae of existence, including diet, taste, leisure preferences and attitudes towards specific issues.

Conscious or more especially unconscious attachment to these world views can lead to entrenchment and prejudice – especially but by no means limited to issues around race, gender, age, ethnicity, sexual orientation and religion.

When dealing with intolerance of other views the following considerations may be helpful:

Resist responding inflexibly: When encountering inflexibility, there may be a temptation to respond in the same way; but this would be more likely to entrench differences rather than allow scope for movement. Even fundamental disagreement can be expressed respectfully.

Use objective criteria: If you have to advise a client with entrenched views that those views may be wrong, it may sometimes be better to refer to an objective third-party source rather than personally challenging his views, for example in the context of a court dispute by pointing out that a judge is likely to take an opposite view to his.

If it matters, examine the alternatives including withdrawal: If the rigidly held views do not impinge on your professional task, you may be able to sidestep having to deal with them. However, if they are integral to the work you are doing, it can help to explore the alternatives, either with the person concerned or as an exercise on your own. Is there a creative way of accommodating the views and doing your job effectively? If not and if you feel that you cannot properly continue, that may be the time to withdraw from your professional role.

Maintain a record: If you have to continue in your professional role following views with which you profoundly disagree, it may be prudent to send a written note of your concerns to the client, in appropriate terms. This may perhaps have a salutary effect – and it also records your reservations in case of any later recriminations.

It's the situation, stupid

Finally, there may be a question as to whether someone might be "difficult" because the situation demands it. Undoubtedly many undemocratic governments view their dissidents as "difficult". Those who have throughout history resisted foreign occupation of their land or who have refused to recant their religion in the face of unimaginable pressures may well have been considered hugely difficult and unreasonable. Public figures who take stands on moral issues may be viewed as difficult by those whose positions have been challenged.

At a more mundane level, people challenge established views, systems and bureaucracies in many ways, whether in the workplace, the family or society generally. It is often through the efforts of such people, individually or collectively, that change is achieved, in small or big ways, and that society moves forward. This, then, is a reminder that difficulty, like beauty, may be in the eye of the beholder.

Further reading

Books addressing the issue of coping with difficult people include Rick Brinkman and Rick Kirschner's *Dealing with Difficult People: 24 Lessons to Bring Out the Best in Everyone* and Roy Lilley's *Dealing with Difficult People*. These tend to identify difficulty by way of metaphor: "the Sherman tank", the sniper, the exploder, the complainer, "the know-it-all" and so on.

For guidance on dealing with difficult people at work ("enemies") there is *Working with the Enemy: How to Survive and Thrive with Really Difficult People* by Mike Leibling; and psychologist Oliver James has written a book on dealing with the "dark triad" of psychopathy, Machiavellianism and narcissism at work in *Office Politics: How to Thrive in a World of Lying, Back-stabbing and Dirty Tricks*. Passive-aggressive behaviour at work is addressed in *Blindsided: Recognizing and Dealing with Passive-Aggressive Leadership in the Workplace* by Paula M. De Angelis.

Chapter 14

Uncertainty, risk and imperfection

Credit: John Richardson

Living with uncertainty

The discomfort of uncertainty

Uncertainty is an uncomfortable phenomenon. As professionals and as human beings, we prefer to have certainty and security in our lives and we do our best to create the trappings, and often the illusion, of certainty around us. Inevitably, so do our clients and patients.

Life, however, is inherently uncertain and insecure. Economic, political and social structures may be fragile and can go awry, whether internationally, nationally or regionally. Conflicting beliefs, ideologies and cultures can lead to intolerance and prejudice that may manifest in violence and disruption. The market economy is based on principles of uncertainty and risk.

At a personal level, ill health can arise and accidents can happen without warning. Marriage vows are "till death do us part" but the divorce rate in many countries exceeds one marriage in three. People involved in litigation cannot be sure what the courts will rule – and 50 per cent of those who go to trial will find that their assessment was wrong. Employees cannot be certain that they will still be in their jobs in six months' time.

By and large, people do not cope well with uncertainty and are ill-prepared for it. We want to feel that we have some control over our lives, that some things are reliably predictable, that the world makes sense and follows some rational set of rules. It is very unsettling to think that these beliefs may be illusory and that much of what may happen in the future is arbitrary despite careful planning, and may not necessarily follow the principles of fairness.

> The best laid schemes o' mice an' men
> Gang aft a-gley,
> An' lea'e us nought but grief an' pain
> For promis'd joy.
>
> (Robert Burns, "To a Mouse, on Turning Her Up in Her Nest with the Plough")

Black Swans

In his book *The Black Swan: The Impact of the Highly Improbable*, Nassim Nicholas Taleb has written about the uncertainty of random events. The title is based on the fact that before the discovery of Australia, people believed that all swans were white, so the discovery that black swans also existed came as a surprise and a shock.

For Taleb, a Black Swan has three attributes. First, it is an outlier – a phenomenon outside of normal experience or, in statistics, an observation falling outside the overall pattern of distribution. It has come to mean something that lies a distance from the norm or a person who is extraordinary – a concept developed by Malcolm Gladwell in *Outliers: The Story of Success*.

Second, it carries an extreme impact. An example that Taleb cites is the attack on the World Trade Center in New York on 9/11, 2001. The third attribute is that although the Black Swan was not predicted, there are many after-the-event explanations as to why it was predictable.

Taleb believes that we are blind to the Black Swan, that human nature is not programmed to see the phenomenon. Rather, we focus on sources of uncertainty that are more familiar and we tend to look for corroboration of what we already believe – giving rise to the confirmation bias. We also have a need to simplify and to impose order on things so as to feel that the world is less random than it actually is.

However, the sources of Black Swans have increased hugely as have their socio-economic consequences. In Taleb's view, sceptical empiricism, acknowledging that we "don't know" and that we can't easily compute probabilities trump "grand" socio-economic theories and an assumption that we can mathematically or scientifically compute probabilities.

Coping with uncertainty

As professionals, we need to be reasonably comfortable with states of uncertainty and insecurity if we are to be able to help clients and patients in those states. This is more easily said than done. In 1951 Alan Watts wrote in *The Wisdom of Insecurity: A Message for an Age of Anxiety* about feeling that "we live in a time of unusual insecurity". That sense of insecurity does not seem to have changed significantly over time. With a background in Zen Buddhism, Watts maintained that insecurity was the result of striving to be secure, and that it was necessary to understand that there is no security.

We do not have to embrace Zen Buddhism to realise that we need to accept the uncertainties and insecurities of life, and instead of railing against them, find ways of being flexible and responsive to circumstances in order to cope with the inevitable changes that we will face, and willing to make decisions in imperfect circumstances. That in turn may help us to work with others who are also facing uncertainty.

Some people find that spiritual practice helps them to cope with life's uncertainties. Spiritual teachers from most traditions tend to foster the letting-go of the need to try to control events and surrendering to whatever happens in life.

That sense of acceptance is broadly the approach taken by Susan Jeffers, author of *Feel the Fear and Do It Anyway*, who has also written *Embracing Uncertainty: Achieving Peace of Mind as We Face the Unknown* in which she provides personal insights, spiritual references and exercises to help achieving peace of mind by accepting uncertainty.

Some practical steps to help cope with uncertainty might include the following:

- Cultivate a frame of mind that is flexible, creative and open to change and new learning. Accept that life has many imponderables and uncertainties and that it can be insecure but that we can be adaptable and can manage change if we need to.
- You may have a hypothesis about the future, but "don't marry your hypothesis". Be ready to change it when you see that it is not correct or appropriate.
- Without paralysing yourself by a multiplicity of options, consider pragmatically what aspects of life or work are more uncertain than others, and have contingency plans in case needed.
- Allow your intuitive capacity to guide you, especially after you have done some initial outline planning of options. When the mind is still, thoughts and ideas are more likely to arise; but before acting on your intuition, review the intuitive biases that can mislead you.
- Adopting some positive daily rituals that enhance good health and rest, such as exercise, a healthy diet, conscious diaphragmatic breathing and stress-relief techniques, can help coping mechanisms.

- Meditation helps many people cope with uncertainty and anxiety.
- Be willing to obtain support from others who can help you and bear in mind also that mutual support between people facing similar challenges can lighten the load.

> The longing for certainty ... is in every human mind. But certainty is generally illusion.
>
> (Oliver Wendell Holmes)

Superstition: illusory control over uncertainty

Superstition is broadly defined as an irrational, illogical and credulous belief in something supernatural or mysterious affecting one's life or luck, with consequent fear or awe. Although many of these beliefs may go back to pagan times, the number of people who currently have some form of superstitious belief or practice is "surprisingly high", according to a survey carried out in the UK in 2003 by psychology professor Richard Wiseman of the University of Hertfordshire. Perhaps that should not be so surprising when one considers anecdotally how widespread superstitious beliefs in one form or another are across cultures, religions and ages.

Even though it may be illusory, doing something that helps to avoid a bad outcome (like touching wood or saying something to ward off the evil eye) provides some feeling of addressing the uncertainty instead of doing nothing and waiting. Also, as observed in Chapter 5, the placebo or Rosenthal effect (which might be called "the transformative belief effect") has its own power: a positive expectation is more likely to produce a positive outcome.

The relationship between uncertainty and risk

Risk is the possibility that an expected or desired outcome will not occur, or that some undesirable or negative outcome will happen. Uncertainty is the state of not knowing what will happen because of future imponderables.

In 1921, economist Frank Knight distinguished "risk", involving a measurable probability with known or knowable consequences, from "uncertainty", which is not measurable and, in effect, has imponderable consequences. This distinction has not been universally accepted, but it does indicate that uncertainty, with its imponderables, is more difficult to manage whereas risk allows one to take a view based on probabilities.

We can perhaps help clients or patients facing uncertainties to identify those aspects that are identifiable and capable of having some kind of risk assessment made – on which they will need to take a considered view – and those aspects which are simply unknowable and unpredictable (on which any view may be an educated guess rather than a risk assessment).

Risk assessment and management

A professional should be able to perceive risk, to make some assessment of it and to manage or mitigate it or to know how and by whom this can be done.

There are of course different kinds of risks. Almost any activity, ranging from work issues through to driving a car or catching a train or plane, or making an investment or deciding on a medical, legal, business or personal course of action, is likely to involve some element of risk. Mostly these do not need to be brought into consciousness: you don't have to assess the level of risk every time you drive your car.

You may need to consider what risks are inherent in any course of action. As a professional in your field, you should be able to draw on your experience to advise what risks can ordinarily be expected; and you may be expected as a matter of law and practice to do so. Failure in some circumstances to warn a client or patient of predictable risks may well constitute negligence.

Risk–benefit analysis

Risk cannot be considered in isolation, but rather in relation to any corresponding benefit. Sometimes the relationship is obvious and explicit: you may invest funds in a secure bank deposit with a low return, low risk and a high likelihood that your capital will not diminish; or you may invest in a high-risk project, with a risk that the funds may be lost or diminished, but with the possibility that you may receive a substantial profit.

Sometimes however the relationship is more difficult to assess, and it is these situations that are particularly challenging for professionals to advise on, especially where there are multiple uncertainties. For example, a patient diagnosed with a severe heart disease may be advised that surgery is necessary for survival in the medium to long term, but that the procedure is risky, carrying a significant risk of death. The patient's risk–benefit analysis is very unclear: the options are to decline the surgery and persevere with the condition, with a high probability of further deterioration and an early death, or having the surgery with the prospect of a better quality of life if the operation is successful, but with a real risk of death during it.

The professional of course cannot make the client's or patient's decision, but in all fields we need to be aware of our supportive role in helping them work through their difficult decisions.

Appreciating levels of risk and benefit

Risk assessment is commonly based largely on a value judgement by the professional, drawing on his or her knowledge and experience. This needs to be quantified in a comprehensible way, often by showing risk as a percentage; but do people readily appreciate the implications of percentage prospects? These are invariably coloured by the context in which they are viewed.

Take, for example, a claimant who is considering litigation. If told that he has 50 per cent prospects of success, he might think twice about proceeding; but if told that he has 60 per cent prospects, he is quite likely to decide to proceed. In his mind, his prospects are significantly better than his opponent who has only a 40 per cent prospect.

Take now someone who is considering heart surgery. He is advised that his prospect of surviving the surgery is 60 per cent. This means that he has a 40 per cent risk of dying in the operating theatre. Very few people would be as ready as our litigation claimant to steam ahead. Most would want to explore all the alternatives rather than simply decide to go ahead. Although the risk factor is the same, the consequence of the downside is so serious that a 60 per cent success prospect is unlikely to feel good enough.

To help the litigation claimant understand the risk better, it means that if the same case were argued before 100 judges, about 60 of them would find in favour of the claimant and 40 of them would find in favour of the other party. Is that a risk that the claimant wants to take?

So people who are given percentage judgements of risk should really be taken carefully through the implications so that they get a better understanding of what the risk really means.

Chance favors the prepared mind.

(Louis Pasteur)

Complexity of risk measurement – decision trees

It is not uncommon for risk assessment to comprise a complex set of factors, rather than necessarily a single consideration. For example, in analysing the risk of taking a case through litigation to trial, a series of questions may need to be asked, each with its own risk assessment. This is the basis of decision-tree analysis, in which a series of consecutive risks need to be assessed in order to decide on the best course of action.

However, specialist advice is needed to construct an effective decision tree. Trying to use one without the complex algorithms that are available from sophisticated and potentially very helpful software could lead to wrong, inappropriate and sometimes absurd results.

However, the principles underlying the decision tree, namely identifying and evaluating the component sequential choices, decisions or factors that go into the total outcome, remain entirely valid; and an approach that the professional can take to assessing risk without decision-tree software is set out in the next section.

The considerable significance of subjective judgement

A decision tree – or any analogous set of sequential questions or choices – involves having to make judgements in relation to each such question or choice. Sometimes, this may involve objective and verifiable data but more commonly the assessment is made on the basis of the professional's subjective judgement. In this event, much depends on the experience, expertise and wisdom of the professional.

So decision-tree software ultimately relies on the judgement of the person feeding in the composite elements. The maxim "garbage in, garbage out" applies here: the outcome is only as good as the data inputted. Sophisticated software may give the impression of scientific accuracy, but ultimately it is only as good as the judgement of the person using the software.

However, whether or not using a decision tree, a professional would need to have regard to all these sequential considerations in arriving at a composite risk assessment that could help guide the client or patient in making a decision as to any course of action.

A lawyer advising on prospects of success of contemplated litigation might use decision- tree software with appropriate algorithms or, using his (or her) judgement, might perhaps provide an assessment of prospects of success of the claim in percentage terms. But other factors might be relevant, for example:

- He would identify and ensure that the client appreciated the risks involved.
- An expert view on prospects of success would be provided.
- He might discuss the client's personal circumstances and establish the implications of a court action for the client, including the client's personal resources and financial ability to sustain an action and to cope if it is unsuccessful.
- It would also be relevant to establish the client's risk tolerance, as outlined below.
- An estimate of the likely range of legal costs would need to be provided. This would be based on a successful or alternatively an unsuccessful outcome.
- Other factors would be considered. Is the client insured or otherwise indemnified for costs? What are the potential effects of publicity for each party? What time scales are involved? How well might each party cope with the demands and stress of prolonged litigation? Are there any other personal considerations?

A sensitive understanding of the client and his circumstances and needs as well as factors peripheral to the actual issues may be critical to many situations involving uncertainty and risk. We may sometimes need to go beyond the strict confines of the actual job to be able to give the advice and support that is needed.

Taleb's "Black Swan" proposition that we "don't know" and can't easily compute probabilities comes back into focus. A 65 per cent probability of success may give a clue to the possible outcome – but ultimately this necessarily has an arbitrary and uncertain element.

Finally, the principle of proportionality will be relevant. The amount of time, resource and cost going into the professional's advice and support would need to be proportionate to the circumstances. A low-level consumer dispute, for example, would not ordinarily need the level of consideration and support that a complex clinical negligence action would demand – though sometimes small issues can have significant implications.

> A decision tree approach requires candid discussion between lawyer and client about the likelihood of each branch on the tree, each twist in the litigation path. That discussion is always worth having. Even if the decision tree is used for nothing more than adding clarity in the conversation of trial alternatives and the client's comfort with attendant levels of risk, the tree has added value.
>
> (Marjorie Corman Aaron, "Finding Settlement with Numbers, Maps and Trees" in *The Handbook of Dispute Resolution*)

Prospect Theory

Individuals react differently in their attitude to risk. To be able to advise and support a client or patient faced with decisions involving risk, it is helpful for a professional to understand some factors at play in this regard.

People who need to make decisions under conditions of uncertainty may be expected to do so by rationally considering the outcome that will provide the highest expected utility and benefit – the Expected Utility Theory.

However, people don't necessarily act rationally. They are affected by biases and prejudices and are commonly bad at assessing probabilities ("probability weighting"). So, rejecting the Expected Utility Theory, Daniel Kahneman and Amos Tversky developed principles known as Prospect Theory, which describes how people evaluate risk in real life. Kahneman was awarded the Nobel Prize in Economic Sciences in 2002 for this work.

Prospect Theory's major features are:

* *Relativity of value:* People tend to take a view relative to some position (or "reference level") that they have in their minds. This may be a comparison with the status quo or it may be the outcome relative to some other person's outcome in similar circumstances.
* *Loss aversion:* People strongly prefer to avoid losses rather than making gains. They will be more persuaded to do something if it might avoid a loss than if it might make a profit. Losing £50 causes more pain than the pleasure of gaining £50; and even if in a set of transactions gains exceed losses, there is a tendency to focus on the losses. Also, people who have things will protect them – and often value them – more than those who are contemplating acquiring them: the aversion to loss is greater than the satisfaction of gain.

- *Certainty:* People strongly prefer a lesser outcome that provides certainty to the prospect of a more beneficial outcome that contains an element of uncertainty. So they may agree to settle a dispute at 75 per cent of what they are claiming rather than face the uncertainty of a trial even if advised that they have a 90 per cent prospect of being awarded the full sum.
- *Weighting extreme probabilities:* People tend to under-react to low-probability events, and may inappropriately discount risk completely where the risk probability is very small, which can result in choices being very risky indeed. At the other end, people tend to underweight outcomes that are statistically highly probable (though in relation to the appreciation of risk, this depends to some extent on context and the actual consequences of one's choice).

Risk tolerance and aversion

The issue of risk tolerance and aversion may be relevant to professionals in relation to their own decision-making, and for their clients or patients who may look to them for guidance. The following are some relevant factors:

Personality differences: The way in which people balance competing considerations is likely to be influenced by aspects of their personalities and how comfortable they feel about taking risks. Some people are readier to "go to the brink" while others would feel very discomforted by this and are inherently more comfortable living with low risk and with a feeling of greater certainty (however illusory the concept of certainty may be).

Some research has been done as to the kind of personality that may be more risk prone, using the Myers–Briggs Type Indicator, and unsurprisingly there are indications that personalities who combine extraversion, intuition, thinking and perceiving are considered to be visionaries who are innovative, seeking new solutions to challenging problems and readier to take risks.

Gender and age differences: Research has, again unsurprisingly, indicated that younger people in general have greater tolerance to risk and that women in general tend to be more cautious than men. However, these findings are of minimal value, since each professional is, and is dealing with, an individual who cannot be expected to fit into some norm.

Relevant considerations: The following considerations arguably apply in most circumstances: (i) Subjectively: What does the person facing the risk feel about the level of risk that he or she can comfortably tolerate? (ii) Objectively: What is the level of risk that a person should take, having regard to objective criteria such as the personal and financial implications and his or her ability to sustain the adverse consequences if the risk fails? (iii) Are there overriding considerations that make the decision clearer? For example, someone facing the need for emergency life-saving but high-risk surgery is not going to weigh up risks and benefits but is going to prioritise staying alive. And some situations may have moral, financial, legal, health or personal imperatives that may override any risk involved.

> Courage is willingness to take the risk once you know the odds. Optimistic overconfidence means you are taking the risk because you don't know the odds. It's a big difference.
>
> (Daniel Kahneman)

Imperfection

If certainty is an illusion, then perfection must be its sibling. We may seek certainty and perfection, but both have a way of presenting as a mirage: you think you see it, but when you get closer you find that it isn't there.

Striving for perfection

As professionals, we will inevitably and properly strive for excellence in our work and lives. That is realistic and achievable; but it is a different concept from striving for perfection, which is generally unrealistic and unachievable.

This striving for perfection may be viewed as having a productive element. Some of the great human achievements, whether in science, literature, art, sport or public life, will have been the product of a striving personality. But this "adaptive" view of such striving is challenged by many psychologists, who see perfectionism as inherently problematical.

Striving for perfection is more likely to reflect problematical personality traits signalling neurotic and obsessive tendencies. It may indicate insecurity, low self-esteem and critical self-judgement. It commonly involves high stress and anxiety levels, and in some cases fear of failure, procrastination, depression and psychological distress, sometimes extreme and with links to eating disorders and mental health problems.

Indeed, Brené Brown, writer and researcher on shame and imperfection, links perfectionism to shame, fear and vulnerability, and believes that we seek perfection "to avoid the pain of blame, judgment and shame". She sees perfectionism as a heavy shield that we believe will protect us from this pain but which actually prevents us from taking flight.

Shame and humiliation, and the fear of these, trigger some very primitive parts of the human brain. Shame, says Brené Brown, is the birthplace of perfectionism.

> Understanding the difference between healthy striving and perfectionism is critical to laying down the shield and picking up your life. Research shows that perfectionism hampers success. In fact, it's often the path to depression, anxiety, addiction, and life paralysis.
>
> (Brené Brown, *The Gifts of Imperfection: Let Go of Who You Think You're Supposed to Be and Embrace Who You Are*)

Living with imperfection

Psychoanalyst D. W. Winnicott wrote about the "good enough mother" and Bruno Bettelheim wrote about "the good enough parent". This concept arises from the proposition that one cannot and should not aspire to be a perfect parent, because, as Bettelheim says: "Perfection is not within the grasp of ordinary human beings." Furthermore, efforts to attain perfection may interfere with a rather more forbearing response to the imperfections of others. What is more achievable is being "good enough".

This principle applies to all aspects of life generally. There is a paradox in that by accepting imperfection, one can let go of unrealistic and stressful aspirations and concentrate on what is realistically possible and hence function more authentically and more effectively.

The following considerations are relevant in this regard:

- Self-acceptance is a critical factor in learning to live with imperfection. This requires awareness of one's inner processes and a conscious effort to change the way that one functions – possible but difficult to do on one's own.
- This means recognising that the striving for perfection is unhealthy and that we need to break our habitual patterns of behaviour and accept our humanness – and the fallibility and imperfections of others.
- Ideas for letting go of perfectionism include locating aspects of one's life where perfection is not sought and drawing on this to guide one in moving off the need to be perfect; viewing one's attitudes from a third-party outsider's perspective; cultivating resilience; and setting and maintaining a realistic time limit for doing work where one might aim for perfection.
- Where the striving for perfection is based on some clinical obsessiveness, including but not limited to any form of obsessive compulsive disorder (OCD), therapeutic support may be needed, and cognitive behavioural therapy (CBT) has been found to help with this.
- One strategy for letting go of obsessive perfectionism is "exposure and response prevention" – consciously and deliberately allowing one's imperfections to emerge and be exposed and tolerated in areas where one would have sought perfection, and gradually coming to terms with the anxiety that this causes. Although this may ordinarily be done with the support of a therapist, it can be undertaken on a carefully planned self-help basis.

Where a choice must be made between two options neither of which is ideal, it is worth remembering that sometimes the right choice may have to be one which is imperfect, and which may simply mean choosing the less bad one. Otherwise one can be paralysed by continuing to seek an ideal outcome that is not available.

When imperfection constitutes professional negligence (malpractice)

For professionals, the message that we are imperfect may have an underlying truth, but this has to be distinguished from undertaking our professional work in an imperfect way. A surgeon who removes the wrong limb from a patient cannot say: "I'm only human, we are all imperfect and we all make mistakes."

The essential element of a claim for professional negligence or malpractice in many jurisdictions is that the professional breached a duty of care. The level of care appropriate to each situation is generally measured against the standard of care that can reasonably be expected from a competent professional. But in some cases a court may go further and test the professional's actions on a more objective basis.

Where it is clear that the duty of care has been breached, causation needs to be established (that is, that any loss suffered was caused by the professional and not by some other factor) and, under English law, that any losses sustained were reasonably foreseeable. It is beyond the scope of this book to examine these principles. The fundamental point, however, is that imperfection may be human, but professionals who claim to function to a high standard will generally be judged by a high standard of care and responsibility.

Imperfection and paradox

The *Shorter Oxford Dictionary* defines paradox as "a statement seemingly self-contradictory or absurd, though possibly well-founded or essentially true". On this basis, one might say that there is an inherent paradox in the proposition that humans are messy and imperfect but that we have an ideal expectation of our professionals, who are only human.

Such paradoxes arise in professional life and indeed in life generally. Professions are generally expected to distinguish themselves from commercial enterprises by their rigorous quality standards and to stand apart from others in the market-place, yet paradoxically they are increasingly being required to compete in the marketplace as businesses. It is also paradoxical that professional specialisation, while positive, may also be negative in that it threatens the concept of generalist professionals who may be competent in all aspects of their profession.

It is paradoxical that in a democratic political system based on "first past the post" electoral principles, where four candidates stand for office and three of them each get 24 per cent of the vote, and one gets 28 per cent, the successful and elected candidate will be one whom 72 per cent of the electorate do not want.

How interesting and paradoxical that so many fictional and mythological superheroes fall short of perfection. With all his superpowers, Superman was vulnerable to kryptonite, Achilles became invulnerable and immortal when his mother dipped him as a baby into the River Styx, but as she held him by the heel, that was where he was vulnerable and mortal; and Popeye had super strength, but deprived of his spinach he was weak and vulnerable. The acceptance of vulnerability in heroic figures is also central to Greek tragedy. The paradox of imperfection alongside strength and heroism is embodied in the stories we tell.

Perhaps we should not be surprised if we find that people who rise to positions of power may sometimes be flawed. That is in the nature of human paradox.

Paradox joins uncertainty and imperfection as an inherent and sometimes uncomfortable feature of the human condition.

I am the wisest man alive, for I know one thing, and that is that I know nothing.

(Plato, *The Republic*)

Further reading

Gert Gigerenzer's *Gut Feelings: The Intelligence of the Unconscious* deals with decision-making. His other works include *Rationality for Mortals: How People Cope with Uncertainty* and *Risk Savvy: How to Make Good Decisions*. Also relevant is Susan Jeffers' *Embracing Uncertainty: Achieving Peace of Mind as we Face the Unknown*; and Bruce Eimer and Moshe Torem, a clinical hypnotherapist and a psychiatrist, have written *10 Simple Solutions for Coping with Uncertainty* which provides cognitive-behavioural techniques to help with uncertainty and change.

Alan Watts' classic *The Wisdom of Insecurity: A Message for an Age of Anxiety* dates back to 1951, but for those interested in a philosophical and spiritual approach to uncertainty and insecurity, it has been highly praised. Going 30 years further back is Frank Knight's *Risk, Uncertainty, and Profit*, which provided the basis for the distinction between uncertainty and risk and has been currently described as "one of the most interesting reads in economics even today".

Nicholas Taleb's *The Black Swan: The Impact of the Highly Improbable* has widespread acceptance of its central theme.

Daniel Kahneman's *Thinking, Fast and Slow* leads one into his ideas about Prospect Theory.

Brené Brown has written a number of books on shame, imperfection and related subjects, two of which are particularly relevant: *I Thought It Was Just Me (But It Isn't)* which addresses the issue of shame, with particular reference to women; and *The Gifts of Imperfection: Let Go of Who You Think You're Supposed to Be and Embrace Who You Are*.

Chapter 15

Negotiation

Negotiation fundamentals

Negotiation may be seen as a basic prerequisite for getting what we need or want as human beings. We will each have our own individual negotiating styles, which will to some extent be a product of individual personalities and to some extent what we have learned, either formally or pragmatically, by experience and observation.

For professionals, the need to negotiate may arise for a client, or with a client, or with colleagues or co-workers, professional or commercial organisations or others. Negotiations may be structured, for example trying to resolve a conflict or dispute or negotiating contract terms, or informal, such as negotiating a weekend contact rota.

This chapter addresses principles of negotiation on the basis of a structured form of negotiation but they may be equally applicable in unstructured and informal circumstances.

To negotiate or not to negotiate – that is the question

Dealing with non-negotiable values

Values that people hold so dear to them that they are not capable of any variation cannot realistically be made the subject of negotiation. People's identities may be intertwined with their values. So, for example, for many devout people, their religious beliefs are generally not amenable to negotiated change; and similarly people with strong ethical or political beliefs would not enter into negotiations that affect those beliefs or values.

Personal values may similarly be non-negotiable. For an individual, personal integrity, dignity, non-discrimination or compliance with a personal moral code may be sacrosanct.

Yet this does not necessarily mean that people with apparently irreconcilable values and beliefs cannot explore areas of agreement and disagreement and to see whether lines of communication can be established, common ground found and attempts made to bridge differences. Northern Ireland and South Africa provide examples of differences that no one thought could be bridged by discussion and negotiation, yet that is exactly what happened.

In *Staying with Conflict: A Strategic Approach to Ongoing Disputes* Bernard Mayer writes about seeking "conflict transformation" where such irreconcilable differences exist, rather than "conflict resolution". This may occur through parties engaging with their differences, establishing sustainable approaches to communication and developing systems of support.

"Bargaining with the devil"

The question may arise as to whether or not to try to negotiate with someone who you feel has behaved badly towards you, has infringed your rights or who has harmed you in the past and you fear may do so again in the future.

Harvard Law School Professor Robert Mnookin has addressed this in his book *Bargaining with the Devil: When to Negotiate and When to Fight*, covering two different but corresponding elements. The one is to identify issues that cannot or should not be negotiated and the other is to identify those issues that appear to be non-negotiable but which can in fact be negotiated. Mnookin warns against two opposing sets of traps. The one is to decline inappropriately to negotiate when it might be better to do so, commonly motivated by anger and demonisation of the other party, and the other is to try to negotiate in circumstances where it is wrong and inappropriate to do so.

Mnookin provides examples of each kind of decision: two people whom he identifies as political heroes of the twentieth century: Winston Churchill, because he refused to negotiate (with Adolf Hitler), and Nelson Mandela, because he agreed to negotiate (with a racist apartheid regime, thereby helping to bring about historical change as a result).

One of the most common reasons for refusing to negotiate is probably mistrust of and antagonism towards the other party, who may be perceived as intransigent/impossible/dishonest/greedy/manipulative or any of a number of other similar descriptions. "You simply can't negotiate with him/her." That may be true in some cases when one may either have to walk away or to have any issues resolved in an appropriate forum such as the court.

However, in the majority of such cases the balance may well lie in favour of negotiating rather than not. Mnookin recommends a rebuttable presumption in favour of negotiation, to counter-balance the negative traps; and he also urges assessing with caution the expected costs and benefits, engaging third-party advice and support in making this analysis. While respecting the client's views and beliefs, the professional needs to step back from the potential traps of demonisation, anger, dehumanisation and the impulse towards fight or flight and take a balanced and rational view of the pros and cons of negotiation.

Negotiation approaches

Fundamentally, although there are many different theoretical and practical approaches to negotiation, three ways of negotiating prevail. They are:

- an interest-based, cooperative approach;
- a competitive approach;
- a "hybrid" approach that draws on both the cooperative and the competitive methods as appropriate.

Each of these will be briefly considered.

Interest-based cooperative negotiation

Cooperative or interest-based negotiation involves an exploration of parties' respective needs and interests, with a problem-solving approach and an aim to find a consensual resolution that meets those needs and interests – achieving what the jargon might describe as a "win–win" outcome.

Working collaboratively and arriving at an agreed resolution that meets everyone's needs and interests is clearly desirable, where this is achievable.

One of the primary principles inherent in the interest-based approach is trying to establish parties' underlying interests, needs and concerns, looking deeper than the issues presented in the negotiations. When one understands these, possibilities for arriving at an agreement that addresses these can be explored.

Having regard to both the issues presented and the underlying aspects, parties will aim for an outcome that is objectively fair and acceptable. In doing so, negotiators will be on the lookout for creating value by taking advantage of differences: people may place different weight on different things, and understanding and taking advantage of this may allow each to have what matters more to them in an agreed outcome. Exploring a range of possible options may help in arriving at some composite solution that draws on these.

Another fundamental principle is to concentrate on the issues and to avoid being diverted by personality differences or antagonisms, which can so easily occur.

These and related principles were outlined in the classic work *Getting to Yes: Negotiating Agreement Without Giving In* by Roger Fisher and William Ury. As the title indicates, cooperation obviously does not mean having to agree to unacceptable proposals.

In *The Power of a Positive No: How to Say No and Still Get to Yes* William Ury recognises the importance of being able to reject unacceptable requests or demands in a way that supports principled negotiation. He provides practical strategies for rejecting inappropriate demands or behaviour, while maintaining a positive approach – for example by avoiding personal blaming, presenting facts objectively, using language with care and giving due respect to the other party. Negotiators need to know what will be done if agreement cannot be reached: this adds power to a negotiating position and removes dependence on gaining agreement.

> Instead of pushing your opponent towards an agreement, you need to do the opposite. You need to *draw* him in the direction you want him to move. Your job is to *build a golden bridge* across the chasm. You need to reframe a retreat from his position as an advance toward a better solution.
>
> (William Ury, *Getting Past No: Negotiating with Difficult People*)

Competitive negotiation

This approach proceeds on the basis that there is a limited resource available and that the stronger negotiator will achieve the better outcome and scoop the greater part of "the pot". In order to do so, the negotiator needs to be tough and skilful, making few concessions or goodwill gestures, going to the brink and being untroubled by the prospect of deadlock.

Competitive negotiation is not necessarily the same as *rights-based negotiation* in which the negotiators are primarily concerned with the law and arriving as close as they can to the outcome they consider likely in the event of a court trial. In practice, many negotiators may have regard to rights as an element in negotiation but this is unlikely to be the only consideration, and parties may well have regard to commercial, personal and other factors.

Gavin Kennedy, author of *Everything Is Negotiable: How To Negotiate And Win*, does not believe that adopting a soft stance is right because it may tend to permeate the negotiator's whole approach to the negotiations. Tough negotiators use shock openings and maintain them, and do not back down in the face of tough opponents. They are not afraid of deadlock. In a personal note to the authors of this book, Gavin Kennedy adds: "I would not recommend aggressive behaviour; more firmness of trading than fighting talk."

Reconciling interest-based and competitive approaches

Negotiators do not have to make a choice between cooperation and competition. David A. Lax and James K. Sebenius consider that both are present in negotiation. In *The Manager as Negotiator: Bargaining for Co-operation and Competitive Gain* they consider that both kinds of process are present in negotiation, and that there is an "essential tension" between the creation and the division of value. Their synthesis of problem-solving and competitive approaches results in one of the most useful models of negotiation available.

Some practical aspects of negotiation

Preparation, design and set-up

Generally, preparation is fundamental to effective negotiation. This includes ensuring you have all relevant information available; reflecting on your goals; considering the potential of the relationship with the other party; thinking about each party's interests and how far these are compatible; listing and prioritising options; reflecting on the alternatives to reaching agreement; being emotionally prepared; and having a clear idea of intended process.

In their work *3-D Negotiation: Powerful Tools to Change the Game in Your Most Important Deals* Lax and Sebenius refer to the three dimensions of negotiation, two of which will be noted in this context (the third relates to negotiation tactics):

Design involves considering how to create value by going behind stated positions and understanding all the interests involved, thinking imaginatively and dovetailing differences.

Set-up focuses on the arrangements for the negotiation, including ensuring that the right parties and their decision-makers are involved in the process; understanding all interests; developing a negotiation strategy, also the alternatives if agreement cannot be reached; and ensuring that the other party understands that one is not compelled to agree at any cost.

Zone of (possible) agreement and the negotiation dance

The "zone of possible agreement" represents the parameters of the range of possible terms of settlement within which a particular dispute may be resolved, given the aspirations of each party and any other relevant factors. It may be found in the overlap between the bottom end of what a claimant would accept and the top end of what the other would offer.

Before reaching a zone of agreement, parties often go through a "negotiation dance" – a metaphor for the way in which cooperative and competitive behaviours wax and wane and proposals and counter-proposals are exchanged during the negotiation process.

The initial stages: anchoring

There are pros and cons about opening the negotiations by making the first offer. Some negotiators prefer not to do so because they would like to establish the other side's thinking first without giving away their own approach. On the other hand, the advantage of making the first offer is that it allows one to establish the initial "anchor" – the level that guides further proposals in negotiations.

Anchoring is a cognitive bias that leads a person to place heavy reliance on initial information provided or proposals made – even when aware of its influence. Leigh Thompson addresses this in her book *The Truth about Negotiations: "You May Want to Make the First Offer"*.

There are ways of overcoming the initial anchoring effect, for example by changing the frame of reference or basis for arriving at proposed terms, which effectively establishes a counter-anchor. This can be reinforced by putting the counter-proposals in writing. It seems that doing so, especially if backed by supporting data, helps to reinforce an anchoring or counter-anchoring effect.

Continuing the negotiations

The following are some general observations about negotiations:

- There is a common expectation that each side will broadly match any concessions made by the other, on the principle of reciprocity, perhaps eventually splitting the difference. However, this benefits a party which starts with an extreme position and disadvantages the party which adopts a moderate position. Looking ahead to that, some negotiators might respond to an extreme demand by making an equally extreme response the other way. If a moderated response is made, this discrepancy should be borne in mind if splitting the difference is later proposed. It may not be appropriate to respond symmetrically.
- A cooperative, interest-based problem-solving approach is desirable, but one needs to be alert to the other side seeking to exploit this by purporting to

agree while seeking an advantageous result. This is the "essential tension" mentioned above. It is possible to maintain a principled approach based on fairness while still standing firm where this is not properly reciprocated.

- Sometimes the other side may employ negative tactics or conduct. This can best be met by maintaining focus on one's objectives rather being drawn into responding in a similar way or being diverted from the primary objective of resolving the issues.

- It is generally prudent to avoid reaching partial agreement where there are multiple issues under discussion, unless it is obviously severable from overall agreement. While having some agreement may give a momentum to discussions and may be desirable in itself, if there needs to be an overall agreement it may be desirable to make the partial agreement provisional and dependent on reaching overall resolution.

- Parties are sometimes quick to refer to their "bottom line" at which they will "walk away" from the negotiations. This should really be kept as a last resort and not used as a bluff. Knowing the range within which agreement is acceptable is a powerful basis for discussion and negotiation so that if it seems that this cannot be achieved, one knows when to end the negotiations. It also helps to deal with the other side's "bottom line".

- This necessitates knowing one's BATNA (Best Alternative to a Negotiated Agreement) and WATNA (Worst Alternative to a Negotiated Agreement) – so as to be able to weigh proposals against these.

Some psychological aspects of negotiation

Emotions and the myth of rationality

Chapter 3 considers the myth of rationality and the influence of the emotions in decision-making. This is particularly relevant to negotiation, which one might expect would be conducted as a rational process. In fact, most decisions involve a balance between rational, emotional and intuitive responses.

US mediator Robert Benjamin refers in his online writing to the

strong visceral and emotional torrents of initial resistance … to negotiation. Logical argument – suggesting, for example, how negotiation might save time and money – while eminently rational, is seldom likely to overcome that resistance and often appear as unconvincing and hollow appeals to people who are hurt and angry.

Roger Fisher and Daniel Shapiro's *Building Agreement: Using Emotions as You Negotiate* addresses this issue and how to generate positive emotions and deal with negative ones. While negative emotions can have a detrimental effect including, for example, on cognitive functioning, they can also inform one about matters that one needs to be wary about; and positive emotions can have a beneficial effect on negotiations. They can reduce fear and suspicion and enhance relationships and the ability to negotiate productively.

Negotiators need to develop an emotional awareness and an understanding of the effects of emotions and the ways in which emotional intelligence can inform and support negotiation.

> We cannot stop having emotions any more than we can stop having thoughts.
> The challenge is learning to stimulate helpful emotions in those with whom we negotiate – and in ourselves.
>
> (Roger Fisher and Daniel Shapiro, Introduction to
> *Building Agreement: Using Emotions as You Negotiate*
> (initially published as *Beyond Reason*))

Perceptions

Many disputes arise from different perceptions of the same facts. It can thus be helpful in the negotiation process to check whether people's perceptions – those on one's own side and those on the other side – are based on reality, insofar as this can be established. Of course, reality, like beauty and truth, may be in the eye of the beholder, hence the scope for misperception.

Perceptions may relate to the issues under negotiation, in which case it may be helpful to have some authoritative information that can help to correct misperceptions. Or they may relate to the negotiators, which in turn may influence the dynamic of the negotiations. If a negotiator is seen as straightforward, experienced and reasonably honourable, negotiations are likely to progress more effectively than if he or she is perceived as untrustworthy and manipulative. The choice of negotiator may therefore be a factor influencing the process.

Personality traits

The respective personalities of the negotiators will be likely to have an effect on the dynamics of the process. If both are aggressive and risk-taking, the negotiations are likely to be more volatile than if both are collaborative, open and agreeable. Research indicates that this is not necessarily always the case, depending on how they manifest their personalities, but there is likely to be some relationship between personality and negotiating style.

It is important to maintain authenticity in negotiations, so we cannot change our personalities. We can, however, understand our personalities and how they may be perceived, and we can learn how to manage our negotiating style and approach without compromising ourselves.

We can, for example, be aware of the need to respect the other party's self-esteem and help them to save face where necessary. We may need to use language sensitively even where the other party does not. We can prepare ourselves for dealing with difficult people while still maintaining our focus, our principles and our objectives. With awareness and thought, we do not need to allow our personality or the other party's to frustrate effective negotiations.

Culture and gender in negotiation

In an increasingly diverse world, an effective negotiator will need to appreciate the influence of cultural diversity on the course and outcome of any negotiations in which such differences exist. He or she will also need to understand with some sensitivity the culture in which the negotiations are taking place, which may well involve a learning process; and it then remains necessary to translate this understanding into a practical strategy.

With regard to gender, some common images and perceptions of men and women as negotiators reflect the gender stereotypes of society. For example, men are perceived as tougher and more competitive, women as more concerned and cooperative. Negotiators need to be alert to stereotypes and generalisations and bear in mind their unreliability and irrelevance in dealing with specific issues and individuals.

Some of the issues surrounding culture and gender are outlined in Chapter 9.

Further reading

The classic work on interest-based negotiation is Roger Fisher and William Ury's 1981 *Getting to Yes: Negotiating Agreement Without Giving In*. Later works addressing some of the book's perceived shortcomings in negotiating with unprincipled opponents include Roger Fisher and Scott Brown's *Getting Together: Building a Relationship that Gets to Yes* and William Ury's follow-up, *Getting Past No: Negotiating with Difficult People*. William Ury also wrote *The Power of a Positive No: How to Say No and Still Get to Yes*.

Two books relevant to the question of whether or not to negotiate are Bernard Mayer's *Staying with Conflict: A Strategic Approach to Ongoing Disputes* and Robert Mnookin's *Bargaining with the Devil: When to Negotiate and When to Fight*.

Those involved in negotiation and in influencing people's views and mind-sets are likely to find David Straker's book helpful and informative: *Changing Minds – in Detail: How to Change What People, Think, Feel, Believe and Do* provides understandings about people's drivers and motivators and how these and other patterns can be influenced and changed.

Excellent approaches to negotiation are provided by David A. Lax and James K. Sebenius in their books *The Manager as Negotiator: Bargaining for Co-operation and Competitive Gain* and *3-D Negotiation: Powerful Tools to Change the Game in Your Most Important Deals*.

Other valuable books on negotiation might include Gavin Kennedy's *Everything Is Negotiable: How to Negotiate and Win*; Roger Fisher and Daniel Shapiro's *Building Agreement: Using Emotions as You Negotiate*; Edward de Bono's *Conflicts: A Better Way to Resolve Them*; Leigh L. Thompson's *The Truth About Negotiations: "You May Want to Make the First Offer"*; and Stuart Levine's *Getting to Resolution: Turning Conflict to Collaboration*.

Chapter 16

Conflict and disputes

Management and resolution

Credit: CartoonStock.com

Conflict and dispute outline

Distinguishing conflict and dispute

As professionals we will inevitably be faced from time to time with conflictual situations and perhaps with disputes. We may need to help our clients or patients deal with these, particularly if we are working in fields such as social work, law, management, mental health, counselling or mediation – or indeed in many other kinds of activity. Or we may need to deal with conflicts or disputes in our own workplace, organisations, families or lives.

Brown and Marriott's *ADR Principles and Practice* (3rd edition) addresses the distinction between a conflict and a dispute.

Conflict is a state of being – within oneself, for example where one has an internal conflict about choosing a course of action; with another or others in any context, including work, family, personal or community; with or between groups, organisations or even countries. It is amorphous and can exist in many different environments and take many different shapes or forms, sometimes overt and sometimes hidden beneath the surface and not necessarily brought into consciousness.

A *dispute* on the other hand is a distinct disagreement about a defined or definable issue that can be articulated and argued and which is capable of being determined by a court or other adjudicator.

This is not just an academic distinction. The approach to the issues may be different for a dispute that can be resolved or adjudicated from say an interpersonal or organisational conflict that may require a different kind of intervention.

The paradox

There is, however, a paradox in the distinction. On the one hand, "conflict" may be viewed as a generic term, with "dispute" as one particular kind or class of conflict that manifests itself in distinct and definable issues. On the other hand, a dispute may well involve some element of conflict within itself (for example, interpersonal antagonism).

So disputes may be found within conflicts, and conflicts may be found within disputes.

Conflict

We have observed that conflict is an integral part of human behaviour and that there can be no movement or change without it. It is when conflict becomes dysfunctional that problems arise. It is in this sense that conflict is now further considered.

> Conflict is first and foremost about people's passions, desires and emotions in collision. The friction of conflict generates heat, which like any form of natural energy, can be squandered or harnessed. The sources could be scarce resources, an inability to communicate or empathize, a moral clash over good or evil, or a power struggle of some variety. Typically, they are inextricably intertwined and sometimes disguised.
> (Robert Benjamin, "Mediators, Tricksters, and the Constructive Uses of Deception", in *Bringing Peace into the Room*)

Conflict may manifest itself in many different ways, including anger, aggression, hostility, contempt, mutual mistrust, intransigence, threats, sanctions, violence and, in the case of conflict between states, war. However, people in conflict may not necessarily show it openly. Their anger may be quiet, their aggression passive and their hostility silent and contained.

The causes of conflict may be as varied as the ways in which it can be manifested and these may not necessarily be rationally based. At a personal or professional level, it may arise from personal antagonisms; differences of values or aims; competition and power struggles; reaction to the perception (or the reality) of being badly or unfairly treated or having one's rights, dignity or well-being abused; misinterpreted communications; and many other causes.

The effects of conflict may be significant, potentially causing stress, anxiety and frustration in addition to reactions such as anger, resentment and mistrust, with consequential effects:

Personal consequences may be both emotional and physical, since unresolved stress has a direct, adverse and corrosive impact on mental and bodily health.

Organisational consequences, where the conflict arises in a workplace context, can result in the diversion of energy and resource in dealing with it as well as potentially negative effects on relationships, organisational cohesion, communications, creativity and productivity.

Professional consequences may include the personal consequences outlined above and in addition may have implications for one's good name and reputation – and, depending on the nature of the conflict, perhaps on one's practice, business or organisation generally.

Family consequences may be the spin-off effect on the family of any conflict in which the professional is involved: families are not immune to the stresses and tensions that continuing conflict has on a member. Or a professional may be personally involved in family conflict – perhaps with a family member or with a spouse or life partner, with profound effects.

Dispute

A dispute is a disagreement about respective views, opinions or rights. The sense in which it is used in this chapter is a disagreement about respective rights or obligations. It may but does not necessarily have the emotional component that interpersonal conflict generally involves.

Whereas a simple insurance claim may not involve any interpersonal conflict, a dispute between neighbours about the position of a boundary fence may well be a symptom of an ongoing conflict about a range of differences including personal antagonisms.

Conflict resolution and management

Because of the differences between conflicts and disputes, the approach to dealing with each of these will be addressed separately, though there is inevitably a process overlap.

When dealing with conflict, the primary objective is usually to try to resolve it. However, it may not be possible to do so and the aim of intervention may just be to manage it effectively. Hence conflict resolution and conflict management will be separately considered.

Conflict resolution

Direct discussion

Where people are in conflict, the first question might be whether direct, sensitive and respectful discussion could help resolve the issues. This may well be appropriate where the conflict has arisen because of misunderstandings or miscommunications that can be rectified or where the causes are unclear and discussion may identify problems that can be remedied.

Much will depend on the nature of the conflict, but the following considerations may help:

- While it is invariably necessary to be open and candid about the conflict, it is also important to maintain a calm environment and to avoid it becoming overheated.

> A soft answer turneth away wrath: but grievous words stir up anger.
> (Proverbs 15)

- Have the discussion at a time and place where you will not be disturbed, where you can speak freely and which feels neutral and comfortable.
- Communication skills will be important, especially active listening without blame or judgement, choosing your words carefully and reframing as necessary.
- As far as possible assumptions and preconceptions should be brought into conscious awareness and put aside.
- While objectivity and rationality will be required, bear in mind that conflict is not always rational and that emotions and irrationality may surface. Accept this as part of the necessary discussion and try to see beyond this to underlying issues and concerns.
- Be careful about using humour. If it is gentle, appropriate and affirmative, it can ease tensions; but it often runs the risk of inflaming rather than cooling the situation, especially if used inappropriately while discussing a serious subject.
- It may be necessary to compromise, or to find creative solutions to difficult situations, for example introducing necessary changes slowly in stages to see how they work out.

- Some people find it easier to plan and prepare for the discussion, trying to anticipate contentions and reactions, while others prefer to be spontaneous. Some pre-planning and thought is helpful and may be essential in many cases, but it should not override active listening and spontaneous responses.

Facilitated discussion

Direct communications may resolve some conflictual situations, but many people need the help of a third party to facilitate their discussions. In *Conflicts: A Better Way to Resolve Them* Edward de Bono suggests that people caught up in a "tension of hostility" generally do not trust one another enough or communicate effectively enough to design creative solutions. His remedy is the introduction of a third party into the dynamic, with the necessary skill to create a design for an optimal outcome: a "design idiom".

Third-party intervention may be manifested in different ways:

- Organisational conflict at work can be addressed by specialist management consultants, who may use facilitative and consultative processes to help develop constructive working relationships.
- In the context of families and couples, conflict may be addressed by various forms of counselling or psychotherapeutic processes including the following models:

  The *systemic* model is based on the understanding that symptoms, problems and difficulties arising in the context of relationships are to be understood as interactive processes, having regard to interactional patterns and dynamics.

  The *cognitive-behavioural* model focuses on how thoughts, beliefs and attitudes affect feelings and behaviour, encourages adaptive responses and teaches coping skills.

  The *humanistic* model adopts a holistic approach which may include attention to body, mind and spirit and focuses on self-actualisation and creativity.

  The *psychodynamic* model looks at the underlying, often unconscious causes of distress and conflict and aims to bring them into consciousness with the development of insight, which leads to the necessary changes being made.

- Conflict resolution intervention can take place in a number of other situations, for example in schools, where peer groups can be taught how to resolve their conflicts; in healthcare, including working with patients and clients; in community-based conflict; and even in addressing conflict between rival gangs that impact on the local community.
- Mediation, dealt with below, can hover between conflict and disputes and help facilitate the resolution of either – or both.

Every conflict happens because someone wishes to effect a change which another someone resists ... If we can manage change, perhaps we can manage conflict ... Managing and resolving conflict means managing and resolving the problems of change.

(Andrew Floyer Acland, *A Sudden Outbreak of Common Sense: Managing Conflict through Mediation*)

Conflict management

Conflict management may well be the starting point for addressing conflict as a step on the way to resolution. However, in some situations resolution of the conflict is not possible and facilitative processes may be geared towards managing the conflict rather than trying to resolve it. This means that the conflict is recognised and acknowledged and that the parties agree, explicitly or implicitly, to find ways to live with it and function alongside it.

In his book *Staying with Conflict: A Strategic Approach to Ongoing Disputes* Bernard Mayer identifies kinds of conflicts where conflict professionals may not be able to help the parties end the conflict, but may be able to help them manage or de-escalate it (or sometimes to help them escalate it where this is necessary to promote engagement). This may be because the conflict is about people's non-negotiable core values; or because of the structure of the situation – for example where the available resources do not lend themselves to agreement about the issues; or because of people's personality traits.

Mayer considers that such ongoing conflicts – also called enduring or long-term conflicts – should still be addressed by conflict specialists, but in a different way. People in this situation may need to recognise the paradox that they may need to approach the issues with hopefulness and optimism but that the likelihood is that the issues will not be resolved, that a slow and patient approach may be needed and that they will be living with uncertainty.

Staying with conflict relies on the ability to remain productively, creatively and even serenely in a state of nonresolution (not to be mistaken for irresolution) ... Staying with conflict ... requires us to live with unsolved problems, unresolved conflict, and more questions than answers. A need for certainty and closure often gets us into trouble; it impels us to act as if we know more than we do and to solve problems superficially or ill advisedly, and it limits our ability to think creatively and broadly about difficult issues.

(Bernard Mayer, *Staying with Conflict: A Strategic Approach to Ongoing Disputes*)

Mediators and other conflict professionals can help people manage their conflicts even if they can't resolve them. For example, they can help them to address issues that they might want to avoid, but which may need to be confronted; to communicate more effectively and authentically with one another; to manage power issues; to convert implicit agreements and understandings into explicit ones; to develop support systems; and generally to arrive at workable and sustainable arrangements.

Modes of responding to conflict

People have different ways of responding to conflict, depending on variables including the nature of the conflict, its emotional impact, how values are affected by the conflict and the circumstances in which conflict takes place. These cannot be measurable or quantifiable.

Another factor in the mix is the personality of the individual and the way in which he or she may be naturally inclined to respond to conflict – though any natural tendency may be overridden by the nature and circumstances of the conflict, so that someone may react in one way to one kind of conflict but quite differently to another.

Nevertheless, one's natural proclivity will have an impact, and people may follow responses that feel natural and comfortable to them more readily than others. This principle led Kenneth Thomas and Ralph Kilmann to develop a form of psychometric testing to measure a person's behaviour when faced with conflict situations: the Thomas–Kilmann Conflict Mode Instrument (TKI). This correlates two dimensions of behaviour, assertiveness and cooperativeness, in different permutations to provide five different modes of response:

Competing: This assertive and uncooperative style follows a competitive and aggressive approach, geared towards winning rather than trying to find a cooperative solution, justified perhaps by a sense of the need to protect one's rights and not to be exploited by others.

Accommodating: The opposite of the competing mode – this concedes one's own position in the interests of satisfying the demands or requirements of others. It may create goodwill and keep the peace but it can lead to unsatisfactory outcomes and possible later resentment.

Avoiding: This involves sidestepping or putting off dealing with the issues. Motives may include delaying matters to reduce tensions or to await a better time to address the issues but commonly it is just an unwillingness to face the issues.

Compromising: The pragmatic objective is to find some expedient, mutually acceptable solution that satisfies both parties though not necessarily completely.

Collaborating: This is perceived as the optimal mode of dealing with conflict: trying to work together to arrive at the best and most creative outcome for everyone.

An understanding of the psychological process in play in any conflict or dispute is an important resource for anyone endeavouring to work towards resolution. In *The Psychology of Conflict: Mediating in a Diverse World*, Paul Randolph draws on existentialist theories to provide a valuable contribution to the theory and practice of mediation.

Dispute resolution: primary processes

Negotiation

This is the primary tool for addressing any kind of dispute. Preparing for negotiation is invariably important, particularly when negotiating in a legal context. In such an event, preparation should include taking legal advice to understand and appreciate the legal position and the strengths and weaknesses of one's case, and the available alternatives to reaching agreement in negotiations, including cost and risk factors.

Litigation – the court process

The default process for resolving legal disputes if there is no other mechanism agreed by the parties is very widely litigation through the civil courts.

Religious courts

In some places cultural or religious principles may prevail and disputes may be dealt with in traditional or religious courts, which may co-exist alongside national courts. So, for example, some orthodox Muslims may have their civil disputes dealt with in the Sharia courts on principles of Islamic jurisprudence and some orthodox Jews may do so in the Jewish religious court, the Beth Din, on principles of Jewish Halachic law. For these courts to have jurisdiction, both or all parties must agree to this, otherwise the national courts will prevail.

Alternative dispute resolution (ADR): introduction

Over the years, alternative dispute resolution (ADR) has matured and it is now part of mainstream practice. Its concept as an "alternative" process relates to the fact that it developed as an alternative to litigation. Some ADR proponents see the acronym ADR as "appropriate" dispute resolution to reflect mediation and other processes as equivalent to litigation.

The court system is critical to the protection of people's rights and freedom, providing the backdrop to ADR processes, in that disputants negotiate "in the shadow of the law", without which many would not feel the need to arrive at a resolution of the issues. Litigation and ADR function in a symbiotic relationship with one another: each supports and enhances the other.

ADR may be divided into three broad types with different third-party roles:

Non-adjudicatory processes: The third party helps parties to arrive at their own resolution by some form of facilitation with no authority to make a binding determination.

Adjudicatory processes: The third party determines the issues between the parties.

Hybrid processes: These provide some combination of facilitation and adjudication.

ADR complements litigation ... providing processes which can either stand in their own right or be used as an adjunct to adjudication ... It gives parties more power and greater control over resolving the issues between them, encourages problem-solving approaches, and provides for more effective settlements covering substance and nuance. It also tends to enhance co-operation and to be conducive to the preservation of relationships. Effective impartial third party intercession can help to overcome blocks to settlement, and by expediting and facilitating resolution it can save costs and avoid the delays and risks of litigation. Sometimes, but not necessarily, it can help to heal or provide the conditions for healing underlying conflicts between parties. ADR processes, like adjudicatory procedures, have advantages and disadvantages which make them suitable for some cases but not for others.

(Henry Brown and Arthur Marriott, *ADR Principles and Practice*, 3rd edition)

Non-adjudicatory ADR

Within a range of non-adjudicatory processes mediation has dominated the landscape. The processes are usually treated as evidentially privileged so that negotiations cannot be referred to in any subsequent court proceedings – with some exceptions such as allegations of fraud or duress. Agreements reached are, however, generally made formal and binding.

Mediation (conciliation)

Mediation is a facilitative process in which an impartial mediator with no authority to make any substantive decision helps disputing parties to try to negotiate an agreed resolution of their dispute. Conciliation has broadly the same attributes as mediation. It is sometimes described as being more proactive and evaluative than mediation; but sometimes the opposite view is taken. There is no consistency of usage of these terms.

The mediation process may vary between different fields of activity, models of practice and styles and approaches of individual practitioners.

Civil-commercial practice varies but commonly there is likely to be an exchange of position statements or case summaries and of relevant documents followed by a substantive meeting which takes place over a few hours or a day or more. After a joint meeting the mediator will commonly move the parties into separate rooms and conduct separate and confidential meetings with each group, shuttling back and forth facilitating negotiations and trying to find common ground and narrow differences.

The mediator may also meet parties without their lawyers, or vice versa, or meet any experts if they are brought to the mediation. The mediator may reconvene joint meetings, may adjourn for any purpose, or may need to contact people outside the mediation. The process is flexible and creative.

Opinions differ as to how far a mediator might go in providing any kind of evaluation of the merits of the dispute. Most practitioners accept that this may include challenging perceptions through questioning and probing, but (in the UK) virtually none will express a view as to the likely outcome in the event of a trial. Practitioners may, in the privacy of a separate meeting, challenge perceptions and/ or help facilitate a better understanding of the legal position.

Where there is deadlock some mediators may suggest pragmatic settlement terms, others would not do so. Mediator approaches to this and to evaluation vary.

Any agreement reached needs to be recorded on a binding basis. Where parties don't reach agreement in the mediation, their rights to proceed to adjudication are ordinarily reserved.

Discourage litigation. Persuade your neighbors to compromise whenever you can. Point out to them how the nominal winner is often the real loser— in fees, and expenses, and waste of time. As a peace-maker the lawyer has a superior opportunity of being a good man. There will still be business enough.

(Abraham Lincoln)

The mini-trial (executive tribunal)

This is a form of evaluative mediation in which a senior executive of each corporate party to a commercial dispute joins an independent third party to form an executive "tribunal" to hear the case on both sides as presented by the respective lawyers on an abbreviated basis. No formal evidence is led or witnesses called, and no decision is made, but the neutral may express a non-binding opinion to the executives, giving them a better understanding of the issues and enabling them to enter into settlement negotiations on a more informed basis, facilitated by the neutral. This process converts the problem to a business one rather than a legal one. The executives can bring their business judgement into the settlement discussions.

Neutral case evaluation (early neutral evaluation)

In this process, the parties appoint an agreed neutral evaluator whose opinion and authority they both or all respect, who evaluates the merits of the case and provides his or her views on a non-binding basis. This may comprise an assessment of the relative strengths and weaknesses of the case. If required, the neutral may go on to work with the parties to facilitate discussions and negotiations and help them get to an agreed resolution.

Adjudicatory ADR

Arbitration

Most countries have arbitration statutes and institutions with prescribed rules and procedures and panels of approved arbitrators. The following are some key features of arbitration:

- The arbitral process rests on agreement between the parties to engage in it.
- The arbitrator or arbitral tribunal can be appointed by the parties either directly, or by some appointing authority agreed upon by them.
- The arbitrator or tribunal has a duty to be impartial and to act judicially, to observe due process (or natural justice) and to provide a fair and unbiased hearing.
- Procedures, which may be more flexible than in litigation, are generally set out in the rules of the relevant arbitral organisation. Subject to this, parties are free to agree the procedure, constrained by basic principles of fairness and due process. They may for example have a documents-only arbitration.
- Parties are free to choose the applicable system of law and the arbitration venue.
- Under some circumstances, issues of law can be reserved to the courts, which also have a supervisory power, for example where there are allegations of irregularity.
- The award should be binding and enforceable.
- There is generally no appeal against the award, though some consumer organisations may allow limited forms of appeal.
- Many statutes and rules provide for the award of costs in arbitrations.

Contractual adjudication

Contractual adjudication ("interim" or "fast-track" adjudication) is frequently used to resolve certain types of commercial disputes, particularly but not only in the construction industry. An adjudicator, agreed between the parties, considers the issues and provides a speedy interim decision that is binding, but allows any party dissatisfied with the decision to have the issues reheard and determined in arbitration or litigation. Pending this, the decision remains binding. The adjudicator may also award interest and costs if the contractual provision allows for this.

Dispute boards

The dispute board is a form of adjudication in which an agreed panel is set up at the start of a project, which can address issues and disputes as they arise. Although initially used in the construction field, dispute boards are now used in a wider range of industries including information technology, insurance contracts and financial and other services.

Boards usually have both informal and formal roles. Informally a board can provide a forum for the discussion of contentious matters, and if required, to help devise practical solutions consistent with their neutral role. In its formal capacity, the board may function in a number of ways, most commonly either making a non-binding recommendation or making an interim binding decision that can be overridden by a later determination.

Expert determination

Expert determination is commonly used in relation to property, share or business valuations and to technical or accounting disputes, issues regarding contractual specifications and contract performance matters. In this process the parties, either contractually in advance or as required on an ad hoc basis, appoint an independent expert in the subject matter of the dispute to resolve the issues between them on a legally binding basis.

The appointed expert will usually decide on procedure, either conducting an enquiry and/or a technical inspection, or sometimes conducting the process on a documents-only basis.

Administrative or statutory tribunals

Administrative tribunals, in the mental health, employment, immigration, social security and other fields, are established by statute, and are based on the principle of having an informal, cost-effective system of dealing with issues arising in specialist administrative areas by engaging people with relevant knowledge and experience to make necessary decisions, rather than generalist judges in the courts. They are required to function on the principles of openness, accessibility, fairness, efficiency and impartiality, adjudicating disputes that people may have in relation to decisions of government agencies.

Hybrid ADR processes

These processes combine different features of ADR.

Med-arb (mediation-arbitration)

In this process, the parties agree in advance that if the matter does not settle in mediation the mediator should change role and become an arbitrator with the task of making a binding determination. This means that the process will produce a resolution, one way or another.

However, there is a concern that the mediator's ability to function in either mode may be compromised by having both roles. A potential solution to this issue is to require the mediator to indicate at the end of the mediation whether he has any confidential information and to allow either party to opt out of the arbitration phase. Another option is to provide for the mediator to give a non-binding and confidential opinion rather than a binding award.

Arb-med (arbitration-mediation)

This is the reverse of med-arb, though not quite a mirror image. Here arbitration takes place first but the award is not published. It is instead sealed and maintained by the arbitrator confidentially, and the parties then move into mediation in an attempt to reach an agreed resolution without knowing what the award is.

Some arbitrators limit the length of the arbitration element, for example to a half-day for each party in order to contain costs. This abbreviated arbitration may well suffice in many cases, but will not be appropriate for those cases that require detailed evidence and probing.

Neutral fact-finding expert

The neutral fact-finding expert, appointed by the parties jointly, may be required to investigate and report on relevant facts and present an opinion, which may be binding, or non-binding but admissible in court proceedings as a factor, but not a conclusive one, allowing each party to adduce any other expert evidence to try to controvert the neutral expert's views. This makes the neutral expert's opinion persuasive without making it decisive.

Ombudsman

An ombudsman is an independent person whose primary role is to deal with complaints against administrative injustice and maladministration, with the power to investigate, criticise and make issues public, and who promotes good administration. Although having no power to alter a decision when a complaint is found to be justified, he or she may persuade the relevant authority to alter its decision, to improve facilities, or to apologise or pay compensation.

Online dispute resolution (ODR)

Information and communications technology (ICT) covers an increasingly wide range of available communications and other information sourcing and usage technologies. The need exists for appropriate dispute resolution mechanisms to deal with issues arising in this environment. Online dispute resolution (ODR) addresses this and is also increasingly available for disputes arising in the real world, alongside and complementary to traditional ADR processes.

So, for example, online ombuds services have been established and some commercial Internet retailers and users have set up their own online dispute resolution services. In addition, online resources are also being made available to facilitate ordinary "real world" disputes. ODR technology can also support traditional processes through case-management programs, case files with multiple collaborative forums, audio-visual teleconferencing, psychometric profiling, data storage and retrieval and an increasing range of other resources.

Further reading

The authors acknowledge Henry Brown and Arthur Marriott's *ADR Principles and Practice* (3rd edition) from which various elements of this chapter were drawn.

A shortlist, geared primarily to civil and commercial processes and not to the wide range of books relating to family mediation or other specialist areas, might include Susan Blake, Julie Browne and Stuart Simes' *A Practical Approach to Alternative Dispute Resolution*; Tony Allen's *Mediation Law and Civil Practice*; and for mediation practice David Richbell's *How to Master Commercial Mediation*; and an update of the now classic *The Mediation Process: Practical Strategies for Resolving Conflict* by Christopher Moore. Also Allan Barsky's *Conflict Resolution for the Helping Professions*; Stuart Levine's *Getting to Resolution: Turning Conflict into Collaboration*; Daniel Bowling and David Hoffman's *Bringing Peace into the Room*; and Bernard Mayer's *Staying with Conflict: A Strategic Approach to Ongoing Disputes*.

Some specialist works would include Mohamed Keshavjee's *Islam, Sharia and Alternative Dispute Resolution*; Paul Randolph's *The Psychology of Conflict: Mediating in a Diverse World*, which addresses psychological aspects based on existential principles; and David Straker's *Changing Minds – in Detail: How to Change What People, Think, Feel, Believe and Do*, which provides detailed understandings of how people interact with one another and how they may be influenced through persuasive methods. For those who work as mediation advocates for clients rather than as mediators, Stephen Walker's *Mediation Advocacy: Representing Clients in Mediation* is well regarded and for lawyers generally Professor Marjorie Corman Aaron's *Client Science: Advice for Lawyers on Counseling Clients through Bad News and Other Legal Realities* provides practical help in guiding clients through difficult decision-making.

Chapter 17

Beyond technique

Beyond technique: the concept

This title is inspired by a workshop of this name run by the US Academy of Family Mediators at their annual conference in Breckenridge, Colorado, in 1989. The concept, here widened to relate to all professionals generally, concerns the need to step aside periodically from issues of expertise, technique, skills and theoretical knowledge, and to take stock of other "non-technique" elements that we bring into our professional lives and practice.

It relates to the need for us to practise self-care, to nurture ourselves as professionals and as individuals and family members, and to maintain our physical and emotional well-being.

It also relates to fact that by being more attuned and sensitive to things around us, experiencing greater mindfulness, having the capacity to relax and minimise stress, and having personal authenticity, we not only enhance our personal lives but we are also able to function more effectively as professionals – consciously and unconsciously. In essence, who we are as people affects what we do and how we relate in our professional lives.

Self-nurturing and establishing calm

As individuals, we may have a multitude of different ways of relaxing and nurturing ourselves – though for some people this may not always be easy to do: personal or work stresses and anxieties may make it hard to relax, or we may be so connected to the work mode and the adrenaline rush that we find it very difficult to shift mode. Or family, financial or work demands may be so great that we feel that we genuinely cannot afford to take time out.

Yet self-care is critical if we are to function to maximum effectiveness. A stressed or exhausted professional cannot function consistently effectively, puts clients or patients at risk, and does not have the necessary resources – of energy, of responsiveness, of cognitive function or of an ability to draw on the unconscious – to maintain excellence.

There is no "right" way to nurture or care for oneself. Everyone may have their own personal preference. For one it may be yoga or meditation, for another it may be listening to music or watching a film, or walking, jogging or gardening. Or it may be participating – or competing – in sport or games, or playing a musical instrument, or cooking, or spending quality time with loved ones, or just peacefully observing a beautiful sunset.

> What is this life if, full of care,
> We have no time to stand and stare ...
> (W. H. Davies, in *Songs of Joy and Others*)

Given the vast and highly personal array of options for self-care and nurturing, it is wholly impracticable to try to list them. However, it may be helpful to highlight a few esoteric approaches to self-nurturing, which have been found to have benefits to health and cognitive awareness and which can help us to establish and maintain a calm presence. They also help us to be centred – maintaining a balanced frame of mind, unflustered and in personal control.

Meditation

Meditation is widely seen as an effective way of reducing stress in a stressful world and to develop a greater sense of calm. It is also a way to reduce anxiety levels, attain some kind of inner peace, help tap into the unconscious more effectively, and enhance clarity of thinking and quality of life. It can help people to focus and to have a greater ability to choose where to place attention without being distracted – a particular advantage for professionals.

There are also claims that it can improve physical health, with much supporting and some ambivalent research, including managing symptoms of high blood pressure, chronic pain and sleep problems, and various other physical and psychosomatic problems.

At a more profound level, meditation has a spiritual significance for many, providing a path to spiritual enlightenment and freedom. Based largely on Eastern techniques and wisdom including Buddhist and Hindu (Vedic and yoga) traditions going back millennia, the spiritual aims of meditation could be said to be to help people to achieve greater insight, clarity and compassion, to be fully "awake" and self-realised, and receptive to their inner voice.

There are some common misconceptions about meditation:

It involves blanking out one's mind and thinking of nothing. On the contrary, you are shifting your mind towards greater awareness and consciousness. You will still have thoughts, but you can just let them pass by.

It is a difficult, esoteric practice. In fact, it is a relatively simple practice that can provide some immediate benefits, which are likely to be enhanced with practice. It may involve no more than 20 minutes a day and could even begin with 5 minutes a day.

Listening to music or conducting other restful activities is a form of meditation. Many such activities can indeed provide relaxation calm and self-nurturing, but they are not the same as meditation, which involves becoming "awake" and providing insight and self-realisation.

There are different kinds of meditation, with overlapping elements. It may be guided, where you are led through the process by a teacher or a recording. It may be concentrative (involving focusing attention on breathing, a mantra or specific thoughts) or non-directive (involving open awareness and allowing the mind to wander while effortlessly focusing on something) or a hybrid of both.

Within these broad categories, the kinds of meditation include the following:

Zen (Zazen) is a Buddhist form, also called sitting meditation. Its minimalist approach involves instruction in sitting and in postures and concentrating on the breath.

Transcendental meditation (TM), initiated in the West by Maharishi Mahesh Yogi, involves the silent use of a mantra (which may be a word, sound or phrase assigned by a TM teacher) in a prescribed manner, using a simple, natural, effortless mental technique.

Vipassana (Insight) meditation: Vipassana means "clear-seeing", "to see things as they really are". It is based on a simple technique of being mindful of the breath or bodily sensations. Its contemplative nature relates to the impermanence and ever-changing nature of things.

Qi gong (Chi Gong): This practice generally combines meditation, relaxation, physical movement and breathing exercises, and involves the coordination of breathing patterns with various physical postures and bodily movements.

Mindfulness meditation: This practice is based on conscious awareness and acceptance of living in the present moment, focusing on the experience during meditation, such as breath flow. Meditation is only one aspect of mindfulness, which is further considered below.

Yoga meditation: As with mindfulness, meditation is a part of yoga.

Mindfulness

Many of us tend to live our lives largely on "auto-pilot" – on patterns of behaviour that feel second nature to us. The idea of mindfulness is to bring us into the present moment by helping us become consciously aware of and attentive to what we are doing in each moment.

Although meditation is an integral part of mindfulness, the concept is wider than this and embraces a way of being and of experiencing life, with greater awareness. One of the foremost teachers of mindfulness, Jon Kabat-Zinn, author of *Mindfulness Meditation for Everyday Life*, regards mindfulness as "the art of conscious living".

One of the problems about describing mindfulness – and this applies to some extent to all esoteric practices – is that it may be perceived as some kind of alternative lifestyle that has no relevance in the "real world". Yet the process has been shown to have significant positive effects for those who adopt its principles and practice, which include the following (adapted from Kabat-Zinn's principles in *Full Catastrophe Living*):

- View things without judgemental preconceptions by adopting a "beginner's mind".
- Let go of the emotions attached to experiences and thoughts.
- Adopt a practice of not striving for a result.
- Trust yourself and your feelings.
- Accept things as they are, which does not mean you have to like them.
- Accept yourself as you are.
- Cultivate patience and "be in each moment".

The UK's National Health Service website says that "Good mental wellbeing means feeling good about life and yourself, and being able to get on with life in the way you want … Mindfulness, sometimes also called 'present-centredness', can help us enjoy the world more and understand ourselves better."

A programme of mindfulness-based cognitive therapy (MBCT) has also been developed, based on Kabat-Zinn's work, which specifically targets people suffering from depression. Comedian and mental health campaigner Ruby Wax, from personal as well as professional experience, strongly supports the practice of MBCT and its techniques of self-regulation and focusing on one's senses.

Scientist and psychiatrist Daniel J. Siegel has explored the practice and neuroscience of mindfulness and has written about its workings and value, for example in supporting internal attunement, the functioning of mirror neurons, neural integration and emotional balance.

> There are deep wellsprings of peace and contentment living inside us all, no matter how trapped and distraught we might feel. They're just waiting to be liberated from the cage that our frantic and relentless way of life has crafted for them.
>
> (Mark Williams and Danny Penman, *Mindfulness: A Practical Guide to Finding Peace in a Frantic World*)

Yoga

Yoga practice involves postures and controlled breathing exercises that promote a flexible body and a calm mind as well as lifestyle practices, which include simplicity and austerity, moderation and a healthy diet. Like mindfulness, it is recommended by the UK's National Health Service (NHS), and is described by it as "an ancient form of exercise that focuses on strength, flexibility and breathing to boost physical and mental wellbeing".

For those who do not feel ready for meditation but prefer a more physical practice, yoga may be a good activity to begin with. As a complement to meditation, there are many different styles, from more traditional practices to very modern interpretations – fast and slow moving. Beginners might benefit from trying different styles and seeing what works best for them.

In considering yoga from different perspectives, physician and consultant psychiatrist Dr Rishi Vivekananda describes it in his book *Practical Yoga Psychology* as "an ancient system of philosophy, lifestyle and techniques that evolves the whole person" including the mind, emotion and ethics. It also enhances the quality of relationships and internal harmony.

Quite apart from its intrinsic value, if yoga or any other practice can enhance and help develop the totality of a professional's life – including the mind, emotions and ethics – then this must be beneficial at a personal, professional and relationship level.

The benefits of yoga have been well documented. The NHS says:

> Most studies suggest that yoga is a safe and effective way to increase physical activity, especially strength, flexibility and balance ... There's some evidence that regular yoga practice is beneficial for people with high blood pressure, heart disease, aches and pains – including lower back pain – depression and stress.

Obviously one should medically check the suitability of embarking on yoga practice or one might need to adapt certain postures if one has physical conditions such as a herniated disc, glaucoma or severe osteoporosis. In any event, yoga should be practised with good sense and caution: it is for each individual to "listen to his or her body" and to be aware of what can be managed without straining.

It is also important to choose the right teacher, approach and level of intensity appropriate to one's age, physical limitations and circumstances.

Purpose and meaning

This topic could raise some existential questions about the purpose and meaning of life, but is limited here to the sense of purpose and meaning we might have in relation to our work.

Of course this varies hugely between individuals, but some common themes are relevant.

Earning a living

Whatever deeper purpose or meaning work may have for anyone, the primary need for the overwhelming majority of people is to earn a living – for themselves and where appropriate for their families. Of course, that is not necessarily its only function, and for many people it has other purposes, but it would be disingenuous to explore meaning at a more profound level without acknowledging this basic and fundamental fact.

Article 23(1) of the Universal Declaration of Human Rights provides that "Everyone has the right to work, to free choice of employment, to just and favourable conditions of work and to protection against unemployment"; and Article 23(3) refers to "the right to just and favourable remuneration ensuring for himself and his family an existence worthy of human dignity".

Having the dignity of work is perceived as a fundamental human right.

Making a difference

We live in an uncertain, challenging and volatile world, in which we observe conflict, hardship, injustice and distress, as well as joy, courage, determination and occasional triumph. Some societies are fragmented by war, conflict, natural disaster and poverty; others are more fortunate and function relatively smoothly – but nevertheless with problems and imperfections, inequities and flaws.

Many of us may want to make some contribution towards helping to create a better world, but for most of us, there is very little that we can effectively do in the grand scheme of things.

But, of course, we can make a difference in our own individual way, whether it is by way of political action, charitable support, social media, joining a collective petition or in a multitude of other small ways. And the scope for making a difference can be particularly significant in our work. The fundamental point is that we don't have to make grand contributions or gestures. By doing whatever we do professionally in a thoughtful and helpful way, we can make life that bit better for someone and "make a difference".

Some professions inherently do this. By definition, those in the helping professions have this potential. So do those in the legal profession. But virtually all other professions also offer the scope for helping people: journalists can do so in what they write, human resources in how they support people, management in how they balance support for organisations and businesses with looking after those working in them, financial, tax, accounting and other advisers by helping people to address their issues and problems, as do those in skilled trades.

The list is endless and universal: we can all make a difference in what we do professionally and how we do it. How we interact with the people we come into contact with in our professional and personal lives makes a difference to the world.

Having a sense of purpose and meaning

A sense of purpose reflects a personal aspiration, a wish to achieve something meaningful to one personally and a belief – even a passion – that pursuing it is worthwhile. It may relate to long-term, overarching goals or to immediate objectives, or of course both. However, it does not necessarily have to be profound: it may just be doing what one enjoys, what makes one happy and what gives a sense of peace and satisfaction.

Research has shown a link between purpose and psychological and brain health and well-being; and further research presented in 2015 to the American Heart Association reflected that a high sense of purpose significantly reduced the risk of heart attack and stroke.

The classic work *Man's Search for Meaning* by psychiatrist Viktor E. Frankl, whose experience in surviving three years in concentration camps informed his book, graphically outlines the existential importance of finding one's meaning and purpose in life. For him, life's purpose and meaning were essential to survival.

Purpose may relate to personal or professional ambition, or it may be altruistic: to help others and to improve society. These may be, but are not necessarily, mutually inconsistent. Indeed, combining personal achievement with idealism can be a positive aspiration.

Purpose may relate to religion or spirituality – to live a life according to the principles of a religious or spiritual belief. One's behaviour and lifestyle and the way one practises one's profession may be geared to or influenced by these principles and beliefs.

In a business context there is a view that the future for organisations lies primarily in the creation of meaning. This view is canvassed in the book *Meaning Inc: The Blueprint for Business Success in the 21st Century* by Gurnek Bains and others. For these authors, a sense of meaning is created when activities are connected to something that is significant and that matters to people. Businesses need to develop and act on authentic core purposes. This has relevance to professionals as well.

> People care about their work. They want the issues that concern them to be tackled. They want to feel good about a part of their life that takes up over fifty per cent of their waking hours. In short they want their work to be meaningful.
>
> (Gurnek Bains et al., *Meaning Inc.: The Blueprint for Business Success in the 21st Century*)

Expressing our humanity

Despite our differences, we all share a common humanity, a compassion for the conditions of others. Of course we know that we cannot ordinarily take on the responsibility for all their needs, and it is entirely right that we should have our emotional boundaries, if only for our own survival – and we are generally socialised to establish those boundaries, while retaining our deep if sometimes submerged feelings of compassion and understanding.

The concept of humanity is incorporated in the Southern African concept of "Ubuntu", which broadly means "I am what I am because of who we all are." We are all bound up with one another and our individual humanity is interconnected with everyone else's.

In our professional work we have the opportunity to express our humanity. Some people may do so in a very significant way, for example doctors and nurses who travel to remote parts of the world to help deal with health crises, teachers who provide education in deprived areas of the world and other professionals who take their skills and expertise to those who do not otherwise have the opportunity to receive them.

But we can share our common humanity in our everyday work. In every field of activity we can be sensitive to our clients' or patients' needs and concerns, we can relate to them in an appropriately empathetic and caring way, we can provide our services effectively and skilfully so that they can feel genuinely heard and well looked after. This is the difference between providing our services perfunctorily or with some personal connection and with humanity.

Working holistically

The concept of holism is the recognition of the interconnectedness and inter-dependence of different parts that make up the whole. That may be practical – as, for example, in medicine, where a holistic practitioner will be likely to have regard to the whole body as also psychological, emotional and perhaps social factors, rather than just the presenting symptoms; or it may also have a more intangible component, of the professional bringing himself or herself into the process and drawing on that sense of self – sometimes described as working with mind, body and spirit.

Working holistically may involve a number of components including applying necessary skills and expertise, exercising judgement and understanding, working with empathy and humanity, maintaining a set of ethics and values and having a fundamental care for and (professionally boundaried) connection with the client or patient – all integrated with personal insights, sensitivity and self-awareness.

Holistic practice requires the mentalising, reflective functions and skills referred to in the context of attunement in Chapter 8 and a readiness to accept the use and management of self in a proper professional way – working with head, heart and gut.

> Holistic law is a form of professional practice where no fixed route is prescribed. It's about lawyers with compassion. Anyone can contribute. We all have our so-called soul task which implies that on the one hand you ask for help and on the other you are able to provide the requested help. We all do this in a certain balanced way based on the path that you have chosen to walk. Clients want to be heard, to connect and feel that what we do is right. I call this the brain-heart connection. Being connected with your client is a new skill that you as a professional need to develop. Not only with your head, but even more with your heart and spirit.
>
> (Lawyer Petra Beishuizen in her Henry Brown Lecture given to the family law organisation Resolution in October 2016)

Enhancing expertise and skill

While some professions have periodical re-certification requirements that may include keeping up to date with developments in their field of work, for example by way of compulsory continuing professional development (CPD), many individuals will in any event want to do this on a voluntary basis in order to maintain their skills at an optimal level. In many fields ways of working are developing rapidly, with new insights and new technology, and people and institutions are finding it necessary to adapt to change at an increasing pace.

Peter M. Senge refers in *The Fifth Discipline: The Art & Practice of the Learning Organisation* to "personal mastery", which he sees as "a special level of proficiency" and of people committing themselves to lifelong learning. Senge sees a relationship between individual and organisational learning and the reciprocal commitments that each gives to the other.

> In *The Fifth Discipline: The Art & Practice of the Learning Organisation* Peter Senge sees "real learning" as fundamental to being human – effectively helping us to rekindle the consciousness of our relationship to the world, allowing us to do things that we previously couldn't and extending our creative and life-generative capacity. He considers that we all have a "deep hunger" for this kind of learning.

Maintaining professional identity and self-esteem

It is hardly startling to observe that for many people, identity and self-esteem are bound up with work and professional standing. There is a direct relationship between having a successful career and having a strong sense of self-worth – and vice versa. Cause and effect are not necessarily clear, but what is apparent is that they are mutually reinforcing.

People commonly define themselves in terms of the work that they do. This may give them a sense of meaning and purpose. This is almost a societal ritual: "So what do you do?" Some people who retire may feel that they have lost some part of their identity; and those whose careers end prematurely and involuntarily commonly find themselves in a depressed state.

While pride in one's work is understandable and appropriate, a note of caution does need to be introduced: it cannot be emotionally healthy to invest one's entire being into one's work identity. Life is uncertain and things change. Work identity tempered with a balance of other qualities and self-awareness may provide greater life equilibrium.

Unconscious competence revisited

Chapter 5 mentions the four-stage progression from unconscious incompetence to unconscious competence, where the practice or skill in question is so ingrained that it becomes "second nature". We have internalised the knowledge and skills of the practice through repetition and understanding so that it becomes part of our unconscious process.

That process can be extended into working with purpose and meaning and self-nurturing so that they too can become second nature. By working in a way that expresses our humanity, that is geared to making a difference, that relates to our clients or patients empathetically or that enhances our learning, we can integrate these ways of working and of being into our unconscious so that they also become second nature. The principles of unconscious competence do not need to be limited only to skills.

Further reading

Peter Senge's *The Fifth Discipline: The Art & Practice of the Learning Organisation* has been mentioned in the context of enhancing expertise and skill.

The Power of Meditation and Prayer offers interviews by Michael Toms with ten thinkers and writers in the field of meditation and spiritual growth including Larry Dossey, John Kabat-Zinn, Sogyal Rinpoche and others. Also highly regarded is *The Art of Meditation* by Buddhist monk Matthieu Ricard.

An accessible introduction to mindfulness is Jon Kabat-Zinn's *Wherever You Go, There You Are: Mindfulness Meditation for Everyday Life*. See also his *Full Catastrophe Living: How to Cope with Stress, Pain and Illness Using Mindfulness*

Meditation. Mark Williams and Danny Penman's *Mindfulness: A Practical Guide to Finding Peace in a Frantic World* also introduces mindfulness practice. Daniel J. Siegel's *The Mindful Brain: Reflection and Attunement in the Cultivation of Well-being* provides fascinating insights. Ruby Wax's *Sane New World: Taming the Mind* is a clear, easy-to-read and often witty introduction to mindfulness and the brain, as is her subsequent work *A Mindfulness Guide for the Frazzled.*

An excellent work on yoga is *Practical Yoga Psychology* by Dr Rishi Vivekananda, which explains yoga teaching and lifestyle practices in the context of psychology and personality.

Fiona Gardner's *Being Critically Reflective: Engaging in Holistic Practice* explores a range of ideas and perspectives on critical reflection and reflective practice, theoretical and practical.

Man's Search for Meaning: An Introduction to Logotherapy was written by Victor E. Frankl in 1946, after his release from concentration camps. His concepts of logotherapy and existential analysis are based on the proposition that happiness and peace of mind are by-products of finding meaning in life. The topic of meaning in a business context is powerfully addressed in *Meaning Inc: The Blueprint for Business Success in the 21st Century* by Gurnek Baines and others.

Chapter 18

Support needs and resources

Professional back-up, teams and networks

Professionals can organise themselves in many different ways: as sole practitioners, in partnerships or groups, in institutions or companies or through other structures.

However they work, professionals will invariably require some form of back-up support to enable them to carry out their roles and functions effectively, or they may themselves be part of a team – to deal with administration, organisation, accounting and communications. Many of those in support teams may well be professionals: accountants, librarians, researchers, nurses, administrators – working together to provide a comprehensive professional service.

Even professionals working on their own may need some form of assistance, whether by way of telephone answering, bookkeeping or the services of a personal assistant (PA). At the other end of the spectrum, larger organisations may, in addition to all the basic administrative functions, also have IT, marketing, financial, research and other support.

And there may be times when professionals may need to go outside of themselves and their structures to get the help that they need, whether professional, practical or personal.

> No man is an island entire of itself; every man
> is a piece of the continent, a part of the main …
>
> (John Donne, Meditation XVII)

Working in teams

Many professional undertakings may involve some form of teamwork, set up on a permanent basis or organised for specific tasks. Managing complex litigation may involve collaboration between lawyers with different specialisations, perhaps also liaising with expert witnesses or advisers, and backed up by researchers and secretarial, administrative and other support. Medical treatment may involve collaboration between general practitioners, specialists in different fields, radiographers, nurses and various others working in healthcare.

Multidisciplinary teams may provide mutual expertise and support (such as providing law and accountancy crossover). The integration of different fields of specialisation can provide a more holistic approach without diluting the expertise of the component parts.

Considerations influencing team effectiveness include:

- a shared goal to which all members of the team can give their commitment;
- clearly defined and appropriately allocated individual roles;
- communications to be conducted openly and with sensitivity, candour and respect;
- a readiness to give and accept mutual support and acknowledgment, and constructive comments and criticism where appropriate;
- acceptance of the authority of the team leader if there is one;
- members of the team to be individually and collectively aware of ego issues that may arise and managing and communicating about these sensitively and firmly so that they do not get in the way of the team effort.

Professional networks and bodies

Networks have different forms. They may be of individual professionals or of firms or organisations, perhaps operating in different places, who may have the same professional background and who offer one another mutual support, the exchange of information, knowledge and expertise and perhaps cross-referral of clients. Or networking may take place electronically through professional networking sites such as LinkedIn. Web-based social networking, particularly through sites with a professional bias, has become essential for professionals for communications and marketing.

Professional networks link professionals with common backgrounds, interests or other commonalities. There is also a professional network – the Professional Associations Research Network – that provides research, consultancy, networking, bespoke services and training support, and promotes best practice among professional bodies.

Quality standards

Of course, the primary bodies providing support are the formal professional organisations in each field. Such bodies are established in most countries and generally serve the mutual purpose of setting standards for their members for the protection of the public and the enhancement of their professional standing, and the representation of their members' common interests – though this may vary from one profession to another.

The primary purpose of any professional body or professional organisation is to promote and support the particular profession. This has two aspects:

– the protection of the interests of the professionals themselves
– protection of the public interest.

(The Chartered Quality Institute website: www.quality.org)

The standards set by professional bodies may be embodied in rules, ethical codes or other publications, sometimes described as "best practice". These standards are designed to ensure quality of service and as such are essential to ensure that all practitioners belonging to those bodies maintain a high quality of work. There is though some paradox in the concept of "best practice" in that it suggests that there can be no better practice possible – nothing can be better than "best" – which in turn precludes any possible development of such practice in the future, no matter what new ideas or developments might arise.

A better concept would be to establish a culture of continual evaluation and improvement of standards – as adopted by the Chartered Quality Institute, which supports business, industry and professional organisations in establishing strong governance with clear management aims and policies, and in giving assurance that services are being properly provided in accordance with those aims.

Supervision, consultancy, coaching and mentoring

Supervision

In its ordinary usage, supervision implies that the task undertaken by one person is being directly or indirectly watched over by another person who is responsible for ensuring that it is properly done. A supervisor will generally instruct a subordinate what to do and will be responsible for ensuring that it is done in accordance with instructions and requirements.

In its professional usage, "supervision" has come to be used as a term of art, particularly within the helping professions. In their book *Supervision in the Helping Professions*, Peter Hawkins and Robin Shohet – drawing on writers such as Brigid Proctor and Alfred Kadushin – outline some of the main functions of supervision, which may be summarised as follows:

Educative: Helping to develop the supervisee's skills, competence and understanding, which may include consideration of work done, with reflective feedback.

Supportive: Helping the supervisee to explore, address and cope with any emotions and distress they may experience from their work and how they have been affected.

Managerial: Helping to ensure that the supervisee's work is of an appropriate quality and ethical standard, and that the supervisee is functioning effectively.

These modes of supervision may well overlap. There may also be different models and ways of carrying out these functions: supervision may be individual or it may be with a group or team, it may involve a senior supervisory role or it may be done on a peer basis. It may be undertaken regularly and frequently, for example weekly, or at wider intervals.

> Supervision must enable and support workers to build effective professional relationships, develop good practice, and exercise both professional judgement and discretion in decision-making. For supervision to be effective it needs to combine a performance management approach with a dynamic, empowering and enabling supervisory relationship.
>
> (Skills for Care, 2007: definition adopted by British Association of Social Workers, 2011)

But although regarded as vital in many of the helping professions and increasingly in the medical profession and gradually in education and human-resource management, this reflective and emotionally supportive model is barely used in most other professions.

Other professions tend to approach these issues in a different way: the notion of periodical supervision meetings as such is replaced by a more managerial type of supervisory process. Also, the quasi-therapeutic element of supervision does not have the same focus (although supervision must be clearly distinguished from any kind of therapy).

So, for example, the Solicitors Regulation Authority for England and Wales has a Code of Conduct (2011) which provides that supervision relates to clients' matters including regular quality checks by suitably competent and experienced people. There is an expectation that support will be provided; but the supportive element is implicit rather than explicit and is likely to take a different shape from counselling or social work supervision.

Consultancy

The usual focus of consultancy is primarily on helping to address tasks and process by bringing specialised expertise to these matters rather than dealing with feelings and emotional needs and issues.

However, some consultancy may be directed towards personal issues such as stress management and developing personal confidence. These may border on coaching. And consultants working in the helping professions are more likely to follow a mode of working more akin to the supervision model, for example working with individuals or small groups, assisting with client problems and helping to provide a framework for addressing similar problems in the future. In *Issues and Ethics in the Helping Professions*, Gerald Corey, Marianne Corey and Patrick Callanan point out that consultancy's primarily focus is on work or caretaking as distinct from personal issues, though it may include learning to recognise and deal with work-related stress that can interfere with work effectiveness.

The distinction between consultancy and supervision can be blurred, as illustrated in the UK family mediation field, which has opted for professional practice consultancy (PPC) – consultancy based on a form of supervision.

> PPCs have an increasing responsibility to ensure they are able to properly support mediators in their career development and in maintaining high standards of practice whether preparing or encouraging mediators towards accreditation or competence assessment, assisting mediators to build high standards of client care or in disseminating information about changes in policy and practice standards.
>
> (Resolution (UK family lawyers' association) flyer
> for seminar in 2014)

Coaching

A trained coach supports the professional in identifying and achieving work and sometimes also personal goals. Coaching is used in a wide variety of contexts, including career decisions, managing work and life transitions and changes, identifying and enhancing management, leadership or other skills, dealing with conflicts in teams, addressing work–life imbalances or generally bridging skills gaps.

One of the underlying principles of coaching is that those being coached have the capacity themselves to deal with their issues and that the coach's primary role is to assist and support them in developing their own strengths and arriving at and implementing their own decisions.

Mentoring

Mentors tend to combine the roles of consultants and coaches, drawing on their personal experience and expertise to provide advice, guidance and support to professionals to help them develop their skills and expertise. Although mentors are generally more senior and more experienced than the person they are mentoring, the relationship should be a collaborative one of mutual respect and caring.

Mentoring tends to be more informal and relationship-geared than coaching, with the mentor having a continuing interest in the well-being and development of the person being mentored. It is also more commonly a longer-term arrangement than coaching. A mentor is more likely to draw on specific and relevant experience, whereas a coach does not need to have that specific and personal background experience but has expertise in coaching.

Some frailties and problems requiring personal support

Professionals may at times need support in their personal lives, whether arising from the stresses and challenges of their professional lives or relating to any of the physical, mental, emotional or spiritual issues that affect them as human beings – or a combination of both.

Sometimes working as professionals may delude us into believing that somehow we should be able to rise above these pressures and "just get on with it". And that may indeed be the case with some transitory issues; but if we are to function effectively in our professional and personal lives, we need to have both the self-awareness as to when we need to engage external support and the courage to do so.

Inevitably, we will carry our work challenges and stresses between our personal and our professional lives, as we do with our personalities, attributes and belief systems. Each will impact on the other and affect us and our relationships.

> Wherever you go, there you are.
> (Confucius (attributed); also book title by Jon Kabat-Zinn)

As complex human beings, we each have our own individual combination of strengths and frailties, which we generally learn how to manage so as to function with reasonable effectiveness in our working and personal lives; but sometimes the balance may skew and we may not be as functional in our lives as we may wish or need to be. At those times support from a counsellor or therapist or other similar resource can be helpful to facilitate our gaining some insights into ourselves and rebalancing ourselves more comfortably.

It is impossible to list all the circumstances that may cause difficulties, but some will be briefly mentioned.

The Achilles Syndrome, self-doubt and the secret fear of failure

In Greek mythology, Achilles was the bravest warrior in the Trojan War. His mother Thetis dipped him into the River Styx, which made him invulnerable – except for the part of his heel where she held him and where he had a secret vulnerability, the point where he could be – and eventually was – slain, his "Achilles heel".

Psychologist Petrūska Clarkson adopted this myth to describe a syndrome in which high achievers, successful in their fields of activity, internally felt vulnerable and insecure, filled with secret self-doubt and the belief that they were lucky to achieve what they did and that they were bound to be "found out" at some stage.

Clarkson called this *pseudocompetency* which does not equate to incompetence but rather the mismatch between a person's self-confidence and the high assessment and opinion that others have of him or her. The underlying self-message runs along the lines of: "Whew, I managed to achieve that last time but I may not be so lucky next time."

Pseudocompetency is neither humility nor dishonesty. It may arise from growing up with unrealistic parental demands; educational mismanagement, where phases of learning or development have been missed out; a cultural tendency in society encouraging people to aspire to unrealistic ideals; or what Clarkson called "predisposing patterns … known as *archetypal pattern, images or predispositions*" which people may adopt as their own story.

There can be huge anxiety or panic each time one faces the required task, with a fear of possible humiliation, and a sense of relief each time it is completed satisfactorily. This self-doubt and secret fear can arise in different environments: not only in the professional and business field, but in all aspects of learning and academia, in the artistic and creative world and indeed in one's role as a parent or lover.

Stress

The UK's Health and Safety Executive has a category of "work related stress", which it says "develops because a person is unable to cope with the demands being placed on them". Protracted stress can result in exhaustion, insomnia, headaches, gut dysfunction (such as irritable bowel syndrome) and peptic ulcers, weight changes, sexual malfunction and depression. It can lead to physical and emotional disorders including burnout – emotional, mental, and physical exhaustion – and addictive behaviour; and it can have damaging effects on relationships, both professional and personal.

In a survey by the Junior Lawyers Division of the Law Society of England and Wales published in April 2017, more than 90 per cent of junior lawyers reported that they felt stressed and under pressure at work, with more than 25 per cent describing stress levels as "severe" or "extreme".

Work-related stress is widespread and is not confined to particular professions. It may be caused by the pressures of the professional situation, but the way in which each person copes with that stress is at least in part a factor of the individual's capacity and personality, so professional stress may be viewed as a combination of the situation and the individual.

From the situational (or environmental) perspective, stress factors need to be identified and assessed, and work organisation and job content need to be planned and managed so as to minimise stress. This may involve reviewing workload, working hours and conditions, processes and organisation, roles and interpersonal relationships. Other stress factors include insecurity; status and recognition (or the lack of these); lack of support or control over situations; unclear or conflicting roles or objectives; and poor management.

From the individual perspective, a lifestyle reassessment can help to establish a healthy work–life balance. There are also self-help options such as meditation, yoga, exercise, diet and taking regular breaks. Where the stress is severe, it may be necessary to seek counselling or therapy support such as cognitive behavioural therapy (CBT) which helps change the way one thinks and behaves, or perhaps hypnotherapy.

Stress may have positive purposes: short bursts may boost the immune system, it can sometimes aid creative thinking and it can be motivating; and physical stress can enhance energy, stamina and body functioning.

Increasing epidemiological evidence indicates that chronic stress not only adversely affects physical and mental well-being, it increases the risk of cardio-vascular and autoimmune disease, asthma and diabetes. Stressed professionals need to take care of themselves.

Whenever we feel stressed out, that's a signal that our brain is pumping out stress hormones. If sustained over months and years, those hormones can ruin our health and make us a nervous wreck.

(Daniel Goleman, "De-Stress: How to Handle
the Holidays", *Psychology Today*)

Anxiety and panic

Feeling uneasy and anxious at times is the body's natural and appropriate response to situations that might generate concern or fear. However, if anxiety is severe, pro-longed or frequent, it may be the symptom of a condition such as a phobia or panic disorder, or it may indicate the existence of a generalised anxiety disorder (GAD).

We know that anxiety increases the production of the stress hormone cortisol as well as the fight-or-flight hormone adrenaline. The fight-or-flight response does not necessarily get quickly deactivated if the perceived threat or concern remains in our mind yet does not materialise. Some people may have a hypersensitive fight-or-flight response, which is activated more readily and for longer periods. They may be more prone to anxiety or panic.

Like anxiety, panic is the activation of the body's fight-or-flight response, but in an immediate, exaggerated and overwhelming mode, with an intense rush of psychological and physical symptoms, which may include feeling faint or dizzy, increased heart rate, hyperventilating, perspiring or having difficulty in breathing.

The national charity Anxiety UK believes that avoidance is the most common behavioural response to anxiety, but that although this may produce short-term relief, it does not resolve the underlying issue. Anxiety and panic are best dealt with by being properly addressed, whether by way of self-help or through some form of professional intervention or treatment.

People suffering from anxiety need to have an understanding about it and its causes and to develop ways of coping and dealing with it rather than avoiding doing so. Strategies include deep-breathing exercises; exercising regularly (particularly aerobic exercise which causes the brain to release endorphins that boost pleasurable emotions and the mood-improving chemical serotonin); avoiding alcohol, which has a negative effect; learning how to challenge and confront worrying thoughts and fears; developing problem-solving techniques; and taking time out – walking around the block, making a cup of tea or having a bath.

Similar self-help techniques exist for panic, particularly slow and deep diaphragmatic breathing, mindfulness meditation, relaxation and exercise, also creative visualisation.

Professional support may well be indicated for severe anxiety or panic, by way of counselling or therapy, including here again CBT. In some cases, medication may be prescribed; and where none of these can budge the anxiety or panic, referral to a psychiatrist or psychologist for assessment, support and help may be appropriate.

Depression

Among the common misconceptions about depression, perhaps the most prevalent is that it is about being sad or unhappy and that one needs to think positively and "get over it". Another is that one shouldn't dwell on it as this merely reinforces negativity; or that it reflects personal weakness – which is in part why there is perceived to be a stigma attached to it.

In fact, depression is an illness, which in its most severe form may make it almost impossible for someone suffering with it to cope with everyday life. In *Malignant Sadness: The Anatomy of Depression*, developmental biologist Lewis Wolpert describes his own depression as being unlike anything he had ever experienced: he suffered from extreme anxiety, could not sleep or work or think properly or go out alone, he had panic attacks and wanted to stay in bed all day. He was self-absorbed and negative and thought a lot about suicide. He is clear that he was seriously ill and that "pulling up your socks" simply doesn't work with serious depression.

This form of serious and disabling depression – clinical depression – should be distinguished from the less serious form that may exist in a more transitory and less severe form in which one may feel "down" for a while. Indeed, the word "depression" is really an umbrella term covering many different things, ranging from this sense of feeling "blue" to major clinical depression, and includes bipolar disorder (sometimes called manic depression) with the experience of extreme highs followed by extreme lows; seasonal affective disorder (SAD) in which the lack of sunlight causes a depression in winter; dysthymia, a chronic, continuing low-level form of depression; and postpartum depression – feelings of fatigue, hopelessness and extreme sadness occurring in mothers some while after the birth of a child.

Depression does not necessarily have a single cause. There is strong evidence of a genetic component. Low self-esteem may be a factor, as may life events particularly loss and bereavement or those involving humiliation and shame and physical illness. In the West, the incidence of depression is significantly higher among women than men.

While there is a dearth of information about the link between occupation and depression, there is considerable evidence of a correlation between high stress levels and depression. Research has reflected a relatively high depression rate among lawyers and doctors, though statistics are not readily available particularly because of the reluctance of professionals – particularly in the medical profession – to disclose their depression because of the stigma attached to this. Other professions with relatively high rates of depression include nurses, social workers, care workers, teachers and administrative support staff.

Professional help is likely to be needed for depression, and certainly for the more severe forms. Various therapies, especially CBT, are likely to be indicated, though other forms of counselling or therapeutic intervention may be appropriate. Antidepressant medication is widely prescribed and can relieve symptoms, though these may also have side effects: a balance needs to be found in each case. Medication is not generally advisable for those with mild depression as the risks may outweigh the benefits.

There are things that a person with depression can do himself or herself, perhaps alongside professional support. These might include joining a support group, undertaking regular exercise (with the positive chemical production this generates), maintaining a careful diet (there is some suggestion that foods rich in essential fatty acids, such as fish oils found in salmon, could relieve some of the symptoms of depression), trying to maintain a good work–life balance and undertaking relaxing activities.

To some extent, depression has come out of the shadows as prominent people in different walks of life have told of their experience with it and it is to be hoped that this pervasive illness will be given the respect and understanding that it needs.

If you know someone who's depressed, please resolve never to ask them why. Depression isn't a straightforward response to a bad situation; depression just is, like the weather.

Try to understand the blackness, lethargy, hopelessness, and loneliness they're going through. Be there for them when they come through the other side. It's hard to be a friend to someone who's depressed, but it is one of the kindest, noblest, and best things you will ever do.

(Stephen Fry, comedian, actor and writer)

Addiction

In November 2011 the UK's *Guardian* newspaper ran an article "Alarm at growing addiction problems among professionals" and subheaded "Urgent action needed to tackle problems suffered by doctors, lawyers and people in other high-profile jobs, say healthcare experts". The story related to the "significant challenge" of rising levels of alcoholism and substance abuse among these and other professionals. Research suggested that 15–24 per cent of lawyers would suffer from alcoholism during their careers, while the British Medical Association estimated that one in 15 healthcare professionals would develop an addiction problem.

Addiction does not, of course, only relate to drink or drugs. Other kinds of addictions include gambling, the Internet, video games, shopping and even work (hence "workaholic").

Self-help and home-based recovery programmes have been found to be helpful, as are support groups; but specialised support is likely to be necessary. This may take the form of organisations such as Alcoholics Anonymous or professional support services such as LawCare for lawyers (an independent support charity part funded by the Law Society). Alternatively, CBT tends to be used because it works effectively with addiction problems.

Other personal issues indicating a need for support

Anger issues: Anger has constructive purposes including setting us up to cope with actual or perceived threats, motivating us and making our feelings clear to others. However, some people find it very difficult to keep their anger under control, which can be damaging to relationships, socially and to health.

Anger may well have other emotions underlying it, such as resentment or more vulnerable feelings such as deep hurt or humiliation, anxiety, helplessness or grief. Past feelings that sparked anger may be rekindled by some unrelated later remark or event, however minor, resulting in a disproportionate and inappropriate expression of anger.

There are different kinds of anger. Chronic anger indicates a need to explore the underlying causes; volatile intermittent anger tends to erupt spontaneously and excessively and may be disproportionate to the cause; repressed anger exists where the unconscious mind represses the emotion which is too painful or difficult to manage, but which manifests itself indirectly or can result in chronic stress or depression; and there is passive-aggressive anger.

Therapeutic strategies for managing anger include individual or group anger-management programmes, counselling or therapy. The symptoms of anger can in some cases be treated with medication, but these do not actually target the anger and rather aim to create a calming effect on the body, and so may be complementary to other therapeutic processes.

> Anybody can become angry – that is easy, but to be angry with the right person and to the right degree and at the right time and for the right purpose, and in the right way – that is not within everybody's power and is not easy.
>
> (Aristotle)

Perfectionism: While realistic striving for high standards is generally healthy and productive, perfectionism involves striving for exceptionally high and generally unrealistic standards and judging yourself based on your ability to achieve them, with a negative, distorted and self-critical judgement if you fall short. It may indicate an obsessive personality, and is a symptom of obsessive compulsive disorder (OCD), though not necessarily linked to OCD.

Perfectionism has links to anxiety and also, ironically, to inefficient work practice, as perfectionists may struggle to complete work to their satisfaction, and thus risk missing deadlines. It may also lead to depression and illness.

Self-help strategies start by understanding perfectionism and establishing realistic goals for change including establishing limited progressive aspirations for change in thinking and behaviour, identifying realistic standards, and accepting and even practising imperfection, uncertainty and making mistakes. Various forms of therapeutic interventions are helpful including CBT, psychodynamic or humanistic approaches or group therapy.

Co-dependency: This describes a dysfunctional relationship in which one subjugates one's personal needs to those of another person and is dependent on the latter's approval for a sense of self-worth and identity, often accompanied by insecurity, shame and guilt. Self-help may involve the mutuality of group support for example through Co-Dependents Anonymous (CoDA) but in any event necessitates developing self-awareness, self-acceptance, and establishing and maintaining assertiveness. Counselling or therapy is also generally helpful.

Relationship issues

Where relationships are under stress or have broken down, external support is often necessary, whether to help try to repair them or to support ending them in a reasonable way.

Couples' relationships: Whether married or not and whatever their sexual orientation or cultural background, couples may face stresses and challenges in their lives. In many cases they may work through these, but where these problems are more than they can manage themselves, they may need to seek professional support and help.

Couples' counselling or therapy facilitates communication and an exploration of the issues. Couples' counsellors and therapists offer this resource and there are also organisations that do so, such as Relate in the UK. Couples' counselling can take place alongside either party having individual counselling or therapy – these are not mutually exclusive.

Family relationships: Conflict within families can sometimes threaten the fabric of a family. It may be inter-generational, or between siblings or other relatives, or with in-laws or others.

Where the issues relate to family conflict generally, family therapy may be indicated. If, however, there is a specific dispute – for example regarding ownership or management of a family business – then mediation may well offer an appropriate forum to help find a resolution that all can accept and which would afford the best opportunities for healing.

Work relationships: These can of course cover a multitude of issues. Stuck issues relating to the running or management of a business or profession can benefit from bringing in management consultants, who can generally help with all aspects of management including human resources, marketing, IT and finance. Alternatively, specialist mediation may be helpful – available from dispute resolution organisations and private mediators, and also in the UK from ACAS (the Advisory, Conciliation and Arbitration Service), a neutral professional public service committed to promoting employment relations.

Personality disorders and traits

People with severe personality disorders may have a distorted belief system, making it more difficult for them to accept the need for self-help. Where, however, disorders, or associated traits, are mild or moderate there are some self-help options, which would generally need to be considered alongside professional help and support.

The nature of support or treatment appropriate in any such case depends on its nature and severity and needs to be individually tailored. Specialist psychotherapy – individual or group – is widely used, which may well be required on a long-term basis (for six months or longer).

In some cases, therapeutic communities, where people with certain personality disorders can stay for a time, may be able to offer support resources. The UK's Consortium for Therapeutic Communities describes these communities as "structured, psychologically informed environments ... where the social relationships, structure of the day and different activities together are all deliberately designed to help people's health and well-being". Many of these are residential but some offer day-care facilities.

There are no medications to treat personality disorders as such, but they may be prescribed to treat some of the symptoms, for example antidepressants or mood stabilisers.

Autism and Asperger Syndrome

Autism is a complex developmental disorder involving brain wiring that is different from the usual wiring (of "neuro-typicals"). It can take different forms along a spectrum and is hence also referred to as an autism spectrum disorder (ASD). While the form and intensity may vary, common features generally involve narrow interests, great attention to detail, difficulty with social understandings, communications and interaction and, in some cases, repetitive behaviour and difficulty in managing change. Some people with autism who are relatively high functioning are able to live relatively independent lives but others may also have learning disabilities and may need permanent specialist support.

Asperger Syndrome is a high-functioning form of autism, usually associated with high intelligence. In *Autism and Asperger Syndrome*, Professor Simon Baron-Cohen describes a young man with Asperger Syndrome who can do maths, memorise facts and understand the laws of physics or chemistry effortlessly, but who "cannot fathom the unspoken rules of human interaction".

There is no "cure" as such for autism, but there are many interventions and treatments, including providing special individualised education for ASD children. Speech and language therapy may be necessary, focusing not just on verbal skills but also social skills. ASD individuals will also need help in learning how to interpret the mental states and feelings of others. Occupational therapy can be beneficial in helping to manage everyday activities, and may be essential where there are difficulties with motor skills.

Adults who have not previously been diagnosed with autism may be able to find helpful local support services, social learning programmes and leisure activity programmes.

I think all autistic brains tend to be specialized brains. Autistic people tend to be less social. It takes a ton of processor space in the brain to have all the social circuits.

(Temple Grandin, author of *Thinking in Pictures* and *The Autistic Brain*)

Dissatisfaction with life path: self-actualisation and meaning

At some point in our lives, some of us may be aware of a need for personal change, a sense that the path we are on is not right, dissatisfaction with its direction and an underlying awareness that it could be different. This may be stimulated by a significant life or death event, a loss or trauma, or it may just be a developing consciousness of unease.

Psychologist Abraham Maslow formulated a hierarchy of eight individual needs and motivations. At the most basic level, individuals have biological and physiological needs such as food, drink and shelter. Then they have needs for safety and security, love and belongingness, self-esteem, knowledge and aesthetics. At the top Maslow placed self-actualisation and the need to help others to achieve this.

Maslow understood that self-actualisation would vary infinitely from one person to another: for one person it might take the form of the desire to be an ideal mother, in another it might be expressed athletically, and in another it might be expressed creatively or aesthetically. Fundamentally it is about fulfilling individual potential.

Personal growth and self-actualisation generally involve developing self-acceptance, learning to be authentic and recognising one's own uniqueness; treating the process as a journey, with a step at a time; increasing one's sense of self-esteem; learning to "think outside the box" and to develop creativity; and, critically, continuing the process of personal growth.

Whether dissatisfied with any aspect of one's life, whether on the journey of personal growth to self-actualisation or whether searching for greater meaning in life (which are not mutually inconsistent) many kinds of support are available, which may relate to one's emotional, physical, spiritual, professional or social needs.

The support may be spiritual – which may be related to a specific religion or may rather refer to a wider concept of spirituality – what Rabbi Michael Lerner refers to in his book *Spirit Matters* as "a celebration of the wonder of the universe – and the cultivation of our capacities for awe and radical amazement at all that is".

Or the support may be emotional and personal: a range of counselling, psychotherapeutic and other options are available to help people move forward in addressing emotional issues and self-exploration and development. Or it may take other forms, such as physical (exercise, diet, lifestyle), professional or social, geared to helping people to do the best for themselves and maximise their potential.

Consult not your fears but your hopes and your dreams. Think not about your frustrations, but about your unfulfilled potential. Concern yourself not with what you tried and failed in, but with what it is still possible for you to do.

(Pope John XXIII © Libreria Editrice Vaticana)

Counselling, psychotherapy and complementary therapies

It may be helpful to outline briefly some options and approaches available in this regard.

Counselling and psychotherapy

The question is often asked as to the distinction between counselling and psychotherapy. The British Association for Counselling and Psychotherapy (BACP) says that it "sees no evidence of any difference between the functions of counselling and psychotherapy" and has not distinguished between them. They are "umbrella terms that cover a range of talking therapies. They are delivered by trained practitioners who work with people over the short or long term to help them bring about effective change or enhance their wellbeing."

While areas overlap, psychotherapists commonly work on longer-term concerns. However, both may work with people on a short- or long-term basis. Counselling is commonly used for specific issues, such as grief, addiction and coping with illness or relationship breakdown.

Psychotherapy commonly tends to address deeper issues on a more holistic basis. However, this may be interchangeable.

There are many approaches to psychotherapy and counselling including the following (and references to therapy may include counselling):

Psychoanalytic or psychodynamic psychotherapy: This approach endeavours to reach the underlying, often unconscious, causes of distress. The British Psychoanalytic Council describes it as "a therapeutic process which helps patients understand and resolve their problems by increasing awareness of their inner world and its influence over relationships both past and present". Although sometimes treatment may be short term, psychoanalytic psychotherapy is generally a long-term process involving considerable commitment.

Cognitive behavioural therapy (CBT): The UK's National Health Service describes this as "a talking therapy that can help you manage your problems by changing the way you think and behave". CBT teaches coping skills for dealing with different problems. It is commonly used to treat anxiety, stress and depression, but is also used for other problems including addiction and eating disorders. It is ordinarily conducted over a relatively short period.

Humanistic therapies: These recognise people's self-healing and self-development capacities and seek to help them recognise their strengths and potential. They include:

Person-centred therapy, originally developed by Carl Rogers and based on the genuineness (or congruence) and empathy of the therapist and the innate tendency of human beings to find fulfilment of their personal potential.

Transactional analysis is based on the proposition that three ego states – parent, adult and child – exist in all relationships, which is used with other concepts and tools to identify the interaction needed to achieve autonomy.

Psychosynthesis is described in the title of a book by Jean Hardy as "A psychology with a soul" – based on psychoanalysis but integrating spiritual as well as psychological aspects to support the self in emerging for each person.

Gestalt therapy, developed by Fritz Perls, is based on the principle of viewing the holistic totality (mind, body, emotions and spirit) and uniqueness of the person in a relational perspective: a relationship with others and with the environment.

Systemic therapy: This approach to couples' and families' issues is based on systems theory, which considers systems in nature, society and human behaviour on a holistic basis, viewing the whole as a system rather than the individual parts, save as to their interaction. Individual behaviour is viewed in the context of the family system and the interconnection with other parts of the system, and also any other systems in which the family functions.

Complementary therapies

These can work alongside traditional Western practice. Among those registered with the UK's voluntary regulator, the Complementary and Natural Healthcare Council, are:

Hypnotherapy: While evidence-based research is inconclusive, hypnotherapy has been found to be helpful for various conditions including the symptoms of irritable bowel syndrome (IBS); anxiety (with variable results), particularly in pregnancy; helping people with cancer to relax and cope better with symptoms and treatment; and childhood eczema.

Craniosacral therapy: Recognising the interconnection between mind and body, this uses sensitive touch to help deal with physical problems such as back pain or emotional issues arising from stress and tension, creating a sense of relaxation and calm.

Reiki: The concept of a life force or energy in Chinese is known as "Chi" and in Japanese as "Ki" – hence the term Reiki, which translates broadly to "universal life energy". Reiki involves the laying on of hands and is based on the concept that this universal life energy flows through us and that when it is low we feel unwell, and when it is high we are better able to feel healthy. The process aims to provide a sense of well-being and calm.

Further reading

The books mentioned in this chapter are all relevant: Peter Hawkins and Robin Shohet's *Supervision in the Helping Profession*; Petrūska Clarkson's *The Achilles Syndrome: Overcoming the Secret Fear of Failure*; Lewis Wolpert's *Malignant Sadness: The Anatomy of Depression*; Victor Frankl's *Man's Search for Meaning:*

An Introduction to Logotherapy; Michael Lerner's *Spirit Matters*; and Jean Hardy's *A Psychology with a Soul: Psychosynthesis in Evolutionary Context.*

Abraham Maslow's *A Theory of Human Motivation* was originally published in 1943, but a new edition edited by David Webb was published in paperback in 2013.

Among the many books about stress, anxiety and panic, a well-reviewed work is *How to Master Anxiety: All You Need to Know to Overcome Stress, Panic Attacks, Trauma, Phobias, Obsessions and More (Human Givens Approach)* by Joe Griffin and Ivan Tyrrell. Also helpful are Patrick Holford's *The Stress Cure: How to Resolve Stress, Build Resilience and Boost Your Energy* and Karen Sullivan's *How to Cope Successfully with Panic Attacks.*

Books about autism and Asperger Syndrome include Simon Baron-Cohen's *Autism and Asperger Syndrome*; Temple Brandin's *Thinking in Pictures* and *The Autistic Brain*; Martine Ives and Nell Munro's *Caring for a Child with Autism;* and Stephen Silberman's *Neurotribes: The Legacy of Autism and How to Think Smarter about People Who Think Differently.*

A brief selection of books on psychotherapy, counselling and complementary and alternative processes might include *The Handbook of Individual Therapy* edited by Windy Dryden and Andrew Reeves; *The SAGE Handbook of Counselling and Psychotherapy* edited by Colin Feltham; Carl Rogers' *On Becoming a Person: A Therapist's View of Psychotherapy* and *Client Centred Therapy: Its Current Practice, Implications and Theory*; Eric Berne's *Games People Play: The Psychology of Human Relationships*; Alan Cooklin, Neil Dawson and Brenda McHugh's *Family Therapy Basics*; John Welwood's *Towards a Psychology of Awakening: Buddhism, Psychotherapy and the Path of Personal and Spiritual Transformation*; David Westbrook, Helen Kennerley and Joan Kirk's *An Introduction to Cognitive Behaviour Therapy: Skills and Applications*; and *The Psychology Book* published by Dorling Kindersley.

Chapter 19

Transitions and endings

Life and work transitions

Throughout life we make transitions: from babyhood to becoming a toddler, from nursery school year by year through infant, primary and secondary school, through adolescence to adulthood, undertaking further learning, ending our formal education and starting work. We may have rites of passage or markers as we pass through each stage, whether formal or just personal to us, or we may slip quietly from one to the other.

In our working lives, we may go through training and learning, gaining qualifications, getting started in our careers and over time experiencing role, organisational and practice changes. As we get older and become more senior we may have increased responsibility or managerial roles, or we may change the way we work or our focus.

Our personal lives are also likely to go through multiple transitions. We may establish personal relationships which may last or may change. We may marry and we may have children and establish families, and as they grow up we may face continuing change and challenges. And throughout all of this, change is inevitable.

Friendships and relationships may end, accidents, ill health or death may result in shifts in our lives or of those close to us.

Change may be motivated by us: we may at some point feel a need to review our lives and to change our way of being or of working; or change may be thrust upon us by circumstances we cannot control. Fate can smile on some of us and sometimes it can be arbitrarily unkind.

This chapter is about the transitions that we make in life, as professionals and as human beings, and about endings including those inherent in these transitions.

Transitions: "little dying" – endings and new beginnings

When a transition takes place from one state of affairs to another, however positive and beneficial it may be, it implicitly involves accepting the ending of one state, letting go of it in order to move on to the next. As obvious as this may be, it can still sometimes be hard to give up what one has become accustomed to without experiencing some sense of loss. The sense of loss occasioned by these transitions or turning points led psychotherapist Stanley Keleman to describe them as "little dyings", ways of learning "how to live our big dying".

> Turning points are the cauldron of our lives, the steps of our birthings our self-formings. There are no turning points that are not accompanied by feelings of dying; no self-forming occurs without endings and loss.
>
> (Stanley Keleman, *Living Your Dying*)

Likewise William Bridges, in his book *Transitions: Making Sense of Life's Changes*, refers to the endings that are an essential part of moving to new beginnings – and in many cases with a period of confusion and sometimes distress in between. He observes that in spite of being in a new situation, a new job or a new home, which we may have looked forward to, we may nevertheless find it very difficult to let go of the old ties and rhythms. While we all may have some difficulty in managing endings, each of us brings to a transition our own style of dealing with endings, whether one of anxiety, being in control or slow and gradual adaptation.

Transitions may contain paradoxical elements: a wish for change and a new beginning and alongside that fear and concern about the change and some regret at losing what is being given up. Fear and excitement are opposite sides of the same coin. Small wonder that transitions can be so stressful while promising the potential of something better.

Between the ending of the old and the beginning of the new there may sometimes be what William Bridges calls "the neutral zone" where one can allow a period, however short, of self-renewal, reflecting on the past to help shape the future, trying to discover what you really want and consider what aspect of your life remains unlived. In this sense, Bridges shares with Keleman the concept of the endings in transitions as "dyings in one sense" so the reflection on what is unlived can help in the writing of the new life chapter. Create, he suggests, your own private ritual, a retreat where you can have your own individual and private rite of passage.

Once endings are managed, new beginnings offer hope and promise: starting again, wiping the slate clean, believing that the next phase will be better than the last. And indeed, a fresh start can offer new opportunities; but the reality may be rather more complex:

- The quote "Wherever you go, there you are" is particularly apt. We tend to follow our old, established patterns and transitions may not effect meaningful change if we simply carry with us all our old baggage. Hence we may need to take meaningful steps to re-examine ourselves and our ways of being and functioning. Bridges refers to this as "a kind of inner re-alignment".
- Given especially the paradoxical nature of transitions and the uncertainties inherent in life and in change, it is not surprising that new beginnings might sometimes be uncertain, untidy and generally imperfect.
- And even if endings have been managed, there can be recurrence of fear and insecurity and perhaps regret. These are not infrequent by-products of fundamental change.

Life and work stages: The Empty Raincoat

The concept of viewing life as a series of stages is not new. The ancient Romans considered that there were five stages of human development, medieval Islam viewed stages of life linked to an astrological system and Shakespeare referred to the seven ages of man.

> All the world's a stage,
> And all the men and women merely players;
> They have their exits and their entrances;
> And one man in his time plays many parts,
> His acts being seven ages.
>
> (William Shakespeare, *As You Like It*)

More recently, many writers have identified views of life stages, including Gail Sheehy, whose 1976 *Passages: Predictable Crises of Adult Life* was very influential in providing a vision of the passages through which people pass each decade and the crises that they face.

A very interesting concept was developed by Charles Handy, a pre-eminent management thinker, in his 1995 book *The Empty Raincoat: Making Sense of the Future*. Handy wrote about a sculpture that influenced him – a bronze raincoat (by Judith Shea) standing upright but with no one inside it. For Handy, that symbolised a paradox faced by society: that while society pursues economic growth and progress, we as individuals, who should be at the centre of that goal, might be lost in its pursuit. We should not be empty raincoats but should find our own individual paths, our own human selves, in a world of paradoxes.

Handy referred to four stages (or "Ages") of life and work. In the first 25 years or so, a person "forms" himself or herself, preparing for life and work with education and qualifications. The second phase, maybe 30 years or so, is the period of working and earning and perhaps bringing up children. In the Third Age people move to doing what they really want to do, rather than what they have to do to earn a living. This does not necessarily mean working unpaid, but rather taking the opportunity to explore doing or being what one wants to do or be – the "opportunity to be another person". Finally, the Fourth Age is one of dependency.

Client and patient endings

As professionals, we will ordinarily want good relationships with our clients or patients and good endings when those relationships conclude.

However, there may be an occasion when a relationship may founder, disagreements may arise and a client or patient may make a complaint or claim against the professional – whether or not justified – leading to an unhappy or acrimonious ending. This kind of ending needs to be further considered.

Managing contentious endings

Professional relationships that end in contention have a number of features that can make them especially difficult to manage:

- The client or patient may feel let down, having placed faith in the professional to deal effectively with the entrusted task. Instead of resolving the original issue, it has been compounded by this additional dispute.
- The professional may feel let down, having put energy and resource into addressing the issue and now feeling that the client or patient is being unreasonable and ungrateful.
- By the time the relationship reaches this stage, underlying emotions may be running high and mutual trust may be fragile.
- Professionals tend to be careful about what they acknowledge in case this may be regarded as an admission of liability, which may vitiate their professional negligence insurance.

Obviously every contentious ending needs to be dealt with on its own merits but some broad general principles may be helpful:

Insurance: If there is an actual or potential claim, for example of professional negligence, any relevant insurance policy terms need to be carefully observed. Insurers invariably need to be notified.

Relevant papers and documents: These should be preserved so that they can be produced later if needed.

Communications: Any communication that may be construed as an acknowledgement of liability may prejudice the validity of an insurance policy so should only be considered on the basis of professional advice. However, in some situations a thoughtful acknowledgement made with the benefit of legal advice may be appropriate and could prevent a dispute from escalating.

Emotional distance and perspective: It can be really useful to view the complaint or claim unemotionally from an objective and independent perspective, or even as seen from the other side. Is there any substance in any element of it? Is any common ground possible, or any way of explaining your position in a way that wouldn't inflame the position but rather help to resolve any misperceptions – subject of course to professional advice on this?

Dignity: A calm and dignified response to a claim or complaint is likely to be more appropriate and stand one in better stead than an angry and defensive reaction. It flows from and supports a balanced emotional response.

Justified complaints or claims: If a professional thinks that a claim or complaint may be justified and that an apology and perhaps some compensatory payment or gesture is appropriate, this should be considered with a professional adviser, relevant colleagues and where appropriate one's insurer. It may have implications including perhaps adverse professional findings and possible financial redress; but it may be the right thing to do. Or perhaps one's belief of responsibility may be misjudged or misplaced, hence the need for independent advice. Where appropriate, an acknowledgement at an early stage may allow matters to be resolved with less serious consequences than going down a contentious route.

Mediation: This can be useful because it allows parties to discuss the issues and explain their respective positions informally and off the record ("without prejudice") and to explore possible ways of finding some mutually acceptable solution.

The UK Legal Ombudsman has published a "guide to good complaints handling" entitled "Listen, Inform, Respond" providing useful guidance about handling and responding to complaints – probably also useful guidance for other professionals facing similar situations.

Preparing for retirement/Third Age

Retirement, like most other things facing professionals, can best be handled from a head, heart and gut perspective. Some financial, emotional and practical preparation for retirement is likely to be necessary to enable it to be a successful transition.

Financial preparation

Financial, investment and tax provisions and options relating to retirement will vary from time to time and from country to country. The following are some relevant considerations:

Timing: Fixed retirement ages have been discontinued in a number of places as being ageist and discriminatory, save in some occupations where age is considered relevant. It is generally possible to receive a pension when one attains pensionable age and yet to continue working in one way or another, though some occupational pension schemes may not support partial or phased retirement.

Long-term planning involves anticipating future needs, assessing likely state provision and making pension plans to provide for any shortfall. An independent financial adviser can provide valuable guidance.

One may not have an option on the timing of retirement – it may be compulsory or ill health or other circumstances may dictate the timing. Insofar as there may be an optional aspect, considerations as to timing may include the following:

- The earlier one draws down one's pension, the lower the income will be – and this is fixed for life based on the drawdown date. This is a factor in favour of delaying it, but this must obviously be balanced against other considerations.
- The level of projected pension capital and income needs to be calculated, and weighed against likely capital and income needs.
- Personal considerations must obviously be put on the scale: health, well-being, quality of life, responsibility for caring for others, level of job satisfaction or of unhappiness and burnout, alternative options in retirement (doing what you want to do).
- Planning is important but (as the poet Robert Burns observed) "the best-laid schemes o' mice an' men gang aft a-gley": things change unexpectedly and it is prudent to have a Plan B – and also to try to live as comfortably as one can with inherent uncertainty.

Attitude to risk: Risk factors, including investment and longevity risks and likely needs in later life such as long-term care costs, can be weighed against the cost of mitigating them. With the help of an independent financial adviser, one can decide to what extent one wishes to accept these risks or transfer them to an insurer via purchasing an annuity or a deferred income annuity (one that begins at a later date).

Adapting to new financial circumstances: Moving onto a pension will commonly involve a drop in income, which may involve a number of possible considerations:

- Creating a new budget may be needed – and learning how to live within it.
- There may be ways of topping up one's pension income, for example by undertaking part-time work, consultancy, training or other occasional activities.
- Dipping into capital, if available, needs some planning as one needs to consider what one will do if and when the capital gets eroded.
- Downsizing is an option for raising capital and perhaps reducing expenditure. Much would depend on individual circumstances, property values and state of the market – and costs of sale, moving and buying can absorb a significant part of any gain.
- An alternative is to enter into an equity release scheme – a loan secured by mortgage and repayable on death, with interest rolled up. Advantages include remaining in one's home until death, while disadvantages include paying interest on interest as well as on capital, so that the loan grows quickly, and any prospective bequest to heirs is likely to be substantially eroded. Products have, however, developed that enable interest to be paid during one's lifetime, rather than being rolled up, thus avoiding the loan being increased in size. It is essential to seek advice from an independent financial adviser before taking up any such scheme.

> As you simplify your life, the laws of the universe will be simpler; solitude will not be solitude, poverty will not be poverty, nor weakness weakness.
>
> (Henry David Thoreau)

Emotional preparation

Retirement still remains one of the biggest transitions of our lives, with all the conflicts, stresses and challenges associated with change that arise in major transitions. However rationally we may welcome it, we are bound to be emotionally affected by it, so some thoughtful preparation in this regard is clearly necessary.

Take time for "inner re-alignment": This involves quiet self-reflection on the past and on the kind of future you would like or what you consider you may need, also how your sense of identity will be affected and how you will find meaning outside of work. William Bridges recommends consciously carving out time to be quiet and alone, reflecting on the experience of the transition and perhaps keeping a record of it.

Therapy or counselling: Given the challenges and some sense of loss, perhaps also anxiety and concern, counselling or therapy might be helpful to manage the transition to retirement. This can be conducted over time or on a brief limited time basis.

Managing uncertainty: We can try to develop strategies for coping with uncertainty:

- It can be reassuring to have some idea of what you aim to do in retirement, some broad plan of activities, be it undertaking a course of study; doing part-time work; caring for someone; or pursuing a particular interest or hobby. This does not mean that leisure – and just "being" – should be relegated to an afterthought. On the contrary, this is a critical component of a good retirement; however, on its own and without some complementary plans it may not be enough for many people.
- Alongside planning, we also need to try to cultivate an ability to focus on our inner selves and to find some inner peace, some still place within ourselves. Some find this by following a spiritual path. Others may find their own individual way of achieving this.
- There is an inter-relationship between financial insecurity and emotional insecurity and uncertainty. Of course, some certainties may be illusory, but there is little doubt that financial planning for retirement is likely to alleviate some of the concerns and uncertainties about a future with a reduced income.

Acknowledging feelings: It is not uncommon to have mixed feelings on retirement, which are healthy to recognise and acknowledge rather than pretending to oneself that everything is positive and upbeat if that is not how one is actually feeling. Having said this, a positive approach to retirement is helpful and constructive and likely to support a good transition more than a gloomy and pessimistic one. But the reality is complex and one can also acknowledge any other feelings that may co-exist such as sadness at the end of an era and on ending relationships, fear about aspects of the future, questions about self-identity and relief from the burdens and responsibilities of work.

Practical preparation

This overlaps with financial and emotional preparation and may include the following:

Make transitional or termination arrangements with your firm or organisation: The following are some aspects that might need to be discussed with your colleagues or employers:

- You might wish to make transitional arrangements such as working as a consultant for an agreed period.
- If you are a sole practitioner, you may need to arrange for your practice to be taken over by someone else on terms to be agreed, for example as

to the continuation of pending work and your remuneration for work done but not yet charged for, if applicable.

- You may need to arrange run-off professional indemnity insurance cover, which covers you after ceasing to practise, should any claim be made.
- If your practice is not continuing after your departure, there will be implications for ending relationships with employees and making any redundancy payments or the like, bringing any leases to an end and generally winding up the practice.

Establish retirement rules from your professional body: Various professional or other relevant bodies may have rules that enable retiring practitioners to remain registered in their field. For example, solicitors can remain on the roll of practitioners after retirement (making it clear that they are non-practising, if that is the case) and doctors can in many cases retain their registration or licence to practise with the appropriate Medical Council.

Leisure and health: The huge range of options for retirement leisure and activities might include further study for pleasure, developing creative activities, undertaking voluntary or charitable work or getting pleasure from gardening, reading, travel, walking or hobbies; and with all of this, spending time with family and friends. Keeping fit in later years is equally important, particularly aerobic exercise that gets oxygen pumping through the body.

Dr David Perlmutter, who wrote *Grain Brain* with Kristin Loberg, and who is an acknowledged leader in the science of brain nutrition, is clear about the benefit of aerobic exercise, which helps to augment brain cells in the memory centre and has the effect of reversing memory decline in older people.

Mental and spiritual well-being: Physical health may be important, but so is mental well-being and for many people also a sense of spiritual connectedness.

Mental well-being can be enhanced by having some sense of purpose in retirement, maintaining good personal and social contacts, having a balanced lifestyle with plenty of rest and also exercising the brain, for example by doing crosswords or Sudoku, playing bridge or chess and generally keeping the mind active.

Spiritual well-being is not necessarily about religious belief, though it might certainly include this, but in a wider context it may involve one's inner life and meaning, having a sense of connectedness with others and with some higher force or power and experiencing harmony with the environment and a sense of inner peace. There are many paths to spirituality and each person may need to find the way that resonates with him or her individually.

> To the best of our knowledge, human beings have always responded to the universe with awe, wonder and radical amazement ... The need to celebrate, to rejoice in creation and in our own existence, and to connect what was perceived as an inner spiritual reality with the outer spiritual reality of the universe seems to be pervasive throughout all cultures and societies.
>
> (Michael Lerner, *Spirit Matters*)

Lasting (enduring or durable) powers of attorney: This is a power of attorney that survives mental incompetence, known in the UK as a Lasting Power of Attorney, and in other jurisdictions variously as "enduring" or "durable" power of attorney. This can be entered into at any time (while one is still competent to do so). Strict formal requirements need to be carefully observed.

Making a will: This is likely to have been done long before retirement, but if not, here again this is the time to consider doing so; or if there is already a will in place, perhaps it may be appropriate to review it in the new retired circumstances.

Transitions and endings

Perhaps the Bible may provide the last word on transitions and endings:

> To every thing there is a season, and a time to every purpose under the heaven:
>
> A time to be born, and a time to die; a time to plant, and a time to pluck up that which is planted;
>
> A time to kill, and a time to heal; a time to break down, and a time to build up;
>
> A time to weep, and a time to laugh; a time to mourn, and a time to dance;
>
> A time to cast away stones, and a time to gather stones together; a time to embrace, and a time to refrain from embracing;
>
> A time to get, and a time to lose; a time to keep, and a time to cast away;
>
> A time to rend, and a time to sew; a time to keep silence, and a time to speak;
>
> A time to love, and a time to hate; a time of war, and a time of peace.
>
> (Ecclesiastes 3)

Further reading

Two books about transitions have become classics: Gail Sheehy's *Passages: Predictable Crises of Adult Life*, written in the 1970s and revised in 2004/06; and William Bridges' updating of his classic work, now called *Managing Transitions: Making the Most of Change*.

Somatic therapist Stanley Keleman, who has written about the links between body, emotions and mind, wrote *Living Your Dying* in 1974, which is described as a book "about dying, not about death ... about learning how to give up what we have embodied".

Charles Handy has written with particular sensitivity about work, society, meaning and purpose. His thought-provoking book *The Empty Raincoat: Making Sense of the Future* followed his *Age of Unreason*, which examines change and the uncertainties that it involves.

Useful books on the subject of life and work change include Robert Keegan and Lisa Lahey's *Immunity to Change: How to Overcome It and Unlock the Potential in Yourself and Your Organization*; Elizabeth Wilde McCormick's *Change for the Better: Self-Help through Practical Psychotherapy*, largely based on the principles of cognitive analytical therapy; and from a spiritual perspective, drawing on the Chinese Tao Te Ching, Wayne W. Dyer's *Change Your Thoughts Change Your Life: Living the Wisdom of the Tao*.

Again there are many books about retirement, including *Brilliant Retirement: Your Practical Guide to a Happy, Healthy, Financially Sound Retirement* by Dr Nic Peeling; *Your Retirement Masterplan 2e: How to Ensure You Have a Fulfilling and Enjoyable Third Age* by Jim Green; and *Ready, Steady, Retire: Plan Your Way to Success in a Redefined Retirement* by Justin King and Martin Bamford.

Perhaps the leading work dealing with issues around uncertainty is Susan Jeffers' *Embracing Uncertainty: Achieving Peace of Mind as We Face the Unknown*. Others dealing with this topic are listed in Chapter 14.

It is impracticable to try to list works about spiritual development, particularly because of the diversity of philosophies, approaches, values and belief systems. Michael Lerner's *Spirit Matters* and Wayne Dyer's works have been mentioned. Among innumerable other authors who might be mentioned are Marianne Williamson and Ram Dass.

Finally, on the subject of endings, death and dying, no list would be complete without mentioning Elisabeth Kubler-Ross and her many books, including *To Live Until We Say Goodbye, On Death and Dying* and *The Wheel of Life*.

Bibliography

Aaron, Marjorie Corman, *Client Science: Advice for Lawyers on Counseling Clients through Bad News and Other Legal Realities* (Oxford University Press USA, 2012).

Acland, Andrew Floyer, *A Sudden Outbreak of Common Sense: Managing Conflict through Mediation* (Hutchinson Business Books, 1990).

Allen, Tony, *Mediation Law and Civil Practice* (Bloomsbury Professional, 2013).

American Psychiatric Association, *Diagnostic and Statistical Manual of Mental Disorders DSM-5* (American Psychiatric Press Inc., 5th edn, 2013).

Amthor, Frank, *Neuroscience for Dummies* (Wiley, 2012).

Argyle, Michael, *The Psychology of Interpersonal Behaviour* (Penguin, 5th edn, 1994).

Ariely, Dan, *Predictably Irrational* (HarperCollins, 2008).

Arnold, John with Silvester, Joanne, Patterson, Fiona, Robertson, Ivan, Cooper, Cary and Burnes, Bernard, *Work Psychology: Understanding Human Behaviour in the Workplace* (Pearson Education Limited, 4th edn, 2005).

Atkinson, Leslie and Zucker, Kenneth J. (eds), *Attachment and Psychopathology* (Guilford Press, 1997).

Babcock. Linda and Laschever, Sara, *Ask for it: How Women Can Use the Power of Negotiation to Get What They Really Want* (Piatkus, 2009).

Babiak, Paul and Hare, Robert, *Snakes in Suits: When Psychopaths Go to Work* (Harper, 2007).

Baines, Gurnek et al., *Meaning Inc: The Blueprint for Business Success in the 21st Century* (Profile Books, 2007).

Baron-Cohen, Simon, *Autism and Asperger Syndrome* (Oxford University Press, 2008).

Barondes, Samuel, *Making Sense of People: Decoding the Mysteries of Personality* (FT Press/Pearson Education, 2012).

Barsky, Allan, *Conflict Resolution for the Helping Professions* (Oxford University Press, 2nd edn, 2014).

Beauregard, Mario and O'Leary, Denyse, *The Spiritual Brain: A Neuroscientist's Case for the Existence of the Soul* (HarperOne, 2007).

Beck, Aaron T., *Love Is Never Enough* (Penguin, 1989).

Benson, Nigel and others, *The Psychology Book* (Dorling Kindersley, 2012).

Berne, Eric, *Games People Play: The Psychology of Human Relationships* (Penguin, 1964–2010).

Blake, Susan, Browne, Julie and Sims, Stuart, *A Practical Approach to Alternative Dispute Resolution* (Oxford University Press, 2014).

Bloom, Paul, *Against Empathy: The Case for Rational Compassion* (Bodley Head, 2016).

Bowling, Daniel and Hoffman, David (eds), *Bringing Peace into the Room: How the Personal Qualities of the Mediator Impact the Process of Conflict Resolution* (Jossey-Bass, 2003).

Bramson, Robert, *Coping with Difficult People* (Bantam Doubleday Dell, 1988).

Bridges, William, *Managing Transitions: Making the Most of Change* (Nicholas Brearley Publishing, 3rd edn, 2009).

Brinkman, Rick and Kirschner, Rick, *Dealing with Difficult People: 24 Lessons to Bring Out the Best in Everyone* (McGraw-Hill, 2006).

Brown, Brené, *I Thought It Was Just Me (But It Isn't)* (Penguin/Gotham Books, 2008).

Brown, Brené, *The Gifts of Imperfection: Let Go of Who You Think You're Supposed to Be and Embrace Who You Are* (Hazelden, 2010).

Brown, Henry, Dawson, Neil and McHugh, Brenda, *Managing Difficult Divorce Relationships: A Multimedia Training Programme for Family Lawyers* (Resolution, 2006).

Brown, Henry and Marriott, Arthur, *ADR Principles & Practice* (Sweet & Maxwell, 3rd edn, 2011).

Buzan, Tony, *Use Both Sides of Your Brain* (Atlantic Books, 1991).

Cameron, Deborah, *The Myth of Mars And Venus: Do Men and Women Really Speak Different Languages?* (Oxford University Press, 2008).

Cash, Adam, *Psychology for Dummies* (Wiley, 2002).

Clarkson, Petrūska, *The Achilles Syndrome: Overcoming the Secret Fear of Failure* (Element Books, 1994; Vega Books edition, 2003).

Collin, Catherine and others, *The Psychology Book* (Dorling Kindersley, 2011).

Cooklin, Alan, Dawson, Neil and McHugh, Brenda, *Family Therapy Basics* (Marlborough Family Service, 1993, 2003).

Corey, Gerald, Corey, Marianne Schneider and Callanan, Patrick, *Issues and Ethics in the Helping Professions* (Cengage Learning, 8th edn, 2010).

Covey, Stephen R., *The 7 Habits of Highly Effective People: Powerful Lessons in Personal Change* (Simon & Schuster, reprinted edition, 2004).

Cozolino, Louis, *The Neuroscience of Human Relationships: Attachment and the Developing Social Brain* (W. W. Norton & Company, 2006; 2nd edn, 2014).

Cribb, Alan and Gewirtz, Sharon *Professionalism* (Polity Press, 2015).

Crick, Francis, *What Mad Pursuit: A Personal View of Scientific Discovery* (Basic Books, 1988 and 1990).

Damasio, Antonio, *The Feeling of What Happens: Body, Emotion and the Making of Consciousness* (Vintage Books, 2000).

Damasio, Antonio, *Self Comes to Mind: Constructing the Conscious Brain* (Vintage, 2012).

Davies, James, *Cracked: Why Psychiatry Is Doing More Harm than Good* (Icon Books, 2013).

DeAngelis, Catherine D. (ed.), *Patient Care and Professionalism* (Oxford University Press, 2013).

De Angelis, Paula M., *Blindsided: Recognizing and Dealing with Passive-Aggressive Leadership in the Workplace* (CreateSpace Independent Publishing, 2009).

de Bono, Edward, *Conflicts: A Better Way to Resolve Them* (Penguin, 1986).

Debiec, Jacek, Heller, Michael, Bartosz, Brozek and LeDoux, Joseph (eds), *The Emotional Brain Revisited* (Copernicus Center Press, 2014).

Dossey, Larry and others, *The Power of Meditation and Prayer* (Hay House, 1997).

Dryden, Windy and Reeves, Andrew (eds), *The Handbook of Individual Therapy* (Sage, 6th edn, 2013).

Dyer, Wayne W., *Change Your Thoughts Change Your Life: Living the Wisdom of the Tao* (Hay House, 2017).

Eddy, Bill, *High Conflict People in Legal Disputes* (HCI Press, 2005).

Eddy, Bill, *BIFF: Quick Responses to High-Conflict People, Their Personal Attacks, Hostile E-Mail and Social Media Meltdowns* (Unhooked Books, 2nd edn, 2014).

Eddy, Bill, *So What's Your Proposal? Shifting High-Conflict People from Blaming to Problem-Solving in 30 Seconds* (Unhooked Books, 2014).

Egan, Gerard, *The Skilled Helper: A Problem-Management and Opportunity-Development Approach to Helping* (Brooks/Cole, revised edition, 2013).

Eimer, Bruce N. and Torem, Moshe, *10 Simple Solutions for Coping with Uncertainty* (New Harbinger Publications, 2003).

Ellenberger, Henri F., *The Discovery of the Unconscious: The History and Evolution of Dynamic Psychiatry* (Basic Books, 1970).

Ellison, Katherine, *The Mommy Brain: How Motherhood Makes Us Smarter* (Basic Books, 2005).

Evans, Dylan, *Placebo: the Belief Effect* (HarperCollins, 2003).

Feltham, Colin (ed.), *The SAGE Handbook of Counselling and Psychotherapy* (Sage Publications, 3rd edn, 2012).

Fisher, Roger and Ury, William, *Getting to Yes: Negotiating Agreement without Giving In* (Houghton Mifflin, 1981).

Fisher, Roger and Brown, Scott, *Getting Together: Building a Relationship that Gets to Yes* (Penguin, 1989).

Fisher, Roger and Shapiro, Daniel, *Building Agreement: Using Emotions as You Negotiate* (Random House, 2007).

Fonagy, Peter, *Attachment Theory and Psychoanalysis* (Other Press, 2001).

Fonagy, Peter (ed.), *Affect Regulation, Mentalization, and the Development of the Self* (Karnac Books 2003).

Frankl, Victor E., *Man's Search for Meaning: An Introduction to Logotherapy* (Hodder & Stoughton, 1964; original German edition 1946).

Freud, Sigmund, *The Standard Edition of the Complete Psychological Works of Sigmund Freud* (Vintage: The Hogarth Press and the Institute of Psychoanalysis, 2001).

Fromm, Erich, *Man for Himself: An Inquiry into the Psychology of Ethics* (Routledge, 2003).

Gardner, Fiona, *Being Critically reflective: Engaging in Holistic Practice* (Palgrave Macmillan, 2014).

Gardner, Howard, *Frames of Mind: The Theory of Multiple Intelligences* (Heinemann, 1984; Fontana Press, 2nd edn, 1993).

Gardner, Howard, *Five Minds for the Future* (Harvard Business School Press, 2006).

Gazzaniga, Michael S., *The Ethical Brain* (Dana Press, 2005).

Gerhardt, Sue, *Why Love Matters: How Affection Shapes a Baby's Brain* (Brunner-Routledge, 2004; 2nd edn, 2014).

Gerver, Richard, *Change: Learn to Love It, Learn to Lead It* (Portfolio Penguin, 2013).

Gibb, Barry, *The Rough Guide to the Brain* (Rough Guides, 2007; 2nd edn, 2012).

Gigerenzer, Gerd, *Gut Feelings: The Intelligence of the Unconscious* (Penguin/Allen Lane, 2007).

Gigerenzer, Gerd, *Rationality for Mortals: How People Cope with Uncertainty* (Oxford University Press, 2010).

Gigerenzer, Gerd, *Risk Savvy: How to Make Good Decisions* (Allen Lane, 2014).

Gladwell, Malcolm, *Blink* (Penguin, 2006).

Gladwell, Malcolm, *Outliers: The Story of Success* (Penguin, 2009).

Goleman, Daniel, *Emotional Intelligence: Why It Can Matter More than IQ* (Bloomsbury Publishing, 1996).

Grandin, Temple, *Thinking in Pictures* (Bloomsbury Publishing, 2006).

Grandin, Temple and Panek, Richard, *The Autistic Brain: Exploring the Strength of a Different Kind of Mind* (Rider, 2014).

Gray, John, *Men Are from Mars, Women Are from Venus* (HarperCollins, 2002).

Green, Jim, *Your Retirement Masterplan 2e: How to Ensure You Have a Fulfilling and Enjoyable Third Age* (How to Books, 2006).

Griffin, Joe and Tyrrell, Ivan, *How to Lift Depression ... Fast* (HG Publishing, 2004).

Griffin, Joe and Tyrrell, Ivan, *How to Master Anxiety: All You Need to Know to Overcome Stress, Panic Attacks, Trauma, Phobias, Obsessions and More (Human Givens Approach)* (HG Publishing, 2006).

Hall, Edward T., *The Silent Language* (Anchor, 1973; Bantam Doubleday Dell Publishing Group, 1988).

Hamer, Kenneth, *Professional Conduct Casebook* (Oxford University Press, 2nd edn, 2015).

Handy, Charles, *The Age of Unreason* (Arrow/Random House, 1989; new edition, 2002).

Handy, Charles, *The Empty Raincoat: Making Sense of the Future* (Arrow Books, 1995).

Hardy, Jean, *A Psychology with a Soul: Psychosynthesis in Evolutionary Context* (Arkana/Penguin Group, 1987).

Hassin, Ran R., Uleman, James S. and Bargh, John A. (eds), *The New Unconscious (Social Cognition and Social Neuroscience)* (Oxford University Press, 2004).

Hawkins, Peter and Shohet, Robin, *Supervision in the Helping Professions* (Open University Press, 4th edn, 2012).

Herbert, Martin, *Psychology for Social Workers* (The British Psychological Society, 1981, 1986).

Holford, Patrick, *The Optimum Nutrition Bible* (Piatkus, 1997; revised edition, 2004).

Holford, Patrick, *The Alzheimer's Prevention Plan: 10 Proven Ways to Stop Memory Decline and Reduce the Risk of Alzheimer's* (Piatkus, 2005).

Holford, Patrick, *The Stress Cure: How to Resolve Stress, Build Resilience and Boost Your Energy* (Piatkus, 2015).

Howe, David, *On Being a Client: Understanding the Process of Counselling and Psychotherapy* (Sage Publications, 1993, 1998).

Ives, Martine and Munro, Nell, *Caring for a Child with Autism: A Practical Guide for Parents* (Jessica Kingsley Publishers, 2002).

James, Oliver, *Office Politics: How to Thrive in a World of Lying, Back-stabbing and Dirty Tricks* (Vermilion, 2014).

Jeffers, Susan, *Embracing Uncertainty: Achieving Peace of Mind as We Face the Unknown* (Hodder Mobius, 2002).

Jung, Carl G., *Man and His Symbols* (Aldus Books, 1964; Laurel Press, 1997).

Kabat-Zinn, Jon, *Wherever You Go, There You Are: Mindfulness Meditation for Everyday Life* (Piatkus, 2004).

Kabat-Zinn, Jon, *Full Catastrophe Living: How to Cope with Stress, Pain and Illness Using Mindfulness Meditation* (Piatkus, revised edition, 2013).

Kahneman, Daniel, *Thinking, Fast and Slow* (Penguin, 2011).

Karten, Naomi, *Managing Expectations: Working with People Who Want More, Better, Faster, Sooner, Now!* (Dorset House Publishing, 1994).

Kay, Susie, *Professionalism: The ABC for Success* (Professionalism Books, 2010).

Keegan, Robert and Lahey, Lisa, *Immunity to Change: How to Overcome It and Unlock the Potential in Yourself and Your Organization* (Harvard Business School Press, 2009).

Keleman, Stanley, *Living Your Dying* (Center Press, 1974; 2nd edn, 1989).

Kennedy, Gavin, *Everything is Negotiable: How to Negotiate and Win* (Random House Business, 4th edn, 2008).

Keshavjee, Mohamed, *Islam, Sharia and Alternative Dispute Resolution: Mechanisms for Legal Redress in the Muslim Community* (I. B. Taurus, 2013).

King, Justin and Bamford, Martin, *Ready, Steady, Retire: Plan your Way to Success in a Redefined Retirement* (MFP Wealth Management/Lulu.com, 2014).

Klein, Gary, *The Power of Intuition* (Currency/Doubleday, 2004).

Knight, Frank, *Risk, Uncertainty, and Profit* (Houghton Mifflin, 1921; Signalman Publishing, paperback edition, 2009).

Lawley, James and Tomkins, Penny, *Metaphors in Mind: Transformation through Symbolic Modelling* (Developing Company Press, 2000).

Lax, David A. and Sebenius, James K., *The Manager as Negotiator: Bargaining for Co-operation and Competitive Gain* (The Free Press, 1986).

Lax, David A. and Sebenius, James K., *3-D Negotiation: Powerful Tools to Change the Game in Your Most Important Deals* (Harvard Business School Press, 2006).

Leibling, Mike, *Working with the Enemy: How to Survive and Thrive with Really Difficult People* (Kogan Page, 2009).

Lerner, Michael, *Spirit Matters* (Walsch Books, 2000).

Levine, Stuart, *Getting to Resolution: Turning Conflict to Collaboration* (Berrett Koehler Publishers, 2009).

Levitin, Daniel J., *The Organized Mind: Thinking Straight in the Age of Information Overload* (Viking, 2015).

Lewis, Richard D., *When Cultures Collide: Leading, Teamworking and Managing across the Globe* (Nicholas Brealey Publishing, 3rd edn, 2005).

Lilley, Roy, *Dealing with Difficult People: Creating Success* (Kogan Page, 2002/2006; 2nd edn, 2013).

Maslow, Abraham, *A Theory of Human Motivation* (original edition 1943; CreateSpace Independent Publishing Platform, 2013).

Mayer, Bernard, *Staying with Conflict: A Strategic Approach to Ongoing Disputes* (Jossey-Bass, 2009).

McCormick, Elizabeth Wilde, *Change for the Better: Self-Help through Practical Psychotherapy* (Sage Publications, 2012).

Meadows, Donella, and Wright, Diana (eds), *Thinking in Systems: A Primer* (Chelsea Green Publishing Co., updated edition, 2015).

Mehrabian, Albert, *Silent Messages: Implicit Communication of Emotions and Attitudes* (Wadsworth, 1972).

Mehrabian, Albert, *Nonverbal communication* (Aldine Transaction, 2007).

Mnookin, Robert, *Bargaining with the Devil: When to Negotiate and When to Fight* (Simon & Schuster, 2011).

Moore, Christopher W., *The Mediation Process: Practical Strategies for Resolving Conflict* (John Wiley & Sons, 4th edn, 2014).

Morris, Desmond, *Peoplewatching: The Desmond Morris Guide to Body Language* (Vintage, 2002).

Myers, David G., *Intuition: Its Powers and Perils* (Yale University Press, 2002).

Ornstein, Robert, *The Right Mind: Making Sense of the Hemispheres* (Roundhouse Publishing, 1997; and Harcourt Brace International, 1998).

Paris, Joel, *The Intelligent Clinician's Guide to the DSM-5* (Oxford University Press, 2013).

Pease, Allan and Pease, Barbara, *The Definitive Book of Body Language: How to Read Others' Attitudes by Their Gestures* (Orion, 2006).

Pease, Allan, *Body Language: How to Read Others' Thoughts by Their Gestures* (Sheldon Press, 1984; further edition, Manjul Publishing, 2014).

Peeling, Nic, *Brilliant Retirement: Your Practical Guide to a Happy, Healthy, Financially Sound Retirement* (Pearson, 2010).

Perlmutter, David and Loberg, Kristin, *Grain Brain* (Yellow Kite Books, 2014).

Piattelli-Palmarini, Massimo, *Inevitable Illusions: How Mistakes of Reason Rule Our Minds* by (John Wiley & Sons, 1994).

Pink, Daniel H., *A Whole New Mind: Why Right-brainers Will Rule the Future* (Marshall Cavendish, 2008).

Ramachandran, V. S., *A Brief Tour of Human Consciousness: From Impostor Poodles to Purple Numbers* (Pi Press, 2004).

Ramachandran, V. S., *The Tell-Tale Brain: Unlocking the Mystery of Human Nature* (Windmill Books, 2012).

Randolph, Paul, *The Psychology of Conflict: Mediating in a Diverse World* (Bloomsbury, 2016).

Reber, Arthur S. and Reber, Emily S., *The Penguin Dictionary of Psychology* (Penguin Books, 3rd edn, 2001).

Restak, Richard, *The New Brain: How the Modern Age is Rewiring Your Mind* (Rodale, 2004).

Ricard, Matthieu, *The Art of Meditation* (Atlantic Books, 2009).

Richbell, David, *How to Master Commercial Mediation* (Bloomsbury Professional, 2015).

Ridley, Matt, *Nature via Nurture: Genes, Experience and What Makes Us Human* (Harper Perennial, 2004).

Rogers, Carl R., *On Becoming a Person* (Constable, 1967–1982).

Rogers, Carl R., *Client Centred Therapy: Its Current Practice, Implications and Theory* (Constable, new edition, 2003).

Ronson, Jon, *The Psychopath Test: A Journey Through the Madness Industry* (Picador, 2011).

Schore, Allan, *Affect Dysregulation and Disorders of the Self* (W. W. Norton & Company, 2003).

Senge, Peter M., *The Fifth Discipline: The Art & Practice of the Learning Organisation* (Random House Business Books, 1990, 2006).

Sheehy, Gail, *Passages: Predictable Crises of Adult Life* (Bantam Doubleday Dell, 1996/97; Ballantine Books, 2006).

Siegel, Daniel J., *The Mindful Brain: Reflection and Attunement in the Cultivation of Well-being* (W. W. Norton & Company, 2007).

Simanowitz, Valerie and Pearce, Peter, *Personality Development* (Open University Press, 2003).

Skynner, Robin, Cleese, John and Handelsman, Bud (illustrator), *Families and How to Survive Them* (Methuen, hardback edition, 1983; Vermilion, paperback edition, 1993).

Solms, Mark and Turnbull, Oliver, *The Brain and the Inner World: An Introduction to the Neuroscience of Subjective Experience* (Karnac Books, 2002).

Solms, Mark, "Neurobiological Foundations" in J. De Gruchy (ed.), *The Humanist Imperative in South Africa* (SUN Press, 2011).

Stern, David Thomas (ed.), *Measuring Medical Professionalism* (Oxford University Press, 2006).

Straker, David, *Changing Minds – in Detail: How to Change What People, Think, Feel, Believe and Do* (Changing Works, 3rd edn, 2014, www.changingworks.co.uk/books).

Strasser, Freddie and Randolph, Paul, *Mediation: A Psychological Insight into Conflict Resolution* (Continuum, 2004).

Sullivan, Karen, *How to Cope Successfully with Panic Attacks* (Wellhouse, 2002).

Sutherland, Stuart, *Irrationality: The Enemy Within* (Pinter & Martin, 2013).

Taleb, Nassim Nicholas, *The Black Swan: The Impact of the Highly Improbable* (Penguin, 2007).

Tannen, Deborah, *You Just Don't Understand: Women and Men in Conversation* (Virago, 1992; William Morrow & Co., 2007).

Tannen, Deborah, *Talking from 9 to 5: Women and Men at Work: Language, Sex and Power* (Virago, 1996).

Thistlethwaite, Jill and McKimm, Judy, *Healthcare Professionalism at a Glance* (Wiley-Blackwell, 2015).

Thompson, Leigh L., *The Truth about Negotiations: 'You May Want to Make the First Offer'* (Prentice Hall, 2007).

Thorpe, Carola and Trowell, Judith (eds), *Re-rooted Lives: Inter-disciplinary Work within the Family Justice System* (Family Law, 2007).

Ury, William, *Getting Past No: Negotiating with Difficult People* (Random House, 1992).

Ury, William, *The Power of a Positive No: How to Say No and Still Get to Yes* (Bantam Dell Publishing Group, 2007).

Von Bertalanffy, Ludwig with Hofkirchner, Wolfgang (foreword) and Rousseau, David (foreword), *General System Theory: Foundations, Development, Applications* (George Braziller, revised edition, 2015).

Walker, Stephen, *Mediation Advocacy: Representing Clients in Mediation* (Bloomsbury, 2015).

Watts, Alan, *The Wisdom of Insecurity: A Message for an Age of Anxiety* (Pantheon, 1951; Random House, paperback edition, 2011).

Wax, Ruby, *Sane New Mind: Taming the Mind* (Hodder, 2014).

Wax, Ruby, *A Mindfulness Guide for the Frazzled* (Penguin Life, 2016).

Welwood, John, *Towards a Psychology of Awakening: Buddhism, Psychotherapy and the Path of Personal and Spiritual Transformation* (Shambhala Publications, reprint edition, 2002).

Westbrook, David, Kennerley, Helen and Kirk, Joan, *An Introduction to Cognitive Behaviour Therapy: Skills and Applications* (Sage, 2nd edn, 2011).

Whalen, Paul J. and Phelps, Elizabeth A. (eds), *The Human Amygdala* (Guilford Press, 2009).

Widiger, Thomas and Costa, Paul Jr. (eds), *Personality Disorders and the Five-Factor Model of Personality* (American Psychological Association, 3rd edn, 2012).

Williams, Mark and Penman, Danny, *Mindfulness: A Practical Guide to Finding Peace in a Frantic World* (Piatkus, 2011).

Wilson, Timothy D., *Strangers to Ourselves: Discovering the Adaptive Unconscious* (Harvard University Press, 2004).

Wolpert, Lewis, *Malignant Sadness: The Anatomy of Depression* (Faber & Faber, 1999, 2006).

Wolpert, Lewis, *Why Can't a Woman Be More Like a Man? The Evolution of Sex and Gender* (Faber & Faber, 2014).

Zeman, Adam, *A Portrait of the Brain* (Yale University Press, 2008).

Index